The IDG Books Advantage

We at IDG Books Worldwide created *God on the Internet* to meet your growing need for quick access to the most complete and accurate computer information available. Our books work the way you do: They focus on accomplishing specific tasks — not learning random functions. Our books are not long-winded manuals or dry reference tomes. In each book, expert authors tell you exactly what you can do with your technology and how to do it. Easy to follow, step-by-step sections; comprehensive coverage; and convenient access in language and design — it's all here.

The authors of IDG books are uniquely qualified to give you expert advice as well as to provide insightful tips and techniques not found anywhere else. Our authors maintain close contact with end users through feedback from articles, training sessions, e-mail exchanges, user group participation, and consulting work. Because our authors know the realities of daily computer use and are directly tied to the reader, our books have a strategic advantage.

Our authors have the experience to approach a topic in the most efficient manner, and we know that you, the reader, will benefit from a "one-on-one" relationship with the author. Our research shows that readers make computer book purchases because they want expert advice. Because readers want to benefit from the author's experience, the author's voice is always present in an IDG book.

You will find what you need in this book whether you read it from cover to cover, section by section, or simply one topic at a time. As a computer user, you deserve a comprehensive resource of answers. We at IDG Books Worldwide are proud to deliver that resource with *God on the Internet*.

Brenda McLaughlin
Senior Vice President and Group Publisher
YouTellUs@idgbooks.com

God on the Internet

God on the Internet

Mark A. Kellner

IDG Books Worldwide, Inc.
An International Data Group Company

Foster City, CA ♦ Chicago, IL ♦ Indianapolis, IN ♦ Braintree, MA ♦ Southlake, TX

God on the Internet

Published by
IDG Books Worldwide, Inc.
An International Data Group Company
919 E. Hillsdale Blvd.
Suite 400
Foster City, CA 94404

Library of Congress Catalog Card No.:96-75005

ISBN: 1-56884-843-9

Printed in the United States of America

10 9 8 7 6 5 4 3 2 1

Distributed in the United States by IDG Books Worldwide, Inc.

Distributed by Macmillan Canada for Canada; by Computer and Technical Books for the Caribbean Basin; by Contemporanea de Ediciones for Venezuela; by Distribuidora Cuspide for Argentina; by CITEC for Brazil; by Ediciones ZETA S.C.R. Ltda. for Peru; by Editorial Limusa SA for Mexico; by Transworld Publishers Limited in the United Kingdom and Europe; by Al-Maiman Publishers & Distributors for Saudi Arabia; by Simron Pty. Ltd. for South Africa; by IDG Communications (HK) Ltd. for Hong Kong; by Toppan Company Ltd. for Japan; by Addison Wesley Publishing Company for Korea; by Longman Singapore Publishers Ltd. for Singapore, Malaysia, Thailand, and Indonesia; by Unalis Corporation for Taiwan; by WS Computer Publishing Company, Inc. for the Philippines; by WoodsLane Pty. Ltd. for Australia; by WoodsLane Enterprises Ltd. for New Zealand.

For general information on IDG Books Worldwide's books in the U.S., please call our Consumer Customer Service department at 800-762-2974. For reseller information, including discounts and premium sales, please call our Reseller Customer Service department at 800-434-3422.

For information on where to purchase IDG Books Worldwide's books outside the U.S., contact IDG Books Worldwide at 415-655-3021 or fax 415-655-3295.

For information on translations, contact Marc Jeffrey Mikulich, Director, Foreign & Subsidiary Rights, at IDG Books Worldwide, 415-655-3018 or fax 415-655-3295.

For sales inquiries and special prices for bulk quantities, write to the address above or call IDG Books Worldwide at 415-655-3200.

For information on using IDG Books Worldwide's books in the classroom, or ordering examination copies, contact the Education Office at 800-434-2086 or fax 817-251-8174.

For authorization to photocopy items for corporate, personal, or educational use, please contact Copyright Clearance Center, 222 Rosewood Drive, Danvers, MA 01923, or fax 508-750-4470.

is a trademark under exclusive license to IDG Books Worldwide, Inc., from International Data Group, Inc.

About the Author

Mark Kellner has been published as a journalist since 1972, when as a high school student he wrote a weekly column for the *Queens Tribune* in New York City. He's written the "On Computers" column for *The Washington Times* since March 1991. During this time, Mark has published more than 250 articles evaluating Windows and Macintosh hardware and software, as well as the Internet and other leading technologies.

Along with the "On Computers" column, Mark writes about technology for many national publications. In the past year, he's been a contributor to *Communications Week, InfoWorld,* and *Nation's Business* magazines, and written a technology opinion piece for the *San Francisco Examiner.* He's also been published in *PC World, InformationWeek, MacWeek,* and *Computer Buyer's Guide and Handbook* magazines. He makes regular appearances on WAMU-FM's "Derek McGinty Show" as one of the "Software Sages," dispensing practical advice to callers.

From 1993 to 1994, Mark was Editorial Director of (and then Editorial Consultant to) *Mobile Office* and *Portable Computing* magazines. For *Mobile Office,* Mark also created, compiled, and edited a special software section. Prior to that, Mark was Editor of "The Report on AT&T," an independent newsletter based in Alexandria, Virginia. He was also Washington Correspondent and later News Editor at *MISWeek* and a Senior Reporter for *Federal Computer Week,* as well as a Senior Editor of *UNIX Today!* He was a general assignment reporter for the *Wilkes-Barre Times Leader* in Pennsylvania, and he has been published in newspapers and magazines in Canada, Britain, and Australia.

Outside of technology, Mark has written on a variety of subjects for *Delta Sky* magazine, *Travel Weekly,* Religious News Service, *Christianity Today,* and *The Detroit News.* An avid stamp collector, Mark is Editor of *The Philatelic Communicator,* the quarterly journal of the American Philatelic Society's Writer's Unit. He is also a member of the National Press Club and for two years served on its membership committee.

Mark currently resides in Reston, Virginia with his wife, Jean, and their cats, Tony and George. *God on the Internet* is his second book; his first, *WordPerfect 3.5 For Macs For Dummies,* was published in 1995 by IDG Books Worldwide. You can contact Mark via e-mail at `MarkKel@aol.com` or through his Internet home page, `http://www.reston.com/kellner/kellner.html`.

Welcome to the world of IDG Books Worldwide.

IDG Books Worldwide, Inc., is a subsidiary of International Data Group, the world's largest publisher of computer-related information and the leading global provider of information services on information technology. IDG was founded more than 25 years ago and now employs more than 7,700 people worldwide. IDG publishes more than 250 computer publications in 67 countries (see listing below). More than 70 million people read one or more IDG publications each month.

Launched in 1990, IDG Books Worldwide is today the #1 publisher of best-selling computer books in the United States. We are proud to have received 8 awards from the Computer Press Association in recognition of editorial excellence and three from Computer Currents' First Annual Readers' Choice Awards, and our best-selling ...*For Dummies* series has more than 19 million copies in print with translations in 28 languages. IDG Books Worldwide, through a joint venture with IDG's Hi-Tech Beijing, became the first U.S. publisher to publish a computer book in the People's Republic of China. In record time, IDG Books Worldwide has become the first choice for millions of readers around the world who want to learn how to better manage their businesses.

Our mission is simple: Every one of our books is designed to bring extra value and skill-building instructions to the reader. Our books are written by experts who understand and care about our readers. The knowledge base of our editorial staff comes from years of experience in publishing, education, and journalism — experience which we use to produce books for the '90s. In short, we care about books, so we attract the best people. We devote special attention to details such as audience, interior design, use of icons, and illustrations. And because we use an efficient process of authoring, editing, and desktop publishing our books electronically, we can spend more time ensuring superior content and spend less time on the technicalities of making books.

You can count on our commitment to deliver high-quality books at competitive prices on topics you want to read about. At IDG Books Worldwide, we continue in the IDG tradition of delivering quality for more than 25 years. You'll find no better book on a subject than one from IDG Books Worldwide.

John J. Kilcullen

John Kilcullen
President and CEO
IDG Books Worldwide, Inc.

IDG Books Worldwide, Inc., is a subsidiary of International Data Group, the world's largest publisher of computer-related information and the leading global provider of information services on information technology. International Data Group publishes over 250 computer publications in 67 countries. Seventy million people read one or more International Data Group publications each month. International Data Group's publications include: **ARGENTINA:** Computerworld Argentina, GamePro, Infoworld, PC World Argentina; **AUSTRALIA:** Australian Macworld, Client/Server Journal, Digital News, Network World, PC World, Publishing Essentials, Reseller; **AUSTRIA:** Computerwelt, PC TEST; **BELARUS:** PC World Belarus; **BELGIUM:** Data News; **BRAZIL:** Annuário de Informática, Computerworld Brazil, Connections, Super Game Power, Macworld, PC World Brazil, Publish Brazil, SUPERGAME; **BULGARIA:** Computerworld Bulgaria, Networkworld/Bulgaria, PC & MacWorld Bulgaria; **CANADA:** CIO Canada, ComputerWorld Canada, InfoCanada, Network World Canada, Reseller World; **CHILE:** Computerworld Chile, GamePro, PC World Chile; **COLUMBIA:** Computerworld Colombia, GamePro, PC World Colombia; **COSTA RICA:** PC World Costa Rica/Nicaragua; **THE CZECH AND SLOVAK REPUBLICS:** Computerworld Czechoslovakia, Elektronika Czechoslovakia, PC World Czechoslovakia; **DENMARK:** Communications World, Computerworld Danmark, Macworld Danmark, PC World Danmark, PC World Danmark Supplements, TECH World; **DOMINICAN REPUBLIC:** PC World Republica Dominicana; **ECUADOR:** PC World Ecuador, GamePro; **EGYPT:** Computerworld Middle East, PC World Middle East; **EL SALVADOR:** PC World Centro America; **FINLAND:** MikroPC, Tietoverkko, Tietoviikko; **FRANCE:** Distributique, Golden, Info PC, Le Guide du Monde Informatique, Le Monde Informatique, Reseaux & Telecoms; **GERMANY:** Computer Business, Computerwoche, Computerwoche Extra, Computerwoche Focus, Electronic Entertainment, GamePro, I/M Information Management, Macwelt, PC Welt; **GREECE:** GamePro, Macworld & Publish; **GUATEMALA:** PC World Centro America; **HONDURAS:** PC World Centro America; **HONG KONG:** Computerworld Hong Kong, PCWorld Hong Kong, Publish in Asia; **HUNGARY:** ABCD CD-ROM, Computerworld Szamitastechnika, PC & Mac World Hungary, PC-X Magazine; **INDIA:** Computerworld India, PC World India, Publish in Asia; **INDONESIA:** InfoKomputer PC World, Komputek Computerworld, Publish in Asia; **IRELAND:** ComputerScope, PC Live!; **ISRAEL:** PC World 32 BIT, People & Computers; **ITALY:** Computerworld Italia, Computerworld Italia Special Editions, Lotus Italia, Macworld Italia, Networking Italia, PC Shopping, PC World Italia, PC World/Walt Disney; **JAPAN:** Macworld Japan, Nikkei Personal Computing, SunWorld Japan, Windows World Japan; **KENYA:** East African Computer News; **KOREA:** Hi-Tech Information/Computerworld, Macworld Korea, PC World Korea; **MACEDONIA:** PC World Macedonia; **MALAYSIA:** Computerworld Malaysia, PC World Malaysia, Publish in Asia; **MEXICO:** Computerworld Mexico, GamePro, Macworld, PC World Mexico; **MYANMAR:** PC World Myanmar; **NETHERLANDS:** Computable, Computer! Totaal, LAN Magazine, Macworld, Net Magazine; **NEW ZEALAND:** Computer Buyer, Computerworld New Zealand, MTB, Network World, PC World New Zealand; **NICARAGUA:** PC World Costa Rica/Nicaragua; **NIGERIA:** PC World Africa; **NORWAY:** Computerworld Norge, Computerworld Privat, CW Rapport Klient/Tjener, CW Rapport Nettverk & Telecom, CW Rapport Offentlig Sektor, IDG's KURSGUIDE, Macworld Norge, Multimedia World, PC World Ekspress, PC World Nettverk, PC World Norge, PC World's Produktguide, Windows Spesial; **PAKISTAN:** Computerworld Pakistan, PC World Pakistan; **PANAMA:** GamePro, PC World Panama; **PARAGUAY:** PC World Paraguay; **P. R. OF CHINA:** China Computerworld, China Infoworld, Computer & Communication, Electronic Product World, Electronics Today, Game Camp, PC World China, Popular Computer Week, Software World, Telecom Product World; **PERU:** Computerworld Peru, GamePro, PC World Profesional Peru, PC World Peru; **POLAND:** Computerworld Poland, Computerworld Special Report, Macworld, Networld, PC World Komputer; **PHILIPPINES:** Computerworld Philippines, PC Digest, Publish in Asia; **PORTUGAL:** Cerebro/PC World, Correio Informático/Computerworld, Mac•In/PC•In Portugal; **PUERTO RICO:** PC World Puerto Rico; **ROMANIA:** Computerworld Romania, PC World Romania, Telecom Romania; **RUSSIA:** Computerworld Rossiya, Network World Russia, PC World Russia; **SINGAPORE:** Computerworld Singapore, PC World Singapore, Publish in Asia; **SLOVENIA:** MONITOR; **SOUTH AFRICA:** Computing S.A., Network World S.A., Software World; **SPAIN:** Computerworld España, COMUNICACIONES WORLD, Dealer World, Macworld España, PC World España; **SWEDEN:** CAP&Design, Computer Sweden, Corporate Computing, MacWorld, Maxi Data, MikroDatorn, Nätverk & Kommunikation, PC/Aktiv, PC World, Windows World; **SWITZERLAND:** Computerworld Schweiz, Macworld Schweiz, PCtip; **TAIWAN:** Computerworld Taiwan, Macworld Taiwan, PC World Taiwan, Publish Taiwan, Windows World; **THAILAND:** Thai Computerworld, Publish in Asia; **TURKEY:** Computerworld Monitör, MACWORLD Turkiye, PC WORLD Turkiye; **UKRAINE:** Computerworld Kiev, Computers & Software Magazine, PC World Ukraine; **UNITED KINGDOM:** Acorn User, Amiga Action, Amiga Computing, Amiga, Appletalk, CD Powerplay, CD-ROM Now, Computing, Connexion, GamePro, Lotus Magazine, Macaction, Macworld, Open Computing, Parents and Computers, PC Home, PC News, The WEB; **UNITED STATES:** Cable in the Classroom, CD Review, CIO Magazine, Computerworld, Computerworld Client/Server Journal, Digital Video Magazine, DOS World, Electronic, InfoWorld, I-Way, Macworld, Maximize, MULTIMEDIA WORLD, Network World, PC World, PUBLISH, SWATPro Magazine, Video Event, WebMaster; **URUGUAY:** PC World Uruguay; **VENEZUELA:** Computerworld Venezuela, GamePro, PC World Venezuela; and **VIETNAM:** PC World Vietnam   10/17/95

Dedication

Writing books is a relatively new thing for me; therefore, I wish to acknowledge a few of those from whose work I have gained much:

Rev. Dr. Norman Vincent Peale, whom I first met nearly 20 years ago and who is now at home with his Lord, and whose writing offers valuable lessons for those willing to learn;

Rev. Arthur A. Caliandro, whose message of positive faith is so ably communicated from the platform, via broadcast and in print;

Dr. Robert H. Schuller, perhaps the most active exponent of vibrant faith, whose words have touched the lives of millions, including this writer;

David Neff, a gifted thinker, analyst and editorialist, and a man for whom I've been privileged to work;

Ruth A. Tucker, Ph.D., whose work is a model of clarity, vision, and charity, while not compromising on principle or doctrine;

Barbara Grizzuti Harrison, whose book, *Visions of Glory,* set a high standard for non-theologians writing about religion. Her sparkle, freshness, and intimacy of writing are at once a delight and a challenge.

Particular gratitude is due my wife, Jean Kellner, for inspiration, encouragement, guidance and support — as well as patience ably demonstrated during countless days and nights of Web-browsing and book writing. Thanks, sweetheart.

My thanks and appreciation to each and to all.

Credits

**Senior Vice President
and Group Publisher**
Brenda McLaughlin

Vice President & Publisher
Christopher J. Williams

Acquisitions Manager
Gregory S. Croy

Acquisitions Editor
Ellen L. Camm

Software Acquisitions Editor
Tracy Lehman Cramer

Marketing Manager
Melisa M. Duffy

Managing Editor
Andy Cummings

Administrative Assistant
Laura J. Moss

Editorial Assistant
Timothy J. Borek

Production Director
Beth Jenkins

Production Assistant
Jacalyn L. Pennywell

**Supervisor of
Project Coordination**
Cindy L. Phipps

Supervisor of Page Layout
Kathie S. Schnorr

Supervisor of Graphics and Design
Shelley Lea

Reprint/Blueline Coordination
Tony Augsburger
Patricia R. Reynolds
Todd Klemme
Theresa Sánchez-Baker

Media/Archive Coordination
Leslie Popplewell
Melissa Stauffer
Jason Marcuson

Senior Development Editor
Erik Dafforn

Editors
Hugh Vandivier
Kerrie Klein

Project Coordinator
J. Tyler Connor

Graphics Coordination
Gina Scott
Angela F. Hunckler

Production Page Layout
E. Shawn Aylsworth
Mark C. Owens
Michael Sullivan

Proofreaders
Michael Hall
Christine Meloy Beck
Gwenette Gaddis
Carl Saff
Robert Springer

Indexer
Sherry Massey

Book Design
Michael Osborne Design

Acknowledgments

Even with one name on the cover, a book is really the product of many hands. I am grateful beyond measure to so many people and organizations whose help and support have made this effort not only worthwhile, but personally rewarding:

Gregory Croy, Ellen Camm, Andy Cummings, and Melisa Duffy of IDG Books Worldwide. These good people are in large part responsible for this book even seeing the light of day.

The incomparable, encouraging, friendly, and persevering Erik Dafforn, editor to the stars — and to people like me. Kim Komando was right in praising you Erik, for you are a super editor!

Hugh Vandivier and Kerrie Klein, who copyedited this tome. Any errors, however, should be charged to me.

Dan Gugler at The Bohle Company, and Mal Ransom and crew at Packard Bell, whose capable, compact, and complete Corner Computer saw me through most of the writing of this book.

Mike Rosenfelt, Matt Gerber, Bob LeVitus, and the team at Power Computer, maker of the best Mac-compatible computers anywhere. Their Power 100 was instrumental in preparing this book, especially the majority of illustrations in Chapter 17.

ADI Systems, Inc. of San Jose, whose MicroScan 17x monitor provided the portrait view seen in many illustrations in this book.

Ed Juge, Rich Baker, Michelle Moran, Andy Boyer, and a cast of thousands at CompuServe. Folks like these just don't come by every day!

Lydia Trettis and Christian Harper of Connors Communications, and Brian Ek and Carol Wallace of Prodigy, all superb when the chips are down.

Margaret Ryan, Karen Jonson, and the America Online team, builders of strong networks and services.

Chris Escher and Susan Marino of eWorld, a service which deserves respect, in no small part because its people respect their clients!

Kristen Fabos and Elaina Dulaney of Waggener Edstrom, Microsoft's PR agency, which cleared the way for me to surf The Microsoft Network.

Brian Muys and PSInet of Herndon, VA, whose Interramp Service is a great way to access the Net.

General Paul A. Rader, Lt. Colonel Peter Dalziel, and Mark Calleran of The Salvation Army, for their collective vision, their implementation of an Internet strategy, and a special thanks to General Rader for his foreword. Also thanks to Robert E. Bearchell and Capt. Kenneth Hodder of the Army's USA Western Territory for their assistance.

Wesley Pruden, Josette Shiner, Ted Agres, Anne Veigle, Harvey Kabaker, Dean Honeycutt, and Anne Marriott of *The Washington Times* — great colleagues all — for their encouragement and support. A special thanks to *Times* columnist Larry Moffitt, whose Internet columns are always well written and always most helpful.

Derek McGinty and Joe Barber of WAMU-FM, for letting me talk about the Internet and software and Mac hardware on the "Derek McGinty Show," and to Cynthia Morgan of *Windows* magazine for being a great radio partner.

Tony Lobl of the Committee on Publication, the Church of Christ, Scientist, for assistance in reporting on their Web site.

Max Bertola of Utah Valley On-Line, for help with the WWW 1st Ward page; and Steve Handy of the *Deseret News* for assistance with the excellent Church News page.

Keith Cowing of Reston Communications, for Web page support and storage. If you need Web space, sent a note to info@reston.com.

Finally, a cast of thousands for their help and inspiration, including, but not limited to: David Coursey, Daniel Dern, Blake Stowell, Lisa Foster, Teri Robinson, Nathan Bergerbest, Tim Gallan, Warren Andreasen, Sattly Atkins, Barbara Reichert, Val Stephen, Dean Rodgers, Keri Walker, Chuck Ashman, Bob Andelman, Jill Ryan, Lesa Davis, Deborah McAlister, and Guy Kawasaki.

(The publisher would like to give special thanks to Patrick J. McGovern, without whom this book would not have been possible.)

Contents at a Glance

Table of Contents

Foreword

Christian faith has always concerned itself with communication and community. At the heart of the Christian Gospel is the affirmation that it is the very nature of God to communicate. For "In the beginning was the Word and the Word was with God and the Word was God" [John 1:1]. That Word took human form in Jesus and "moved into the neighborhood" so that our world could see and grasp His grace and glory. The outcome was the birth of a community — a global network of networks, made up of those who through faith have become the children of God.

Perhaps there is an analog in the phenomenon of the Internet with its incredible capacity for facilitating communication and creating community that transcends political and social boundaries. The technology in itself is arguably morally neutral, without particular spiritual value or moral peril. It can become a vehicle for moral injection that may call for the emergence of a new epidemiology of evil. On the other hand, it can and has already proved its potential for the dissemination of positive Christian truth and resources for spiritual awakening and nurture on a global scale. God and the Gospel are very much alive on the Internet.

Mark Kellner has ably explored the exciting profusion of rapidly burgeoning sources of potential spiritual enrichment and rewarding interaction available on the Internet. Given the exponential growth in the numbers of locations on the Net, a reliable guide is invaluable. Kellner is just such a guide. As with most Web sites, one has the sense this valuable volume, complete as it is, is unavoidably "under construction" even as it goes to press. Having savored what he gives us here, we will be looking for more. That discovery mode is the essence of the Internet — and of the life of faith — found, finding, and yet ever questing for more of God.

General Paul A. Rader
International Leader
The Salvation Army
London, England

(Author's note: General Paul A. Rader is the first American-born international leader of this 131-year-old church, which is perhaps as well known for its social and humanitarian services as it is for its public preaching of the gospel. He was educated at Asbury College, Southern Baptist Seminary, and Fuller Theological Seminary, from which he holds a Doctorate in Missiology. General Rader has pioneered The Salvation Army's entry to the Internet, which is discussed in Chapter 17.)

A Pilgrim and a Stranger

An Unusual Computer Book

I'm a pilgrim, and I'm a stranger;
I can tarry, I can tarry but a night.
Do not detain me, for I am going,
To where the fountains are ever flowing,
I'm a pilgrim, and I'm a stranger;
I can tarry, I can tarry but a night.

— from a hymn by Mary S.B. Dana Shindler

Welcome to *God on the Internet*, which I believe you will find to be a rather unusual computer book. It is intended as a road map to the "information superhighway" for spiritual pilgrims. If you read most other books about computers, software, or especially this "brave new world" of the Internet, you'll find lots of technical jargon. Those new to computing can find this new lingo confusing — to say the least — and even intimidating sometimes.

You'll find relatively little computer lingo in these pages, almost the barest minimum necessary. Instead, I designed this book to be a *resource*. If you're the only Baha'i in Ames, Iowa (and you're probably not), you'll learn how to connect, literally, with others of like mind around the world. If you're a Jew searching for a deeper understanding of your faith, this is the place to begin your exploration. And if you are either unaffiliated or looking for a spiritual home, I hope this volume will help you on your way.

This book isn't only for those on a religious pilgrimage, however. You might be a high school, college, or seminary student who needs to research religions. You might be a rabbi, priest, or minister who needs to know about another tradition's teachings. Or you might be a missionary, at home or abroad, who wants to gather information about the religions found in the area where you are headed.

This book will serve as your introduction and will offer information on a *variety* of religious traditions and spiritual paths. I do *not* intend to bash any religion or proclaim one faith superior to another. Respect for both freedom of religion and the views of others undergird, I hope, every page in this book.

As you'll read elsewhere:

> **The references in this book are for informational purposes and are not an endorsement of any theology, philosophy, or tenet expressed by any organization.**

The views expressed by participants in the online services and Internet Web sites, discussion groups, and mailing lists *may not* reflect those of this writer, IDG Books Worldwide, or its editorial staff.

If you are reading this book, I assume that you are mature enough to make your own decisions about religion. If you are a minor, you should discuss what you find with a parent or guardian. Regardless of your age, please carefully weigh the claims of *any* movement before committing time, resources, or money.

Above all, keep an open mind as you explore this book and the sites you encounter along the way. You do not necessarily have to become an adherent of any religion or group in order to appreciate something that you find within their beliefs or practices. Also, there's no law to keep you from privately adopting some aspect of a given belief system in your own life, if you so desire.

Whether you find anything new in which to believe or even if you use this book just as a stepping stone to explore your own tradition more fully, please know that the journey is part of the fun. In the months I've spent writing this book, I felt as if I was on a world tour. Indeed, with online stops at the Vatican, Jerusalem, India, China, Japan, and all over the United States, I often feel as if I've been on a rather long journey. It's been intriguing, educational, and informative, and I look forward to continuing my spiritual trek for subsequent editions of this book and other projects.

How This Book is Organized

Like Gaul, this book is divided into three parts, or main sections. Part I, "Looking for God in All the Right Places," will give you a sense of what people are finding, spiritually, online in this age. You'll also learn the basics of what you need to go online and some pointers on how to best take advantage of the online world, including some opinions on proper "netiquette."

Part II, "The Major Online Services," deals with the online services that you may have heard the most about, or with which you are most familiar. You'll get the inside story on America Online, CompuServe, eWorld, Prodigy, and the Microsoft Network (among others), and you'll learn what spiritual resources are available on these services. Included is the latest news about AT&T's new Interchange service (which it bought from Ziff-Davis) and about the recent changes in America Online's religion section.

Part III, "Finding Your Faith On The Internet," is the largest section of this book. In this part, you'll take a look at major communities of faith online, as well as some smaller ones. Did you know that the online services helped foment a schism in a 60-year-old denomination? Have you heard about the church that some believe is trying to "break" the Internet? Where can you go to find out if your aura is more than just a pleasant personality? Check out this section and you'll see.

In this section, I've tried to include a representative, but not exhaustive, series of links to various locations on the Internet. Why not print every single location I could find? For one, I figure that you probably have a phone book or two in your home and little desire to add another. For another, the links I've selected represent what I consider to be among the best available, *and* they often have links to other locations. Add the capability to interactively search the Web to the other links, and this book, like a compass, will point you in the right direction, ready for plenty of hiking.

What You'll Find Here

In short, you'll find just about anything in these pages. A lot of personal opinion, based on more than 13 years of online computer experience, from the days when CompuServe was a text-based wonder at 300 baud up to today, when Windows 95 and a 28.8 modem are almost standard issue. My views also stem from a lifelong fascination with religion, which has led me in a variety of directions. I've written about religious news stories for daily newspapers in Pennsylvania and Washington, D.C., for Religious News Service, *Charisma* magazine, and *Christianity Today*.

This dual track of interest in technology and religion led to the development of this book. I believe — and have seen — that the power of religious faith can sustain and change people's lives, including my own. If one single force contributes to the stability of a society, the development of a culture, and even the flourishing of art, it has been that of a culture of faith, freely expressed. This book aids those who are interested in expanding their spiritual horizons.

You'll also receive some background information on both the online services discussed here and the faith communities described. These sketches may, of necessity, be brief, and such brevity is designed to keep the focus on the technology used by a group. It is not intended to slight any group. For the greatest volume of information on a given movement, you are likely to find it at the source — that group's Web page.

I've also included many illustrations of Web pages. These have often been "captured" from a 17-inch portrait display monitor to show the greatest amount of the given page. Obviously, sites change and designs change, so please understand that what you see in this book may not exactly match what you see on the Net.

A Personal Word and Warning

Some people will read this book and wonder why I included site A but not site B. Others will ask why I didn't "bash" this or that religious group because, obviously, *they* are not as right thinking as *we* are. Still others may question my sanity for saying something *nice* about group X or sect Y.

If the largely nonjudgmental approach I've taken here offends you, my apologies. I know what I believe, and I am happy to enter into a dialog with any reader who desires one (see next section), but I just don't see my place as being that of judge, jury, and executioner. The tragic events of this century — the anti-Catholic bias still extant in early Twentieth Century America; the horrors of Nazism; the tragedy of religious strife in the Middle East, Northern Ireland, and now Bosnia — should convince most people that religious prejudice is not the way to achieve stability or maintain freedom.

I may or may not agree with a given religion, but outlawing it or persecuting it will not make life easier for me. Instead, it could easily make life more difficult because someone will very likely come along and object to *my* beliefs. Thus, I must defend the freedom of others to help preserve my own.

If you're looking for a critical evaluation of religions, an "us versus them" approach, plenty of books, both good and bad, are available for you to read. If you're looking for a prism through which you can view the broad spectrum of religious thought available online today, keep reading.

Let's Communicate

In his kind foreword to this edition, General Paul A. Rader, international leader of The Salvation Army, was prescient in sensing this as a work in progress. I hope that subsequent editions will contain additional resources, more information, and greater usefulness. For that, I would welcome your help.

You may write to me in care of IDG Books or send electronic mail to MarkKel@aol.com. In addition, you can visit my home page (http://www.reston.com/kellner/kellner.html) and send a message from there. However you do it, please keep in touch, and please know that I am interested in your opinions, corrections, criticisms, and comments.

May God bless you today!

Mark A. Kellner
Reston, Virginia
March 1996

Looking for God in All the Right Places

What Is God Doing Online?

Saving a Man from Death, Online: A True Story

One October evening in 1994, two people — a Florida home-maker and a Virginia computer specialist — reached out to save the life of a third man, someone they'd never seen, met, or even knew.

The event began when Sharon Herbitter logged on to the CompuServe Information Service, one of the oldest and largest online networks in the U.S., to check messages posted on a special electronic "bulletin board," the Christian Interactive Network.

Herbitter read a message from a man called Bill (not his real name): "Please pray for us. Last night Sue said that she had no love left for me, and money was the only thing stopping a divorce." Further, Bill said that he had "tried to end it tonight" by locking himself in his truck and breathing carbon monoxide fumes. A Christian radio station brought him back, but he wrote, "I don't know how long I can resist the need to be free from the hurt."

At that moment, Herbitter took action. Checking with other CompuServe subscribers logged into the Christian Interactive Network section, she tried to find out who "Bill" was, and failing that, she started an online prayer session, typing in words of supplication and intercession in a group conversation with others.

Soon, the group was joined by Kevin Tupper, a 28-year-old computer consultant in the Virginia suburbs of Washington, D.C. Tupper had also read Bill's plea, and while acknowledging the need for prayer, he decided to take action as well.

Using an online directory service, Tupper soon found the location of the potential suicide. Tupper called the local county sheriff's department and had to convince a dispatcher his call was not a hoax and that someone several hundred miles away was in danger of dying.

The deputy, however, soon discovered that it wasn't a hoax. Dispatched to Bill's house, he saw lights on but no movement. Prying open a garage door, he confronted billowing clouds of exhaust. Bill was unconscious. He later awoke confused. Hospitalization and counseling followed.

In the weeks that followed, Bill joined an online chat with Herbitter and Tupper, and thanked them for saving his life.

"He was making a cry for help," Tupper told *People* magazine, "and he got some. Now he thinks God must have some sort of reason for him to be alive."

The Phenomenal Growth of Religion Online

This story is true. The potentially tragic outcome was avoided because two people used their computers, their brains, and their hands to reach out to someone in need. If there's a better reason for believers to find fellowship with others online, I can't think of it.

In the roughly 15 years that online services have been available to the public, millions of people have discovered their computers as a place for communication and interaction, and not just a way to crunch spreadsheet numbers. Fast forward to the last two or three years and you'll see multiple millions of people signing up for Internet access and online services such as CompuServe, America Online, and Prodigy. In the past 18 months, Apple Computer and Microsoft Corporation have jumped into the online fray, launching eWorld and the Microsoft Network. Even AT&T, which in the early part of this century brought the nation's disparate phone systems into a single unified network, purchased Interchange, an online service.

For many of us, electronic mail, online networks, and the Internet — best described for the moment as a network of computer networks — form an integral part of our daily lives. When I arise in the morning, before I go out to get the newspaper, I check my desktop computer for e-mail messages and news that has come in overnight. During the day, every 20 minutes, a special software program checks my electronic mailboxes on three services and beeps to let me know if a message has arrived.

If you work in an office or at a university, you may well have a desktop computer hooked into a local-area network. In turn, that network hooks into a *mail server*, through which you can send and receive electronic mail to and from anywhere on the planet. In one office I know about, many of the workers start each morning with a "Word of the Day" message, a scripture verse selected and sent by one man in Redwood City, California, to an international mailing list. It's an encouragement for those who receive these daily bursts of inspiration.

As you will see in the following pages, online services and the Internet are worth more to religious-minded individuals than a crisis intervention service or a neat way to receive a daily spiritual vitamin. Electronic communication has created a digital "Speaker's Corner" where, as at the real one in London's Hyde Park, anyone can have his or her say on issues of the day. Unlike the British version, however, the online forums are available 24 hours a day, seven days a week — not just on Sunday afternoons. These services have also linked members of large and small churches in ways previously unimaginable: people discover shared interests and exchange ideas.

Further, for those people who want to research the basics of their faith, learn about the beliefs of others, or get help in a special area of research, today's online technology offers manifold opportunities for those interested in reaching out to a world of information from their desks or dens.

In short, using a computer to reach out for information and fellowship is no longer an odd or unusual practice. It's commonplace, yet it provides an uncommon capability to reach far beyond local resources.

Will this trend wane? Most likely not. Almost half of all American households (46 percent) now own a computer, according to a mid-1995 study conducted by Casey Communications/Shandwick in cooperation with EPIC-MRA. American consumers are also increasingly becoming wired to the Internet: Of all computer owners, 16 percent subscribe to on-line computer services with Internet access.

According to SIMBA Media Information, Inc., a research firm that studied the growth potential for the Internet in 1995, the picture through the end of the century is bright: Internet usage will grow by 62.4 percent each year through the year 2000. Other studies indicate that 20 or 30 million people worldwide are connected to the Internet (although these figures are disputed), which means that a 62 percent annual rate of growth would give us an Internet community of nearly 250 million people worldwide by 2000, using the lower estimate. That's a population roughly equal to that of the United States.

Even if the growth figures aren't that prodigious, the advent of larger groups of online users means more opportunity for us all to connect and interconnect. To those searching for fellowship, information, and inspiration, that has to be good news.

What's Available: An Overview

If you wanted to ask questions of a noted religious leader, say the Archbishop of New York, Evangelist Billy Graham, or Tibetan Buddhist leader the Dalai Lama, where would you go?

Perhaps you wanted to get the latest on the Dead Sea Scrolls, look up a reference in the Vatican Library, or check out key Islamic texts and teachings, where might you turn?

In the old days — say, back before 1993 — your first stop would likely have been your local public library, or better still a college or university library. There, you could consult a book written by one of these luminaries or perhaps consult write-ups on the Dead Sea Scrolls. If you had the time and money, you might take a trip to visit, say, the Vatican or the Jewish Museum in Jerusalem, where the Scrolls are on display. The most adventurous might go to India to hear the Dalai Lama lecture.

Today, no such expensive travel is required. You can approach many of these leaders online or tap into the research resources you need. You can begin with the top online services, America Online, CompuServe, and Prodigy. (This isn't to neglect the other online providers. I'll cover them elsewhere in these pages. Also, you should know that each of these three online services, among others, provides connections to the Internet, which lets you explore more than their content alone.)

America Online (AOL)

Billy Graham, who has preached the Christian gospel message to more people than anyone in history, was the first major religious figure to go online, in a 1993 conference with *Time* magazine on America Online. The event drew thousands of digital spectators, who asked the renowned evangelist dozens of questions.

Since that time, AOL has hosted conversations and appearances of other religious leaders, among the most recently notable being His Holiness, the Dalai Lama, who is the leader of Tibetan Buddhists. During his visit to Harvard University, the Dalai Lama's remarks were covered, live, by AOL, which had reporters typing in the remarks in real-time.

Two forums dominate AOL's religion coverage, as we'll see in Chapter 4. One, the Religion Forum, contains messages, files, and other items for people of all faiths. This is a home of heated debate on all sides of theological issues and a resource for files of information, graphics, and software.

The other, Christianity Online, is a product of *Christianity Today* magazine, the leading evangelical journal. Christianity Online includes the text of each issue of *CT*, plus text of other magazines published by the company — and *Christian Computing*, which is independently owned.

In addition, Christianity Online includes the following:

◆ message boards for church members and church leaders

◆ advertising of Christian products

◆ job opportunities

◆ regular conferences discussing Christian issues and personalities (the contemporary Christian singing group Point of Grace is a popular online guest)

◆ a software library full of goodies to download (as with the Religion Forum)

America Online is running neck-and-neck with CompuServe for the title of "largest online service," with both groups claiming in excess of 3.5 million members as of this writing. AOL will tell you that its membership is almost exclusively based in the United States, whereas CompuServe's total membership includes many people around the world. By the time you read these words, however, AOL's picture may well have changed: the company expects to launch its service into Britain and Europe, with an eventual presence in Asia and elsewhere.

CompuServe

The oldest commercial online service (established in 1979), CompuServe started life 11 years earlier as a time sharing service for businesses, which tapped into large computer systems to process tax returns and the like. When the system's owners — H&R Block, the income tax people — discovered that the computers were idle for a certain percentage of the time, the idea of reselling *that* time to consumers was born, and so was CompuServe.

CompuServe boasts 3,000 separate services in its portfolio, and while I haven't visited them all, there is certainly something for everyone. In the religion area, CompuServe's forums might well be the "mother of all bulletin boards," featuring discussion areas for believers — and non-believers — of every stripe, as well as software libraries galore.

While CompuServe does not have an alliance with a major religious publication, it does have important affiliations. The Christian Interactive Network is geared towards evangelical users and was the place where Sharon Herbitter found out that Bill was in trouble.

For members of the Roman Catholic Church, the world's largest Christian denomination, Catholic Online provides a place to meet, greet, grow, and learn.

On Catholic Online, a specialized area on the CompuServe Information Service, you can, for example, research ancient church documents, network with Catholics worldwide, and discuss modern-day issues affecting the Catholic faith. Catholic Online (GO CATHOLIC) is dedicated to bringing information, assistance, and an online community to the worldwide membership of the Roman Catholic Church. Catholic Online organizers say that it offers the largest and most extensive Catholic resource available for today's personal computer user.

"Our success the first month has been phenomenal," says Michael Galloway, Catholic Online's founder. "We have enrolled thousands of subscribers from more than 100 countries, including presidents of several Latin American nations. Catholic Online not only tells members about current topics facing the American and international church, but also catalogs the resources that address these issues."

Another good resource on CompuServe is extensive access to a variety of news and information sources, from *People* magazine and *U.S. News & World Report* (where Jeff Shaler does extensive religion reporting) to the Dialog Information Services database of newspaper texts, available through the NewsSource USA service on CompuServe. All of these research tools cost varying amounts of money, but if you need to find just about everything on a given topic, this is a good place to start. (Other online services also offer extensive news resources, and these will be discussed elsewhere.)

Prodigy

Two areas highlight Prodigy's involvement in religion: substantial online chat forums that evoke much user participation, and innovative guests.

Prodigy's proudest moment so far has been its role as the online debut spot for John Cardinal O'Connor, the Archbishop of New York, who for one hour in 1995 answered questions from a multitude of participants. Some of the questions were flippant, others were serious, all were challenging. News reports indicated that Cardinal O'Connor was impressed by the human emotion evident in the questions posed.

The group's religious forums maintain much of the vigor found in similar forums on the other major services. Surprising results often result from messages posted online. One young woman was seeking help as she prepared to leave a group she described as a religious "cult." Almost instantly, she received messages of support and encouragement.

Like the other services, Prodigy also offers access to many publications. One worth particular mention here is *The Los Angeles Times*, whose religion reporting — by Larry Stammer and John Dart, among other staffers — never fails to impress me for its scope, depth, and even-handedness. When I lived in Los Angeles and even now, this newspaper's religion news was and is something I find well worth reading. With Prodigy's TimesLink, you can access this award-winning newspaper easily.

The Internet and Specialized Religion Nets

By now, very few people who use or know of online service are not aware of the Internet. Not since the days of Gutenberg — whose printing of the Bible with movable type sparked a communications revolution of its own — has there been a communications revolution to equal that found on computer screens around the globe. The Internet, a "network of computer networks," is linking upwards of 20 million people, globally, in an electronic community, where all kinds of information can be found and exchanged.

Originally the brainchild of defense and research scientists, the Internet has grown from a mere forum for such specialists into a massive "town square" that operates on a 24-hour, seven-day basis. The Internet is a collection of computer networks that have been designed to interconnect with each other using standardized communications protocols. These protocols allow computers attached to these networks to "speak," or exchange data, with each other. The most common protocol is TCP/IP (Transfer Connection Protocol/Internet Protocol), which evolved out of the Unix software community.

With this common data language, Internet-linked computers can then share graphics, text, audio, and video clips in common formats. The combination of these elements came into focus four years ago with the introduction of the *World Wide Web* (also known as *the Web*, or *WWW*). The Web was created by Tim Berners-Lee and a programming team at CERN, the European Particle Physics Laboratory in Switzerland. The standards created there allowed physicists to organize and access research data.

These standards compose a text coding system, or markup language. With this language, you can use special codes to display a graphical document on a Web browser. You can also search for it using *hotlinks*, which are cross-references to other Web sites. The browser software, of which Netscape and Mosaic are the most popular, allows users to search the Web by topic and find those sites that are of personal interest. Figure 1-1 is an example of a religious site on the World Wide Web.

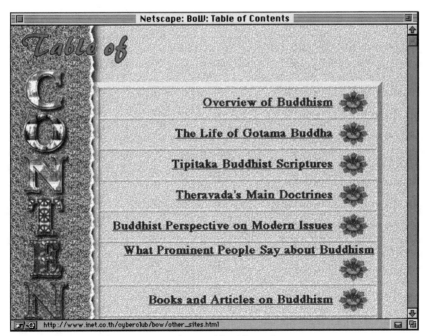

Figure 1-1: A Buddhism site on the World Wide Web.

All this has given rise to a variety of specialized Web sites that meet individual needs. For example, the Lubavitcher branch of Orthodox Judaism maintains branches, known as *Chabad Houses* all over the globe. Now, one of these is in Cyberspace, and the Lubavitch rabbi who runs it says it is the only Chabad House where he can always find observant Jews, but where he can never reach a *minyan*, the assembly of 10 Bar Mitzvahed (confirmed) Jews required for a prayer service.

Within the online world, Christian denominations have set up their own shops online. The Assemblies of God, Church of the Nazarene, Baptists, and Episcopalians have each established special areas on one of the major networks, and some have Web sites as well. Followers of Islam have Internet sites of their own, with some offering audio clips of prayers and readings from the Holy Q'uran, their sacred text.

Religious movements that are newer to the West have also become an online presence. Buddhists have several Web sites and "mailing lists" through which information is communicated. Followers of Soka Gakki, the Nichiren Buddhist sect based in Japan, have their own Web site. The Baha'is, a group whose origins go back to Islamic and Persian religious tradition, are also online in various forums and on the Web.

What all of these locations — and dozens more — have in common is a dual focus of outreach and fellowship. For those who are interested in these movements, the outreach offers an entree that is painless and private. For those who find themselves isolated from a given religious community — you're the only Baha'I in Clark County, let's say — the Internet and online services provide a link to those of like mind.

The value of these services, as we'll see, is virtually priceless. In a world where even spirituality is pressed by an "instant" culture that favors the microwave over the slow-cooker, acquiring information online quickly is most helpful. When it comes to connecting with others, the value of the online world is not only speed, but a collapsing of time as well as distance.

You could, for example, post a request one evening before going to bed. Overnight, readers in other time zones would see that message and respond, while you sleep. The next morning, your answer could well be in your e-mail inbox, thanks to those who answered while you rested, at a speed far greater than air mail and for a cost (usually free) that is less than faxing.

Perhaps the greatest benefit of these forums, as you shall see, is that you can expose your ideas and questions to people whom you have never met. By posting a message electronically, literally thousands of individuals will read it, and one of these readers might well have an answer or comment that you need. If the writer of Proverbs was at it today, "Cast your bread upon the waters" might well be rendered "Post your message on the Net and it shall return to you after a few hours."

CyberWorship Now! Online Services and Study Groups in Real-Time

One Sunday in October, 1995, the supreme pontiff of the Roman Catholic Church, His Holiness John Paul II, celebrated Mass at Camden Yards Stadium in Baltimore, Maryland. Tens of thousands of people packed the home of the Orioles for the solemn celebration. The place where, a few weeks earlier, baseball star Cal Ripken shattered Lou Gehrig's record of consecutive game appearances became an open-air cathedral.

It also became an online cathedral, as thousands of people locked on to America Online and a Catholic site on the Internet for live coverage of the Mass. Just as AOL did for the Dalai Lama, the service used on-site reporters to type in the ceremony as it happened.

On the Internet, however, the Mass was transmitted live in both audio and video to those whose computers were equipped with high speed connections to receive the massive amounts of data involved. While the service was also carried on cable TV networks, this computer transmission brought the event to interested people around the world, as well as within the United States.

The Papal Mass in Baltimore, brought to your computer in real-time, is just one example of online worship taking place every day. Informally, Christians meet for prayer sessions, typing in their requests as opposed to saying them verbally. Jews gather to study and debate the Talmud, with commentary on the scriptures that is pondered by observant Jews worldwide. Buddhists gather to exchange ideas in online groups as well.

You can find some of these discussions in regular places on CompuServe, AOL, and Prodigy. Others are ad hoc: using a computer-based "CB" feature called Internet Relay Chat, you can log onto the Net and connect with fellow believers around the globe in real-time.

In Montclair, New Jersey, the Central Presbyterian Church sponsors an online church, where you can log in to read sermons, participate in discussions, and hear religious music clips. Some wags have dubbed it the "First Church of Cyberspace."

"This is a whole new frontier for religion," said Rev. Charles P. Henderson, pastor of Central Presbyterian and founder of the online venture, in *The New York Times*. "We can find a whole new constituency in cyberspace."

The Amazing Results of Religion Online

It's too early to measure all of the results of online religion, but one thing is clear: the electronic world has opened up new vistas of communication and fellowship among believers and across denominational lines.

The Salvation Army, for example, is not only a social welfare organization but a church with 1.4 million members worldwide. For months, many American pastors and leaders in the church have been sharing ideas, as well as prayer concerns, on America Online. Many victories have been reported, and leaders say they have gained new ideas.

Captain Raphael Jackson, who coordinates activities in several Salvation Army centers in New Jersey, exchanged ideas with other workers in North Carolina and Arizona. In several messages, Captain Jackson wrote of his appreciation for this help, which would not have come otherwise.

For others, the revelations have been less profound, perhaps, but equally real. New friendships have emerged, inquiries have been answered, and faith has been strengthened.

In a world of greater fragmentation and isolation, the arrival of electronic services can bring millions of us together and spark exchanges that build communities and nations. When people of faith use this medium, the message gains strength and resonance, as you'll see in the ensuing pages.

What You Need to Get Online

Getting on the Internet — or beginning to work with online services — sounds like fun. It is. And you've seen, in Chapter One, that those people who engage in spiritual pursuits online can often find great personal rewards.

But how do you get from point A, where you're interested in accessing these resources, to point B, where you're actually online? The answer can be simple or complex, depending on several factors, not the least being whether you own a computer.

I'm not trying to be "smart" here, by the way. I hope that some people reading this volume will not yet be computer veterans and that the promise of online connection to spiritual information will then motivate some people to buy their own equipment. Even without a computer, though, you can sample the Internet at least, thanks to many "free" or "public" Internet connections available around the country, as I'll discuss later in this chapter.

For now, let's look at the things you need to do to get online.

What to Do if You Have a Computer

If you are already the proud owner of a computer, hooking up to the Internet and to online services is very easy. For most computer owners who've bought machines since, say, 1992, the most basic components of computer connectivity are already included.

For the rest of us, or for those of us who have perhaps older or different equipment, we may need to *upgrade* what we have before we're able to take the greatest advantage of the online world.

What are the rock-bottom essential items you need to connect online?

Computers

Generally, either an Apple Macintosh (or clone) or a Windows-compatible (80386 or greater Intel chip or compatible) machine, running a current version of the proper operating system. For Mac owners, this means System 7.1 or greater, and preferably System 7.5. On the Windows side, it's either Windows 95 or Windows 3.1 or 3.11, along with MS-DOS 6.22 or higher.

Having these components will give you a generally fast system that can keep up with the massive amounts of data being pumped in from the Internet or an online service.

Modems

Short for *modulator/demodulator*, a modem converts the bits and bytes of computer code into an electrical impulse that can travel across a telephone line or direct connection to the modem of an online service or Internet Service Provider.

Fifteen years ago, a 300 baud modem was considered fast enough for most uses. Today, most new computers arrive with either a 14,400 bits-per-second or 28,800 bits-per-second modem built in. The former speed is sufficient for most Internet connections; the higher speed, also expressed as 28.8 kilobits-per-second (or 28.8 Kbps), is more than adequate for Internet use.

Faster connections are available using the Integrated Services Digital Network, or ISDN, service provided by many telephone companies. Other possible options include direct satellite feeds of an Internet connection (which AT&T Corporation is expected to offer in 1996) and connections via cable television hookups.

In these instances, users can experience super-fast hookups to the Internet, which means even shorter waiting times to access a Web site. (If all this sounds like Greek, this means, simply, that you can spend less time waiting for information you want with these high-speed connections.)

Regardless of which connection you have, you will almost certainly need a corresponding modem to handle the data flow. Dial-up modems generally top out at 28.8 Kbps in speed; ISDN modems can double that. Modems for cable and satellite connections can reach 10 Megabits per second, a truly massive amount of data. Prices for modems can range from around $50 (yes, $50) for a 14.4 Kbps modem to over $400 for an ISDN modem. Prices for the cable and satellite modems haven't been determined as of this writing, but I would not be surprised to see these range up to $1,000, or conversely, to be much less expensive.

Jim Rohn, one of my favorite inspirational authors, once said that, "It's not what something costs, it's what it's worth." He could well have been speaking about modems. It may seem daunting to spend $200 or more for a computer connectivity device, particularly if your home computer came equipped with a modem.

The "worth" of such a device is seen by what it can accomplish. If you're using a 28.8 Kbps modem, you will achieve much of what you want twice as quickly as with a 14.4 Kbps modem. That means you'll spend either less time online or that you will be able to do twice as much in the same time frame. Either way, you'll save money and time, making the investment in a faster modem very worthwhile.

At the same time, don't feel as if you're a second-class citizen if you have "only" a 14.4 Kbps modem or even a slower one. You can do many things with these modems, and, if you don't mind the wait (or if you have a "flat rate" Internet access account and/or cheap local calling to your Internet provider), you can use a slower modem to dip your toe in the online world. There is one caveat, however: most Internet connections require a minimum of 9,600 baud to work properly, particularly if *any* graphics are involved. As mentioned, however, you can buy a 14.4 Kbps modem for as little $50, so it shouldn't be a major problem.

The other big question modem buyers face, particularly on the PC side of things, is whether to purchase an internal or external modem. This depends in part on the kind of PC you own, and on your own tastes. If your PC has sufficient internal *expansion slots*, you can install an internal modem (or have your dealer do it for you). If you're using Windows 95, the "plug and play" feature of that operating system will recognize and configure itself to work with many modems available on the market.

Macintosh users — and many PC users — will most likely want an external modem, which connects via a serial communications port. These modems generally require a separate power supply, but otherwise are similar to internal modems. One advantage is easy portability between machines, and the external modem is a favorite of many users.

Either way, you'll need a modem. Think about what you need, see the guidelines elsewhere in this chapter, and happy shopping.

Software

Users of America Online, CompuServe, eWorld, AT&T Interchange, Microsoft Network, and Prodigy receive their software *free,* either preloaded on a computer or from the online supplier at sign-up, among other means. The Microsoft Network, for example, is included with Windows 95; AOL, CompuServe, and Prodigy have all included their software in a variety of computer magazines and general interest publications. Each of the services also has a toll-free telephone number in the United States and Canada from which you can request software and information.

In short, the online services, like Uncle Sam in the James Montgomery Flagg poster of years ago, *want you.* They want you badly, and they'll make it easy for you to become a customer.

Internet connections are a bit trickier. Mac and Windows users can access the Net, as it's known, with free software from America Online and Prodigy. CompuServe offers free Internet browsing software to Windows users, whereas Mac users receive free browsing software from eWorld. The Microsoft Network supports Microsoft's Internet browser, which comes with the Windows 95 Plus Pack software, and is also available online. Netcom, among other direct-connect Internet services, offers free software as well.

As you'll see, the most popular Internet browser is quite possibly Netscape. Retail versions of Netscape are available for Windows, Windows 95, and the Macintosh, and, as of this writing, Beta and trial versions of the Netscape software are freely available from Netscape's host computers.

Once you have your software and an Internet connection (see the following sections), you're ready to begin.

What to Buy if You're New to Computers and How to Buy It

If you're a newcomer to computing and you want to buy a system, plenty of options are available. Guiding you through each step of the process is beyond the scope of this book, but some general guidelines may help.

Computers

Whether you buy a Macintosh or a Windows-compatible machine, you will want something with the horsepower necessary to perform the tasks you want. That most likely means a PowerPC processor on the Macintosh side (it's the latest Mac chip and prices on some PowerPC-based systems are low) or a Pentium chip if Windows is your choice. You'll want a color monitor and the kind of display that supports it. Your hard disk should be at least 540 megabytes, and you may want to consider one of the larger 1.2 or 1.6 gigabyte drives. They're not that expensive, and believe me, you'll appreciate the storage space.

Multimedia accessories such as a CD-ROM drive, sound card, and speakers are also becoming common accessories for new computers. (Mac users will gloat a bit, however, stating that *their* brand of computer has always had sound built in.) These accessories will help you enjoy other activities on the computer and even some Internet features such as RealAudio, which will be discussed elsewhere.

The most important advice that I can give anyone who's buying a new computer is to purchase a machine with enough random-access memory, or RAM, to operate the various programs that you plan to use. In fact, if your budget allows, buy a bit *more* RAM than you might think you need. In the computer world, RAM is power, and tomorrow's programs may need more power than you have today.

The *absolute minimum* you should consider for RAM in any new system is 8 megabytes, but 16 megabytes is better still. The extra memory will let many of your programs run faster, and the results will be well worth the effort and expense.

RAM is almost *never* as cheap to buy as when you are buying a new machine. You can add RAM later, but usually the cost is higher.

Modems

See the discussion of modems in the previous section. If your system has a modem built in or included, you should know the speed and capabilities that you're getting. All you *need* for an Internet connection is a data-capable modem, but having fax send-and-receive capabilities is a nice addition for those who work at home. Some newer systems include speakerphone and/or voice mail features with their modems (these offer added communications power).

Software

Many new machines have communications software preloaded. Many also ship with Internet browsers included. From there, you need to sign up with an Internet provider. Many manufacturers are cutting deals with these firms so that their customers receive special offers. Again, note the details of these offers as you shop because any personal preferences may influence your buying choice.

As to the online services, almost every home computer sold in the United States today is supplied with *at least* one software package from an online service, as noted earlier. Most of these packages also come with a free time offer, usually 10 or 20 hours, to let you explore the service in question.

Again, these are *basic* guidelines for buying a computer. You will also want to check out a book such as Dan Gookin's excellent *Buy That Computer!* (published, coincidentally, by IDG Books) for more useful computer-shopping advice.

How to Access the Internet without Owning a Computer

No, I'm not suggesting "channeling" or another esoteric procedure. You *can* access the Internet without owning a computer. In fact, it's rather simple to log on the net from various public access sites.

A *public access site* is, simply, a location with computers connected to the Internet that is open to the general public, or segments of the public. Often, people will be there who can give you assistance in logging in to the Internet and negotiating around to the sites you're interested in seeing. In some instances, this access is free (with limits), but other sites will charge by the hour. In either case, it's a great way to check out the Internet without making a major investment.

Some of the most popular of these sites are *Internet cafés*, coffee shops that have one or more live Internet connections for users. You can find these in New York, San Francisco, Washington, and other major cities, and apparently demand is growing. It's entertaining, to say the least, to be able to come in, have a café latté, and browse Internet sites. Check the phone book or a local weekly such as the *Village Voice* in New York City or the *San Francisco Guardian;* they'll point you in the right direction.

Your local college or university — state or private — can be another source of free or inexpensive Internet access. Either in the school's computer lab or its library, you may be able to access the Internet. If you're a student at such a school, your access will likely be free.

Similarly, call your local public library — especially a larger regional library or a center-city location — and see if it has access to the Internet. Many libraries do, and more are adding the capability as an extension of their research and reference capabilities.

When you're planning a trip to one of these facilities, keep these thoughts in mind:

✦ **Know the ground rules.** Unless you already know the ground rules for the public site you're planning to visit, *call ahead* or stop by *before* you plan to do your research so that you will know what the rules are ahead of time. This will avoid confusion and ill feelings. For example, be sure you know what fees may be involved, what time limits may exist, and whether facilities exist for you to print out selected pages or to *download* them to a diskette that you can take home. If printing is available, find out what the cost per page is to avoid surprises.

✦ **Plan your work.** Check out the listings in this book for what you're interested in seeing, or seek recommendations from others. Bring a list along to aid your searching.

✦ **Keep an eye on the clock.** Even if you're paying for your access by the hour, watch to make sure that you don't blow your budget — or the "cool" of others who may be waiting for your terminal. And, if you're using a *free* Internet access site, be especially considerate of the needs of others, won't you?

✦ **Work on the down times.** If you must work for a super-extended period of time, ask the operators of the access site when it's most convenient for you to come by. They may be less busy early in the morning, or late at night, or on Sunday afternoons. Fit your schedule to the site's "down" times, and you can work with less stress.

Other "rules of the road" may be peculiar to each public access location. You may need to be a member of the public library or have "interbranch loan" privileges from your hometown library or college. By investigating this in advance, however, you will be able to make your soiree into the Internet an easier one.

I truly like and admire the concept of a public place where you can test drive the Internet before you buy, as it were. Even if you spend $50 or $100 in the process — and at most public sites, the cost would be much less, or even free — you will gain your experience for far less than it would cost to buy a computer and get up to Internet speed, while being undecided as to whether you want the Internet to be your online home.

How to Choose the Best Modems and Software

What brands of modems and software do I recommend for users? That's a loaded question in some respects: only you can best judge your needs and interests. However, I can share some thoughts, based on more than a decade of working with data communications as a user and as a computer columnist for the *Washington Times*.

Modems

I have had very good success with modems from US Robotics, MultiTech, and Global Village, the latter designed for Macintosh computers. In each case, the modems are well-made, sturdy, and easy to use.

Prices for these modems fit just about every budget. US Robotics, for example, has some very reasonably priced modems at the 14.4 Kbps speed, and the firm also offers 28.8 Kbps and ISDN modems. The MultiTech range is a bit more upscale, but is extremely reliable, something to be desired in a modem.

For Macintosh users, there's just nothing better than a Global Village modem. The TelePort series connects easily to a serial port, is supplied with *excellent* communications and fax software, and generally works superbly with Macintosh and Power Macintosh computers. I use the 28.8 Kbps TelePort Platinum modem and have had no problems with any of the TelePorts I've owned since 1991. By the way, I'm not alone in endorsing the Global Village modem line: Apple Computer supplies models from the Global Village series with several of its Performa computers.

Software

These days, most modems arrive with communications software, and as noted, the online services have their own software which is generally free for the asking. To make life even more exciting — or confusing — an operating system such as Microsoft Windows 95 comes with communications software of its own, called HyperTerm.

What you select is your own decision, but my advice is generally to try the software you get for free — with your operating system or modem — before buying another program. Also, be aware that most standard communications software allows you to access a service such as CompuServe or MCI Mail (but *not* graphically based services such as America Online or eWorld) on a terminal level, which means you won't see the graphics that you can see with the client software provided by CompuServe and others.

Internet software, on the other hand, is another story entirely. Most services will, as mentioned, give you free software when you sign up. In most cases, this software is sufficient, at least for your initiation.

For those looking for something more online, however, here are some thoughts. For communications software, I like Procomm for Windows and Microphone for Macintosh, as well as Z Term, another Mac program. Two of these programs — Procomm and Microphone — are available in computer stores and range in price from around $50 to $150. Z Term is sold as shareware: you can obtain it from a bulletin board or user group and send a payment to the author. It pays to shop around for your best deal on the retail programs, by the way, because prices can vary widely.

What is my favorite Internet software? I'd have to say Netscape, which costs around $40 in most stores.

You can download a current version of the Netscape navigator software for free, and it isn't too difficult to accomplish. If you're using CompuServe, AOL, Prodigy, eWorld or the Microsoft Network (with Internet access), use the FTP, or File Transfer Protocol, elements of these services to visit the `ftp.netscape.com` site and select the version of the software your system needs. Or, you may find the software posted on one of these services. Or, you can use the Web browsers supplied by these services to go to `http://home.netscape.com`, where you can download a version of the program.

It's also worth noting that many ISPs, when you sign up for their service, offer free software with which you can access the Internet and the Web, read newsgroups, participate in Internet Relay Chat, and finger, (a way of locating people).

Along with Netscape, you will need to install two bits of system software extensions and control panels, specifically MacTCP and MacPPP, before you can run Netscape on your Mac.

MacTCP is a control panel created by Apple Computer. It's available either as a standalone piece of software, in the Apple System 7.5 operating software, or on disks supplied with *The Internet for Macs for Dummies Starter Kit* (another IDG title, I must admit). The bottom line, though, is this: you *must* have MacTCP to run Netscape in a dial-up mode.

That's because MacPPP, which I heartily recommend, requires MacTCP to run. You can download MacPPP from an online service such as CompuServe and configure both programs to fit the needs of your Internet Service Provider, or ISP, whether it is a local company or an online service. (You'll need to call that ISP for information, I'm afraid.)

Windows users of Netscape will need certain other extensions, such as WinSock, to run the browser on their systems. To accomplish this, check with both your Internet provider and on the Netscape disks that you may purchase. As always, your ISP should be able to guide you through the technology.

How to Sign Up for Internet Service

If you're a subscriber to CompuServe, America Online, eWorld, or Prodigy, you're already able to access the Internet. Check with these services for the how-to instructions that you need. Again, the online service will supply most of the required software and tools.

If you're picking a local Internet service provider, here are some points to keep in mind:

+ Check what pricing plans are available. Are there hourly charges? Are there blackout periods when you either can't access the service or have to pay a higher price? Are there other surcharges? Investigate all these in advance, and get offers in writing.

+ Investigate which services are offered. Can you dial up and get on the World Wide Web, for example? Will your provider offer Web page storage for you?

+ Are discounts offered for annual prepayment of a contract? Some services charge a certain fee per month, but offer a 10 percent discount — or more — for annual prepayment.

+ What are the costs for dialing up your provider? Is it a local call, always? Do they provide a toll-free number to access while you're traveling?

Once you find the answers to these questions, make your decision based on the best price and performance you can find. It's that simple.

Walk before Running

The Importance of Starting Sensibly

More than almost anything else on the Internet, one issue seems to grab the attention of new users — and those who have to deal with them. Call it "Newbie" syndrome, the somewhat annoying tendency of some newcomers to the Net to dive into discussion groups and electronic mailing lists and dash off opinions at will, but without giving much thought to what is said or how it's phrased.

Not a few of those people studying Internet culture suggest that the online world is one where some inhibitions and societal conventions easily fall from sight. What we write online is divorced from the kind of polite conversation most of us carry on every day at work or school. You're sitting at a keyboard, after all, and what you're "saying" isn't being spoken: you don't hear the words, nor does anyone else. Instead, you're typing them in an e-mail message or as a bulletin board posting.

To make matters even more complex, many of these messages are written in response to equally controversial messages that someone's read. It reminds me very much of comic Emo Philips, who once told the story of an exchange he had with another Christian. After determining they were both Baptists of a particular stripe and had much in common, it all came down to a single point:

"Finally I asked, [are you] Northern conservative fundamentalist Baptist, Great Lakes Region, Council of 1879, or Northern conservative fundamentalist Baptist, Great Lakes Region, Council of 1912?"

His new friend replied, "Northern conservative fundamentalist Baptist, Great Lakes Region, Council of 1912."

Said Philips, "Die, heretic!"

You might chuckle at that anecdote, as I do, but it underscores a point: we often split hairs over religious opinions, even within our general faith community or system of belief. However, when taken to the Internet or other online services, such as America Online, CompuServe, or Prodigy, it can be anything but a laughing matter.

That is why I believe it's important for new Internet and online users to proceed carefully, slowly, and sensibly before plunging into a debate. And whatever you do, I would sincerely urge gentleness instead of dogmatism.

I would sincerely suggest that those starting out in the online world consider learning to walk before they run. There's a great deal to explore online, yes, and your opinions and insights will be welcome, I assure you. It's best to know what you're doing *before* jumping in.

As you'll see in this chapter, some of the ways to do this would seem obvious: spend some time online and see what others are saying and how they do it. Others may seem less obvious: read the posted rules of the road before changing lanes from the on-ramp to the passing lane. Think more than once about what you write and how you write it, and above all, don't be discouraged if someone rejects your message.

Practice Makes Perfect, or at Least Experienced

You will doubtless notice that most online services and Internet providers offer 5, 10, or even 20 hours of free connect time to new customers. Other services are flat-rate utilities, making it just as easy to use 100 hours in a month as it is to use 10.

Either way, you should be able to take some time to practice and move your way around a new service. During this time, you can (and should) explore the new territory to see what you can learn.

Most services will offer a guided tour, online, of their facilities. You will be able to tour interactively the various segments of a given service and practice using them. The major online services take this one step further, offering free practice areas of their own. No matter how long you've been a customer, you can always drop by the free areas of the major services to take a refresher course in the basics, or in any other topic of interest.

But wait . . . As they say on the knife commercial, there's even more! If you're the proud owner of a new computer, you will not only have software for online services preloaded on your machine, but you may well have an interactive software tour of the services built-in as well. I recently tested a computer from Packard Bell that featured demonstrations of CompuServe, Prodigy, and America Online, each of which you could use without a minute of connect time to the services.

With these practice sessions, either online or using a software simulation, you'll gain something more than a rudimentary sense of how to negotiate an online session. You'll get a feel for the new, virtual community you have joined. You can see the rules of the road and how to get along with everyone else in the digital sandbox.

In fact, it's somewhat easier and friendlier online than in those sandboxes where we played long ago. Because even though some people commit faux pas of varying kinds online, most users are rather forgiving if approached in the proper spirit.

Let me share one small example: I was participating in an online conference one evening, and an individual joined, WHO STARTED TYPING ALL HIS COMMENTS IN UPPERCASE LETTERS LIKE THIS. Now that probably looks a bit odd on a printed page — it also looks unusual on screen — but someone who may not be a regular online user, or even a regular typist, may not know that in cyberspace, TYPING IN ALL CAPITAL LETTERS IS THE DIGITAL EQUIVALENT OF SHOUTING. You are heard, yes, but it does become annoying after a while.

As the conference continued, I dropped out of the main discussion and sent an "Instant Message" to the person involved. I gently suggested that the user would gain more attention by using both the upper and lower cases of the keyboard.

"Thanks," came the reply, "I didn't know that, and I'll keep it in mind."

Back in the Old Testament, there's the assertion that, "A soft answer turns away wrath" (Proverbs 15:1), and nowhere might it be more true than in the online world. If you can disagree without being disagreeable, you will go far in your online pursuits.

You may wonder why I devote so much emphasis to this notion of debating reasonably while online. I have two reasons:

✦ It seems to be a continuing problem. More than once I have heard complaints about how a given discussion group can break down into a so-called "flame war" where people toss invectives as if they were volleyballs.

✦ This is such a new area for people. You or I might not walk into a meeting room or conference and start to shout and disrupt the proceedings, but stick us behind a computer screen and our temperaments can change dramatically.

It's perhaps obvious, but as in real life, discussions of religion, politics, and professional sports — online and offline — can tend to result in rather heated arguments and misunderstandings, along with some less than complimentary language. It's sad, but hopefully it will change as people online grow and mature in this new environment.

This is why I sincerely believe that it's useful to look around a given service *before* diving in. You'll be glad you did.

Just the FAQs, Ma'am: Read Messages and Bulletins before Jumping In

Where do you find the ground rules on the Internet or online? Why, just look for the FAQs, as Joe Friday used to say on the old *Dragnet* TV show.

OK, OK, Friday really asked for the *facts*, not the *FAQs*, but you'll soon see that there *are* some similarities. A *FAQ* is a list of "frequently asked questions" about a given Internet site or discussion group. Here, the organizers spell out the rules, set boundaries, and clue users in on what is and isn't permitted. This is especially important when getting involved in an Internet mailing list or other discussion group.

I need to provide some definitions:

✦ A *mailing list* is an automatically maintained electronic subscription to a topic of mutual interest. The "list" is a collection of e-mail addresses to which you can subscribe.

✦ The mailing list — and the messages for that list — are usually maintained on a *server* computer attached to the Internet.

✦ A mailing list can be *moderated* or *unmoderated*. As these words suggest, this means that there's either someone who reads each message submitted to the server computer for distribution to the mailing list, or there isn't. In the former instance, that moderator can decide if a given message is or is not permissible for distribution. (Messages containing libel or slander, using text which would create a copyright violation, or posting obscenity are things that moderators of a mailing list typically trash.) In the case of an unmoderated list, there is still likely to be someone who maintains, or oversees the list. In this latter case, the list "owner" can either remove a message about which complaints have been received or, in extreme circumstances, bar an individual from posting further messages if he or she doesn't abide by the rules of the mailing list.

That's why you should get the FAQs before starting. If you're subscribing to a mailing list, you will probably receive these rules from the server computer when your subscription is approved or acknowledged. The welcome message may contain a host of rules or simply instructions on how to post messages and how to remove your name from the subscription list.

With the online services, many of their discussion areas also post rules for newcomers to review. In addition, these discussion areas are governed by the general rules of the online service, which again officially frown on bad language and poor behavior. The online services are especially hard on users who use abusive language constantly or who harass others with unwanted e-mail. (I once had my name included in a book of e-mail addresses and received all sorts of weird mail from people. The good news is that a press of a button on the keyboard dispatched the unwanted mail to the electronic dead-letter office. The bad news is I did lose a little bit of privacy in the process.)

Another useful thing to do is to read a few of the messages that are posted in a given online service or Internet forum. From this, you can get a sense of what's important and what isn't, how people communicate, and what their main interests are.

Once again, I would emphasize that when you join a newsgroup, get a copy of the FAQs, so you know what the "score" is about permissible conduct, messages, and the like. A little advance planning *will* save you heartache!

As you peruse some Internet discussion groups (also known as *newsgroups*), you may find some rather raw language, even in so-called religious topics. This isn't always the nicest part of Cyber-town, but it's also true that these same groups can contain valuable messages that will be of interest. That's why it's important to know two things:

+ You can usually see the "subject" of a message before reading it. If the message appears obscene or unappealing, you can skip over it.

+ You can erase an unwelcome message from your screen with the click of a button.

By reading sample messages along with the rules of a given mailing list or discussion group, you'll have a good sense of what is out there before you begin.

Phrase Your Messages Carefully

It should go without saying that messages posted on the online services or in Internet discussion groups should reflect civil discussion of controversial issues. It *should* go without saying, but as you'll see in some corners of the Internet, it would appear that such a rule has never been spoken.

So, I'll say it: be gentle in your postings. That's difficult to do in the heat of comment and controversy — how *could* someone actually believe that such-and-such is true? — but in these moments, it is most necessary to keep a cool head and be reasonable in what you say and how you say it.

In advising how to conduct one's self in debate, Abraham Lincoln — no slouch in the debating department — said it best: "A drop of honey catches more flies than a gallon of gall." Some 70 years after Lincoln's death, Dale Carnegie offered the view that "A man convinced against his will is of the same opinion still."

Both bits of advice might well apply here in cyberspace. You can disagree, but without being disagreeable. Phrases such as "Would you consider . . .," "It seems to me . . .," or "I may be incorrect, but have you thought about . . ." are excellent ways to phrase what could be a controversial posting.

Another strategy to employ when you come across a posting that rubs you the wrong way is to send a private e-mail to the offending person. I've done this on more than one occasion and have often either gained some insight from the other person or won agreement from him or her. Again, realize that what we post in cyberspace would sound much different if spoken face to face. We would probably change the way we say something. That's why I've taken this space — and your time — to emphasize the importance of online etiquette. The nicer we all are out there, the better it will be for all of us.

Don't Be Discouraged

Apparently, some people see the Internet as an electronic Crusade ground where they feel obligated to contend earnestly for the faith once delivered to the saints of old. That's their privilege — the online world is a real haven of democracy where anyone can say anything; it's up to you to accept or reject it.

The same applies, of course, to anything you post, or e-mail, to other people. They may agree with you; they may not. They may or may not appreciate what you have to say. They might not even respond. I've had all sorts of reactions to the messages I've posted online, ranging from very nice to, well, very nasty.

The negative reaction to messages from others can be a desire to shrink from the debate. Indeed, in more than one online forum, I've read the complaint that all the "serious" commentary has been driven out by the "fluff" or "vitriol" posted by the allegedly non-serious. This often brings a flurry of messages saying, "Oh, no, we're serious people," which are countered by other messages saying, "Oh, no you're not!"

The key is to keep trying. You may not win others to your way of thinking — indeed, you own attitudes might change — but by interacting with those with whom you don't agree, you can often learn the most. After all, if you only talk to those with whom you have total agreement, that's not very broadening, is it?

"Anyone who takes the time to disagree with you is interested in the same things you are," Dale Carnegie once said. It's a thought worth pondering.

 All this is *not* to argue that you must abandon all convictions when you enter the online world, or that you need to view cyberspace as a place in which you can change your deeply held beliefs. You can restrict yourself to conversation with those of like minds without worrying too much. What I'd suggest, however, is that if you *do* go into this as a missionary for your views — again, an acceptable enterprise — you should be prepared to stay in the arena for a while.

The Major Online Services

America Online

CHAPTER 4

America's Largest Online Service?

The numbers vary — and they're subject to interpretation and dispute by competitors — but at the writing of this book, late in 1995, America Online had proclaimed itself as the largest online service in the United States.

America Online has advertised its services extensively in just about every magazine around as well as on television with spokesmen as diverse as *Batman* TV star Adam West and boxer Peter McNeely, whose defeat by Mike Tyson may have been the highlight of his career. These promotions — along with the bundling of software for the service with almost every new computer sold in the United States — have brought millions of new customers to AOL's door. When those customers arrive on AOL's front porch, they'll see something similar to what is shown in Figure 4-1, a welcome screen tailored to who they are and where they live.

Just how many new subscribers does America Online have? On November 7, 1995, AOL (as it's known in the industry,) said that it had more than tripled its membership in the previous 12 months, to an excess of 4 million members, and said that a study by Odyssey, an independent market research firm, indicated AOL had as many subscribers as Prodigy and CompuServe combined.

"As the market for online services continues to grow, consumers are picking AOL as their online service of choice," said Steve Case, Chairman and CEO of America Online, in announcing the membership gain. "Our success continues to be from the support of our member community and our ability to continue to make AOL easy-to-use, with a broad range of content, presented in an even more engaging context, with a strong sense of community — all at an affordable price."

Figure 4-1: A member's welcome screen, seen when signing on to America Online. If you live in northern California, you'll see this screen, which offers text from the *San Jose Mercury News.*

Beyond the hyperbole — at about the same time, CompuServe said that *it* had more than 4 million subscribers worldwide — AOL *does* offer its customers a wide variety of services, including electronic mail, conferencing software, computing support, interactive magazines, newspapers, and online classes, as well as easy and affordable access to services of the Internet. Established in 1985, AOL's managers have formed strategic alliances with dozens of companies, including ABC, CBS, Knight-Ridder, the Tribune Company, *The New York Times,* Hachette magazines, IBM, and American Express. These alliances allow AOL to offer a wide range of information content, from ABC Radio sound bites (both of today's news and yesterday's events) to the contents of many general interest magazines. You can access the latest news from Reuters and the Associated Press.

Newspaper buffs can receive text from the *San Jose Mercury News,* as well as the *New York Times,* which is the closest thing America has to a "newspaper of record." The *Times'* news area, with a new separate Page One section, is updated nightly at around 11:30 p.m. EST with articles from the next day's paper.

AOL, though, isn't just all news, valuable as that is. It offers a wide range of reference features, from online encyclopedias to the text of the Bible (Figure 4-2).

Research Resources

You'll notice, right up front, that one of the AOL reference services is a look-through of the Bible. From here, you can enter a word, press a key, and see a range of Bible references that relate to that word. For example, look what happened when I entered the word *faith* in the lookup screen (Figure 4-3).

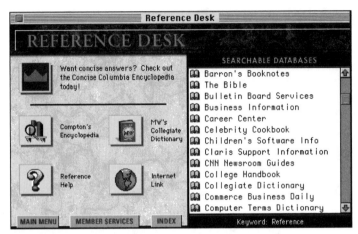

Figure 4-2: The AOL Reference search screen. From here, a user can search a variety of reference services.

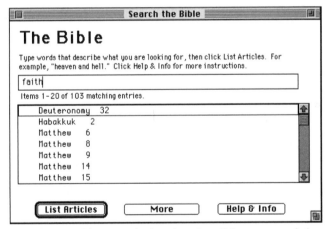

Figure 4-3: Faith comes by hearing, the Bible says — and via this lookup feature in America Online.

All the basic items in AOL's roster of services are designed to attract a variety of users. In addition to these services are very specific ones aimed at the spiritual needs of a wide range of people.

Religion and Ethics Forum

One of the main meeting places for believers — and plenty of non-believers — in AOL-land is the Religion and Ethics Forum (Figure 4-4). It was established several years ago and is maintained by Jerry White, who goes by the screen name of "Sermoner1." Mr. White is a friendly, cooperative person who seems to go out of his way to accommodate the differing needs of religiously minded people on AOL.

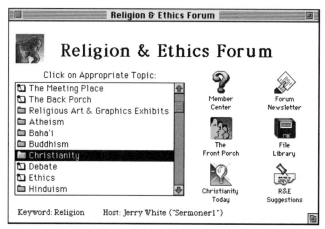

Figure 4-4: The main screen for AOL's Religion and Ethics Forum, your entry point to this section.

This forum is one of the most popular on AOL, and that's largely because it is a "big tent" which has room for just about every shade of religious belief around.

As you can see from the main screen in the section, there's more than Christianity here — and as you scroll through the left side of the welcome screen, you'll see folders (or areas) representing everything from atheism to Islam, Judaism and even pagan religions. Each of these folders contains message boards of varying stripes, where you can post and view messages relating to topics within the general category, as well as pursue other electronic links.

For example, take a look at the areas available in the Judaism area of AOL (Figure 4-5). The categories are typical of those in all the folders, although the contents will obviously vary according to the specific folder.

You can explore the Judaism Boards, which are (currently) three message boards where you can find answers to questions or post comments on relevant issues. Next on the list are the Judaism Libraries, in which software of various stripes is posted. This includes Torah portions and discussions about them, as well as other educational items.

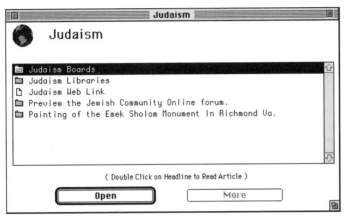

Figure 4-5: There are several links to areas of interest for those who open the Judaism folder in AOL.

You'll also notice something else here, which you may not find in the other Religion area folders: one-button access to Web links related to Judaism. You will need to have AOL's Web browser software to access the World Wide Web, but with it, you'll see a page of links to other Jewish areas of interest, courtesy of the Yahoo search engine (Figure 4-6).

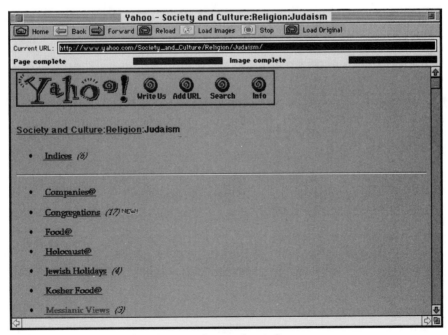

Figure 4-6: Judaism Web links, seen via America Online.

From these Web links, again using the AOL browser, you can jump to a variety of locations. That it is integrated with the main AOL software is, in my view, a neat option.

Weekly Conversations

Many of the areas on the Religion and Ethics Forum sponsor weekly online gatherings of people with similar interests. These discussions take place in *real-time*; in other words, everyone is "talking," through their keyboards, in the same session. These conferences are held in the Front Porch, a chat area (Figure 4-7).

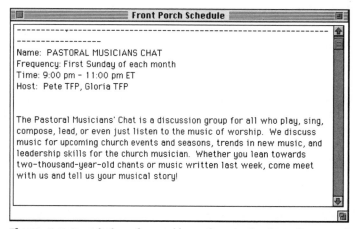

Figure 4-7: Description of a weekly conference for those interested in pastoral music. Many other conferences take place in AOL's Religion and Ethics Forum.

As you can see from Figure 4-7, the description tells you what the theme of this conference is, when it takes place (almost always listed in Eastern time), and who the hosts are.

How do you participate in these conferences? First, of course, you need to show up. When you reach the Religion and Ethics area, you'll see an icon for the Front Porch. Click on it, and you'll see the Front Porch room icon, which brings you into the discussion.

The discussions tend to be a little free wheeling, and can range all over the lot. My best advice to newcomers is always to hang back a little bit and see where the conversation is going before diving in.

As mentioned in Chapters 2 and 3, maintaining a good sense of propriety in online dealings is important. Be respectful, be courteous, and don't shed your sense of humor, and you'll enjoy your times hanging out on the Front Porch.

You may not be an evangelical Christian and therefore may be tempted to skip over this section on Christianity Online. Please don't. You don't have to be a Christian — or a believer of any sort — to visit this area. Also, I sincerely believe the way Christianity Online has been organized may provide useful ideas for others who want to approach AOL about creating special online areas.

Christianity Online

Established in 1994 by the publishers of *Christianity Today* magazine, Christianity Online is a very popular electronic gathering place on AOL for evangelical (and other) Christians. Heavily promoted in *CT* magazine (to which I have regularly contributed), Christianity Online blends text services from several magazines with message boards, discussion forums, and classified ads (see Figure 4-8).

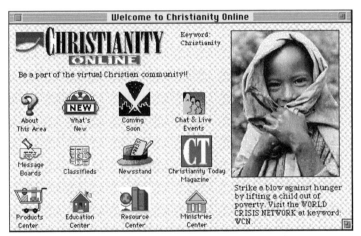

Figure 4-8: The Christianity Online welcome screen, part of the America Online service, often includes appeals from charitable groups.

Also known as CO, the service's opening menu features a wide range of choices. There's an About this Area section that contains answers to frequently asked questions about CO. It notes that although CO is sponsored by an evangelical Christian magazine and is part of a non-profit organization, the group cannot keep members of groups evangelicals would consider "cults" out of the forum. The About this Area section also reassures those who have become comfortable with the paper version of *CT* that the company expects to keep the print version for some time to come, alongside its new venture into electronic publishing.

Among the 11 other areas found in the CO welcome screen are those that offer news (the Newsstand and *CT*'s online version), message boards, and classified ads, among other resources (see Figure 4-9).

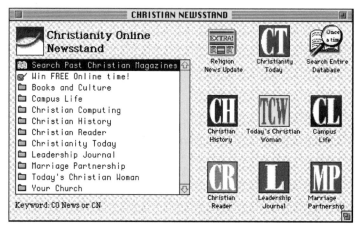

Figure 4-9: This Newsstand is always open. Here, you can select from topics listed at the left and icons for major *CT* publications at the right.

At the Christian Newsstand, you will find a variety of publications. Most are from the stable of Christianity Today, Inc. periodicals, but some — such as *Christian Computing* magazine — are not. Click on one of the icons, or the topic at left, and you're transported to an electronic table of contents for a given title (see Figure 4-10). For the person interested in an evangelical Christian viewpoint on computing, there's no better publication out there today than *Christian Computing* magazine, which features incisive reviews, commentary, and loads of tips. You can find the publication in many Christian bookstores, online via AOL, or at their Web site, `http://www.ccmag.com`.

In such a table of contents, you can select from the articles in the current issue of *CT* and read these online — or save them for future reference. You can also send electronic letters to the editor that may appear in both versions of the magazine. In short, just about everything that is in the print version of *CT* is available online, at or just before the cover date.

As you will note in several places in this book, the capability to *download* something, or save it to your hard disk, does not mean that you have permission to circulate copyrighted materials at will. Copyright law in the United States — which includes some hefty fines, by the way — says no. You cannot do this without the express permission of the copyright holder. What you *can* do, the law says, is download an article for personal reference and reading. (Of course, this is a very brief view of copyright law. For real answers, consult a reference book on copyrights or an attorney who knows about them.)

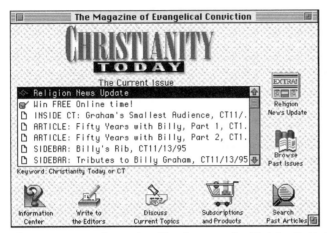

Figure 4-10: An electronic table of content for *Christianity Today* magazine.

The usefulness of having articles online is the ability not only to read them at will but to search current and past issues of the magazine for a given keyword. Enter a topic such as *Easter* or *Seminaries*, and you'll find any number of articles centered on these topics. This kind of searching, which now goes back well over a year's worth of *CT* issues, can also extend across all the publications and news sources available in CO. Try to do that with even a bound volume of a year's issues, and you'll see how valuable the search service can be.

Beyond the articles lie other useful features in CO-land. The Classifieds are a collection of advertisements for various services, products, and even job opportunities. If you work in Christian ministries, or would like to, you may be able to get your next job here.

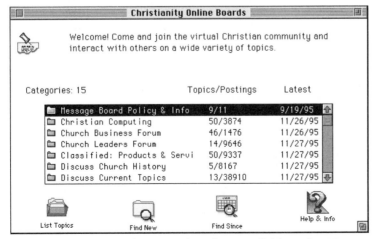

Figure 4-11: A variety of message boards are available to the CO user.

Another feature of the CO service are message boards, with some categories listed in Figure 4-11. The boards, as mentioned elsewhere, are free wheeling places where you can discuss just about anything. Some of these message categories are organized by topic, others, such as the Church Leaders Forum, by denomination (see Figure 4-12). Within a given folder, the topics can be serious — such as missionary work — or humorous. Some messages in a recent folder talked about an online "beauty contest" for members of a given denomination, which gently poked fun at the attire that many of those members wear.

Other message boards are more serious-minded, which is in part determined by the nature of the organization and the attitudes of the participants.

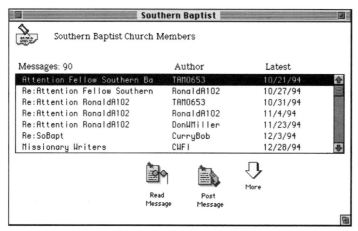

Figure 4-12: Topics seen on AOL's Southern Baptist message board.

If you have a thin skin, or have misplaced your sense of humor, tread softly in the message boards. On the other hand, if you can laugh at yourself and others, dive in. You'll find a lot of fun and fellowship — and this form of electronic networking can pay great dividends.

There's a tremendous amount to explore in Christianity Online, and frankly, I can only scratch the surface here. If the evangelical world is of interest to you, plan to spend some time here, see what's available, and enjoy.

AOL's Internet Connection

One of the other nice things about America Online is how the service integrates Internet access with the basic AOL service. You can download a free Web browser and fire it up as part of an AOL session or as a prelude to one. If you are unsure about which version of AOL software you have, check either the About feature, which is found — when the AOL software is active — under the Help menu button in Windows and under the Apple menu on the Macintosh. You should also check with AOL's tech support, which is available online, to determine which version of AOL you need to browse the Web.

 As this book went to press, reports indicated that discussions between AOL and Netscape were taking place; these meetings may result in your being able to use the Netscape browser to access the Web via AOL.

You will need a computer that is powerful enough to access AOL and the Web with this software. That generally means a Windows 3.x or Windows 95 computer on the PC side, and a Macintosh running System 7.1 or greater on that platform. With these computers, you should have enough memory (8 megabytes would be my personal recommendation) to run both the AOL client software and the Web browser.

The good news about the AOL Web browser, in my view, is that it is *integrated* with the AOL software. This means you can switch from regular AOL services to Internet browsing, and back again, without having to disconnect from AOL and fire up a "Brand X" Internet service (see Figure 4-13).

The AOL browser is certainly adequate for an introduction to the Web, and many users rely on it as their only browser. At this writing, AOL is not set up to accommodate other browsers on its Internet links.

Once downloaded and installed, running the AOL browser is a simple matter of switching to it from within the AOL service. You must be connected to AOL first in order to open a Web link with the browser, however.

Figure 4-13: The Switch to Browser command.

When you open the AOL browser, you will need to enter a Uniform Resource Locator, or URL, address, to go to a Web site. One of the best ways to start exploring the Web is to go to the AOL home page, `http://www.blue.aol.com/`, and start your adventure there. Or, you can enter one of the URLs found elsewhere in this book.

Enter a URL, and you'll soon see a Web page display, as shown in the example in Figure 4-14. The AOL software, as noted, is *not* a Netscape browser, so be aware that some Netscape-based pages may not display as well here.

Figure 4-14: A church Web page, viewed through the AOL browser.

One final note about the AOL browser: it is integrated with AOL's e-mail service. When you click on a response button on a given Web page, the AOL e-mail form pops up, making it easy to send a message to whomever you want to contact.

CompuServe

America's Oldest Online Service?

When you think about the origins of CompuServe, think of income tax returns. CompuServe started as a computer time-sharing service in 1968 and then became an online information service in 1979, which qualifies it as America's oldest public online service.

The time CompuServe originally shared was on computers used by the famous H&R Block firm, which touts itself as the world's leader in tax preparation. In 1995 alone, H&R Block Tax Services handled almost one in every seven returns filed with the U.S. Internal Revenue Service, serving 17.1 million taxpayers in more than 9,500 offices worldwide. However, the large mainframe computers the firm was using during the day to process tax returns were sitting idle during the night.

Nature abhors a vacuum, it is said, and the vacuum created by the idle time on H&R Block's computers represented an opportunity to serve the needs of a soon-growing community of computer users. By offering that unused computer time — and storage space — to other organizations, such as businesses and universities, those computers, which were "up" on a 24-hour basis, became a potential profit center.

I first signed on to CompuServe in 1983. I had a 300 baud modem, which was fast for that time. The service's main menu was a character-based display with many levels needed to reach the various services. That modem was 1/96th the speed of the 28,800 baud modem that I use to access CompuServe these days, with a much more graphical menu and display. What a difference 13 years can make!

Today, according to the firm, CompuServe operates the most comprehensive online network in the world, with 3.8 million members. CompuServe's Internet Division is a leading developer of Internet access applications for the office, home, and publishing markets. In addition to providing online and Internet access from more than 140 countries, CompuServe Network Services provides value-added network services to more than 800 companies worldwide.

Figure 5-1: The CompuServe main menu, as seen on the latest version of WinCIM, version 2.0.1.

One of the big differences for consumers between CompuServe and America Online is that CompuServe has had an overseas presence for several years. It is strong in the United Kingdom, Europe, and Australia, and can be easily accessed from Japan. (In 1995, two weeks after the Hanshin earthquake in Kobe, Japan, I was there with a team of volunteers, one of whom signed on to CompuServe from neighboring Osaka with a local call. It really does work from all corners of the globe!)

This has allowed believers in various countries to get in touch with each other more easily than might be possible otherwise. Information flows from the United States to Europe and back, both within various denominational forums and across such lines.

Another difference is that CompuServe is one of the few large online services that does not require you to have special graphics software in order to access most of its services. Some interactive games and other graphically oriented features will be excluded, but by and large you can reach any text-based area of the service using just about any terminal software package. You'll see a straight ASCII display of menus and this should be good enough for most tasks. Pretty it's not, but if you need to jump on quickly to retrieve or send e-mail, you'll appreciate the difference.

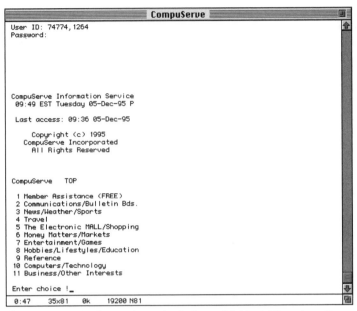

Figure 5-2: How CompuServe looks in straight text. It's not pretty, perhaps, but it'll do the job.

This text-based access is also good news for those who are trying to compute at bargain-basement prices. If you have a more "ancient" computer, say an 80286-based PC or one of the original Macs, you'll appreciate this method of communication.

At this writing, I don't know how long CompuServe — or anyone else — will want to maintain a text-based service. The computing world, for better or for worse, is moving to a graphical system of displays. You should also be aware that you can use many Internet systems as text-only services, also at low cost and with access to newsgroups and mailing lists, as you shall see later.

Indeed, CompuServe itself is changing the way subscribers can access the service. In December 1995, the firm announced a new open standards strategy to help members keep up with the Internet explosion.

CompuServe said it is the first online service in the industry to allow its members to use any World Wide Web browser (the software that lets users see into cyberspace) with no restrictions and no limitations. As part of this move, the CompuServe Information Service is launching a unique online area called WebCentral (SM).

"While others are creating Internet confusion with proprietary software and exclusive arrangements, we are making sense of it for the average consumer," says Rob Mainor, CompuServe's vice president of product marketing and business information services. "Instead of picking sides in the intensifying war between browsers, we are giving our members the right to choose.

"We do offer a browser to our members free of charge, but we recognize that many other outstanding browsers can be used with our value-added services and open network," Mainor adds. "Without services and content, a browser is worthless. The open standards strategy enables us to combine our outstanding online content, the best Internet access, and the ability to use every browser in the market to create a powerful venue for our members in the competitive new world of the Internet."

In any case, the versatility of the CompuServe service appeals to many people. That's why the firm has the subscriber base it enjoys, and why it is likely to remain strong in the face of stiff competition from AOL and other services.

The Religion Forum and the Worship Center

CompuServe's Religion Forum is one of the oldest places online in which believers of varying stripes can come together to discuss their ideas. The introductory message from the forum spells it out with clarity:

"WELCOME TO RELIGION FORUM

"The Religion Forum is made up of people with diverse backgrounds and beliefs who share one thing in common: an interest and a concern for the religious, spiritual and ethical dimensions of life.

"Our MESsage Board, LIBraries and CONference Rooms are divided into 23 sections, the names of which should give you a sense of the breadth of our interests: General Topics, Christianity, Judaism, Hinduism, Islam, Interfaith, Limbo, Pagan & Occult, Taoism, Worldwide Church of God, Catholic & Orthodox, Jehovah's Witnesses, Latter-Day Saints, Free Thought, Native Americans, Evangelicals, Youth Line, Anglicans, Baha'i, Sabbatarians, Buddhism, Messianic Believers, and Miracle Studies.

"We are primarily a discussion forum whose main purpose is to provide an opportunity for people from many different religious traditions and from none, to share their thoughts, ideas, beliefs, practices, and customs with each other in open discussion and debate. It is therefore an exciting opportunity for dialogue, especially interfaith dialogue, to take place across many religious barriers [that] traditionally have been uncrossable. There is on this forum also the chance to discuss contemporary issues related to religion and ethics: separation of church and state, abortion, bioethics, prayer in schools, and many others."

CompuServe's Religion Forum is unaffiliated — there's no denominational connection whatsoever, and none is needed to participate. However, forum operators require that you respect the views of others, and avoid "Lack of respect, bigotry, intolerance, name calling or any other forms of harassment." Amen!

What you'll find in the Religion Forum

The short answer is that you'll find just about anything you're looking for in terms of religious information and news. Some of it will likely be right on target for your needs whereas some of it will strike you as being rather wide of the mark.

The first thing you'll find is a status screen that resembles Figure 5-3 (if you're using a Macintosh, that is). The basic news here will be an indication of any messages waiting for you, any news flashes from the system operator (or sysop) you should read, as well as information on available conferences, messages, and file libraries. You can also find out who else is visiting the forum with the click of a button.

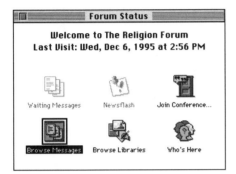

Figure 5-3: The main status screen of CompuServe's Religion Forum, as Mac users see it.

What's the difference between a message posted to a message board and one which is "waiting for you"? The key difference is that those messages which are specifically waiting for you are ones posted in response to a message you've left. This allows you to follow items of particular interest without having to dig through oceans of other messages (unless, of course, you want to do so).

As you can see from Figure 5-4, the Religion Forum's messages are organized into sections. Each section usually has one (or more) leaders, who manage the flow of traffic by making sure that messages are properly posted in a given area. They also make sure that the messages avoid obscenity and slander, and they have the power to curtail such messages and their posters.

This may sound like the public square run amok, but there's good reason for this kind of monitoring. One is that without such moderation — as we'll see in the chapters on the Internet — you can end up with rather unsavory messages that you don't want to bother handling. The other is that for those new to a given topic, having a section leader well versed in that area is a help. Most section leaders — I must stress — aren't afraid of vigorous debate and will allow a wide range of opinion from participants. They, and CompuServe, want to make sure that those debates are framed in cordial and correct terms.

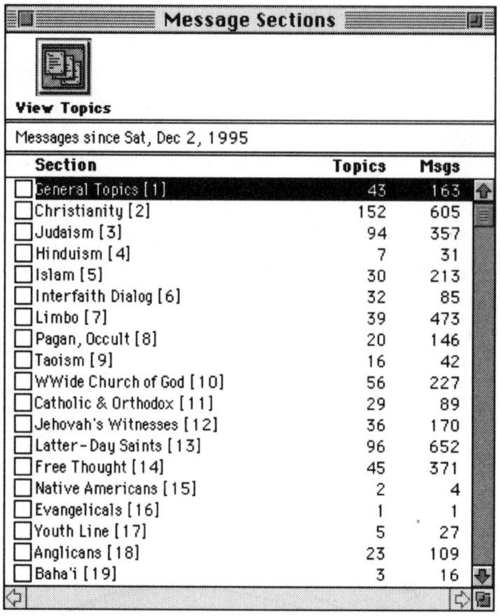

Figure 5-4: The Religion Forum organizes its rich store of messages into sections, each of which has a leader who manages the traffic flow.

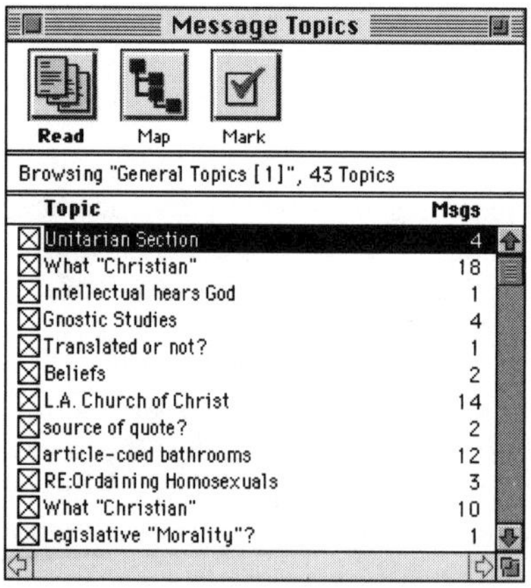

Figure 5-5: Message topics in a given section of the Religion Forum can range over a wide area.

Within each section, message topics are diverse and sometimes even bizarre. (One which mystified me was a discussion of so-called "coed bathrooms" in college dorms, by virtue of its placement in the forum and the heated debate that attended the subject.) But with some searching — and through your own efforts at posting messages — you can find and create useful and interesting topics (see Figure 5-5).

Conferences held in the Religion Forum often center around denominational concerns and issues. These are usually scheduled by the section leader of a given area, which again makes sense. This way, you can know that every Wednesday at 8:30 p.m. Eastern Time Catholic parents meet, let's say.

The conferences themselves usually take one of two directions. Either they're a free flowing exchange on a variety of current topics, or they are based on a given subject established by the section leader or someone else. It could be a continuing study or an introductory series but the discussions are often lively and offer a great way both to learn more about a subject and to meet people of like mind.

File Libraries in the Religion Forum

The file libraries in CompuServe's Religion Forum are, like the message sections they're patterned after, diverse, both in terms of subject and content (see Figure 5-6).

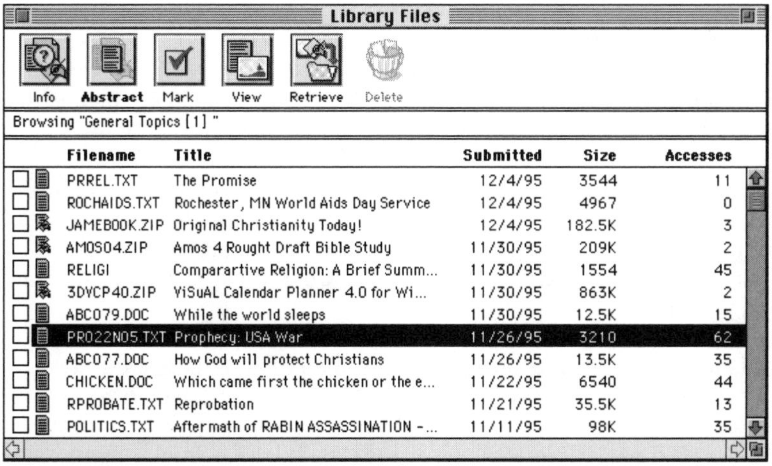
Library Files
Info
Abstract
Mark
View
Retrieve
Delete
Browsing "General Topics [1] "
Filename Title Submitted Size Accesses
PRREL.TXT The Promise 12/4/95 3544 11
ROCHAIDS.TXT Rochester, MN World Aids Day Service 12/4/95 4967 0
JAMEBOOK.ZIP Original Christianity Today! 12/4/95 182.5K 3
AMOS04.ZIP Amos 4 Rought Draft Bible Study 11/30/95 209K 2
RELIGI Comparartive Religion: A Brief Summ... 11/30/95 1554 45
3DVCP40.ZIP ViSuAL Calendar Planner 4.0 for Wi... 11/30/95 863K 2
ABC079.DOC While the world sleeps 11/30/95 12.5K 15
PRO22NO5.TXT Prophecy: USA War 11/26/95 3210 62
ABC077.DOC How God will protect Christians 11/26/95 13.5K 35
CHICKEN.DOC Which came first the chicken or the e... 11/22/95 6540 44
RPROBATE.TXT Reprobation 11/21/95 35.5K 13
POLITICS.TXT Aftermath of RABIN ASSASSINATION -... 11/11/95 98K 35

Figure 5-6: Look familiar? The file libraries generally follow the section format used by the message boards.

A key difference between the message boards and the file libraries is that you can at once find items even more useful (and those which you view as even more inane) than the messages posted on the forum. That's because the file libraries contain rather valuable text, graphics, and program files — and they can contain rather banal ones, too!

Within a given category, there's a rather wide latitude of subjects with files that can be uploaded. They can range all over the lot, as you can see from Figure 5-7.

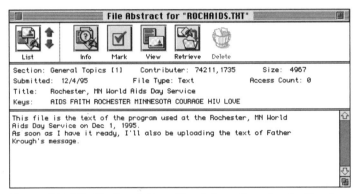

Figure 5-7: This file description offers information about a file of material concerning a service for people with AIDS.

In this figure, the description gives details on the program materials used for a memorial service for people who have died of AIDS. By downloading the text discussed here, you may find ideas for a similar service in your own community.

The key to file downloading is to take a look at the descriptions before you take on a file. If it's a compressed file, be sure that you have the tools with which you can expand it; if it's a program, make sure the program will run on your system. Above all, make sure that the file is something in which you are interested. Disk space is not free, after all, and you need to be selective.

When downloading files, what's more important than disk space is a question of disk security in terms of computer viruses. Files uploaded to CompuServe are supposed to be checked for viruses, but no system is 100 percent foolproof. Therefore, the best thing you can do is have virus-checking software installed on your computer and use that software to check new files before using them. Check a good computer reference book (one of the basic titles for your brand of computer in the ...*For Dummies* series might be a good start) and follow the leads given there.

Rev. Robert Schuller and CompuServe

He began his ministry in California atop the concession stand of a drive-in movie theater. That concept of accessibility hasn't left the Reverend Robert Harold Schuller, who at a very young age knew he was called to be a preacher. Since those early days in Orange County, Schuller's message has gone around the world. For more than 25 years, his *Hour of Power* television program has taken a message of positive Christian living (Schuller gladly claims the late Norman Vincent Peale as an inspiration) to the airwaves.

Schuller is perhaps most famous for his "Possibility Thinker's Creed," which reads: "When faced with a mountain, *I will not quit.* I will either climb over it, go around it, tunnel through it, or stay and turn that mountain into a gold mine, with God's help."

To promote his most recent book, *Prayer: My Spiritual Journey*, Schuller took his accessibility into cyberspace, answering questions from CompuServe subscribers.

If your searching extends beyond CompuServe's Religion Forum, the "Find" command will let you search, by keyword, the entire CompuServe network. A search based on the keyword "religion" turned up over 20 different forums, including New Age, Catholic Online, Religious Issues and others, including a UFO forum. The reach is very broad, as you can see, and you can then narrow your selection to the area or areas you need.

CompuServe's Internet Browser and Spry Services

This section is almost irrelevant — but not totally, so please read it. As I was writing this book, CompuServe announced a change in its operations to become more Web-based and to support all Internet browsers. (Mac users, by the way, have this advantage already. CompuServe advocates the use of outside browsers by its Mac-based Internet users.) In turn, this means there may be a diminishing need for CompuServe's Internet browser.

But for those totally new to the Internet and those who like Mosaic, the Spry Mosaic browser offered by CompuServe is worth a look. It's a handy, useful, and usable browser, and best of all for Windows users, it's now integrated with WinCIM, which makes Internet access on CompuServe easier than before.

By way of explanation, you should note that CompuServe bought Spry, which is a developer of Internet software and services, for $100 million early in 1995. Spry's principal product was *Internet in a Box*, which bundled Spry's version of the public-domain Mosaic software with various guides to the Net and offered Internet access through Spry's dial-up network. That network, by the way, was supplied by CompuServe, which is how the two firms first got together.

We interrupt this chapter for a special announcement: Yet another change may be in the works for CompuServe's Internet services. On December 7, 1995, the firm said it would license Microsoft's Internet Explorer and include that browser — which is also based on Mosaic — in the *Internet in a Box* kits sold by CompuServe's Spry division, as well as with the next revision of CompuServe Information Manager (CIM), which is due in 1996. This may or may not mean potential demise for the Spry Mosaic browser, so stay tuned. We now return to our regularly scheduled chapter.

The current version of WinCIM includes the Spry Mosaic browser, as noted, and lets users switch between the Web and CompuServe. As shown in Figure 5-8, the browser features several buttons at the top of the screen that allow users to navigate easily both the Internet and — by clicking on the WinCIM button — CompuServe.

Figure 5-8: The CompuServe Internet Home page, viewed with the Spry Mosaic browser.

Most useful to note about the Spry Mosaic browser is that the "Web Page" field just below the button bar is where you can enter the Universal Resource Locator (URL) for a given web page. In Figure 5-9, you see the Project Genesis home page as viewed with the Spry Mosaic browser.

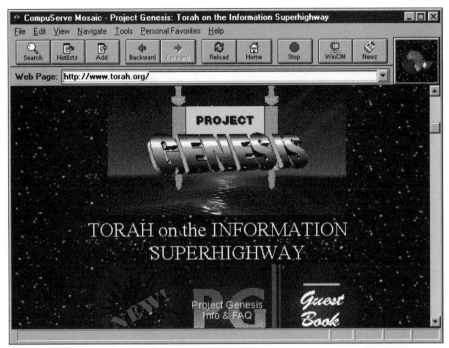

Figure 5-9: Project Genesis home page (`http://www.torah.org`) as seen with the CompuServe Spry Mosaic browser.

Some or all this may well change as WebCentral takes hold within CompuServe. The firm is also lowering its pricing to remain competitive with other Internet providers, and that's good news for end users.

One final note about CompuServe's Internet services. That's the news that you can add your own Web page — up to 1 megabyte's worth of data — to CompuServe's web storage site. The firm will even provide web-authoring software for you to use.

According to CompuServe, their Home Page Wizard uses advanced technology to eliminate many of the hassles associated with designing and submitting a *home page,* the document on the Web that people access for information on certain topics. It offers drag-and-drop editing, templates, and helpful hints to help design attractive, personalized home pages. It provides the capability to add hot links that can jump to any other site on the Web, the capability to insert images, and numerous other features. Once members design their pages, they can automatically test it in the browser of their choice to ensure that it looks exactly as they intended.

eWorld: The New (and Changing) Kid in Cyber-Town

The Growth of eWorld — and its eVolution

In June 1994, Apple Computer did something audacious: it became the first computer manufacturer to launch an online information service, which it called "eWorld." Like the Macintosh computer the service supports, eWorld is quirky and Mac-like in both its look, feel, and attitude (see Figure 6-1). This is not your father's online service!

Apple's audacity came from not only jumping into the online world as the brainchild of a computer maker but also because it launched as a Mac-first service, with plans for a Microsoft Windows "client" software package "later." As of this writing, at the end of 1995, the Windows version of eWorld has yet to appear. Instead, eWorld is going to, well, "eVolve" into an Internet-based service sometime during mid-1996, if not a little later. For now, only Mac users can access *all* of eWorld's features and services. Windows users, however, can access Apple's WebCity, which is an Internet site offering a taste of where eWorld is going.

This audacity wasn't really arrogance, however. Apple already had the basics of an online service in its internal e-mail system, AppleLink (which for a good 10 years or so had been the internal network of Apple Computer), its developers, and select other individuals in the Apple/Macintosh community. The service was limited in its popularity and was expensive, but it helped the Mac fraternity develop close bonds.

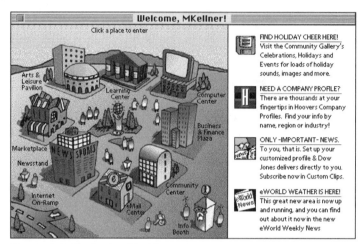

Figure 6-1: The main eWorld screen.

Couple that online experience with another need Apple faced — and solved — in creating eWorld. Apple, like most computer makers, wants to support its users and keep them as customers. In the early days of computing, support meant sticking someone at the other end of a phone line — with a toll-free 800 number, if possible — and having that person wait for you to call. Of course, because you might be calling at 3 a.m. on a Sunday morning, that meant the computer maker had to have someone available at 3 a.m. on a Sunday morning or else risk both your wrath and you buying another computer.

As people became more experienced with computers and as manufacturers built up a base of information that could be used in supporting customers, the search was on for ways to provide at least some of that support in less costly ways. After all, if you know enough to plug in a computer and modem, you probably know enough to find answers to your computing questions without having to dial up a person and ask, "Now, how do I format a floppy disk?"

That's where eWorld began taking on usefulness as more than just "another online service." The world was full of those, executives reasoned, but it was *not* full of an Apple-supported service that provided value to customers on several levels. eWorld's life as an additional support vehicle for Apple — which I *must* note still maintains a top-flight customer support department for buyers of Mac hardware — is one of its most important functions. Moreover, by pre-loading eWorld software with each and every new Macintosh sold in most parts of the planet, Apple was creating a community of demand for the service, and, yes, potentially a profit center for itself.

Those of us who are partial to the Macintosh as a computing platform (although, ironically, I'm writing *this* chapter on a Pentium-based system) will note that Microsoft Corporation apparently took another page from Apple's book when, about a year after eWorld's debut, it launched the Microsoft Network (MSN). Of course, some industry people suggest that Microsoft *first* began aping Apple when, about two years after the Mac was launched, Microsoft rolled out the now-forgotten version 1.0 of Windows!

Back to the real world — or, for the moment, back to eWorld. I mentioned before that eWorld is more Mac-like in its approach than other online services. By this I would suggest that, unlike CompuServe and America Online, which are rather imposing services — and rightfully so, with about 4 million members in *each* camp — eWorld is more relaxed and casual. If CompuServe or America Online are big and somewhat business-like, eWorld is like "casual day" at work. Leave your necktie at home, don't worry about putting a crease in your trousers, and, ladies, slacks are just fine when visiting eWorld.

That's not to say that eWorld lacks substantive information or that it is not a structured service. eWorld includes news from Reuters and a bunch of other publishers. It's structured very well, thank you: the computer stuff stays in the computer area and the community items stay in the community area.

For all that structure, though, eWorld is, well, friendlier than some other online services. A friendly voice welcomes you to eWorld. Instead of an overpowering graphics display, you're greeted with soft, cartoon-like illustrations of a town square. Even the idea of a "community center," while sounding a bit hokey, is actually quite pleasant. It all makes the user — novice or experienced — feel at home and not threatened, which is pretty nice.

At this writing, eWorld has well over 120,000 members worldwide and will probably pick up tens of thousands of new members after the last quarter of 1995, in which many computers are expected to be sold for home use. eWorld is planning to grow further, but in a different way than in the past. Instead of being just a client-based service, where the host computers store information that is supplied to your computer using a software "client," eWorld is transforming itself into a service that bases itself on the Internet.

This means users will enter eWorld via a World Wide Web browser, which will enable Microsoft Windows (and UNIX users, among others) to access the service. eWorld is expected to retain electronic mail services and many of the subject areas that it has today. However, my sources at Apple admit that not everything is settled yet, so stay tuned.

eWorld is evolving even as this book is being prepared. As such, what is reported here may — or may not — be available when *you* roam around eWorld. However, what we're discussing here will give you a good picture of what is available on the service and maybe provide an historical "snapshot" of this noble experiment.

Religious Resources

You can find eWorld's religious resources in the Religions and Spiritualities Forum, part of the service's Arts and Leisure pavilion. One obvious difference between eWorld and other online services is that eWorld's spiritual focus is broader than some others in that Christian topics do not initially dominate the eWorld scene in the same way as on other services. From the start of the Religions and Spiritualities Forum, eWorld has endeavored to structure the service as *inclusive,* with room for everything spiritual or anti-spiritual, as atheism is also a welcome topic here.

Upon entering the Religions and Spiritualities Forum, you see a welcome screen (Figure 6-2) that offers five main areas. For example, consider The Sharing Scrolls, where users can post just about any writing related to religion or spirituality.

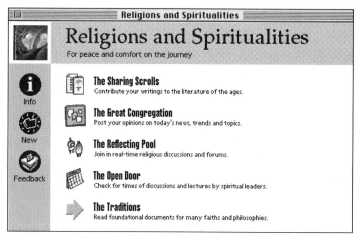

Figure 6-2: Religions and Spiritualities main screen.

"We welcome all kinds of contributions to this area," the eWorld announcement says. Forum leader Roy Sniffen (screen name "Pulpiteer") will screen postings for abusive or hateful language — which are prohibited by eWorld rules — but otherwise, just about any opinion goes. In a recent foray, I found Buddhist documents; a copy of the eulogy prepared by Noa Ben-Artzi for her grandfather, Yitzhak Rabin, the late prime minister of Israel; the "Suhamaraan Scrolls," a New Age document that claims to be the views of a many-times reincarnated being; as well as an issue of a newsletter discussing Bible prophecy.

As you can see, you can find a fair amount of diversity here — and that's something you'll find elsewhere in the forum, too.

One of the most active areas of eWorld is The Great Congregation, (see Figure 6-3) the electronic message board that has 11 main categories — from atheism to eastern and western religions — and 82 sub-topics within those categories. Thousands of messages attest to the popularity of this area.

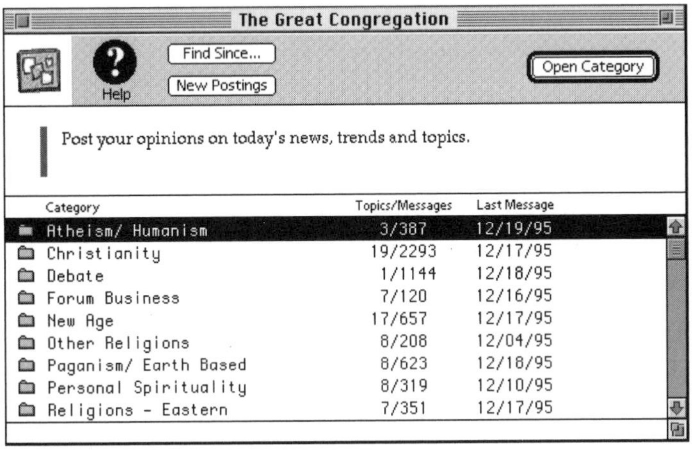

The Great Congregation

Find Since...

New Postings

Help

Open Category

Post your opinions on today's news, trends and topics.

Category	Topics/Messages	Last Message
Atheism/ Humanism	3/387	12/19/95
Christianity	19/2293	12/17/95
Debate	1/1144	12/18/95
Forum Business	7/120	12/16/95
New Age	17/657	12/17/95
Other Religions	8/208	12/04/95
Paganism/ Earth Based	8/623	12/18/95
Personal Spirituality	8/319	12/10/95
Religions - Eastern	7/351	12/17/95

Figure 6-3: The Great Congregation.

Christian topics dominate the message board, with the Christianity section hosting the greatest number of topics and messages. However, there are a fair amount of non-Christian message topics as well. In fact, those interested in non-Christian religions will find a great deal of information and discussion here.

To find religious resources on eWorld, you can look through the Religion and Spiritualities forum, but you can't search by keyword either for groups or for religiously oriented software. At the time of this writing, these searching features had not been implemented.

Responsible Chat Areas

The Reflecting Pool (Figure 6-4) is the covering name for the Religions and Spiritualities Forum's conferences. These weekly chat sessions offer exposure to a variety of topics as wide ranging as the forum itself.

By "responsible," I mean that these areas are ones where tolerance and respect are valued most highly. They allow people to express views without rancor.

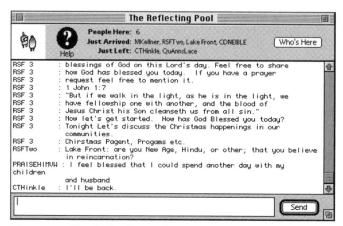

Figure 6-4: The Reflecting Pool.

I should note that along with the wide range of religious discussion, you'll notice something else here that is different from other online services. The general tone of messages and online conversations in the forum is, shall we say, kinder and gentler than that found in some other services. That's because eWorld does not permit "anonymous" screen names — your screen name is created when you sign up and it is linked to your real identity. This way, if you sign on as "John Wesley," eWorld, at least, will know that you're really Horatio Jones. This allows eWorld to track anyone whose postings become abusive. You do not have to list your screen name/real name connection in eWorld's member profiles, but you cannot create an untrackable persona.

I'm not suggesting that this approach is necessarily better than that of America Online, where you can create a separate screen name and post messages with it. AOL could track you down, of course, but the basic premise of eWorld — that you can't hide online from the online service — is a comforting one. It lowers the heat of the flames you sometimes find on other services. (And though all of the online services have tightened things up to help protect children who access their services, another purpose of the eWorld policy is clearly to help protect kids from adult predators who might masquerade as kids themselves.)

I'm of two minds on this practice, to be honest. One of the nice things about the Internet and online services is that you *can* offer your opinions, somewhat anonymously if you like, and leave them out for others to see. However, in too many cases some have turned this liberty into license, and what could be a "normal" or rational discussion degenerates into name calling and shouting. (Here come those messages IN ALL CAPS again!) It's a tough balance, but I applaud eWorld's commitment to keeping some tabs on its members in order to minimize potential abuse.

You can find the real-time discussions by checking the next area listed on the forum menu, The Open Door, which lists the various conferences and their times. As you can see from the illustration (Figure 6-5), there's a wide range of discussions held here weekly.

Figure 6-5: The Open Door window.

Last up on the eWorld Religions and Spiritualities Forum menu is The Traditions, which offers "foundational documents" from many religions and philosophies. Some of these are profound — you can download the text of the Bible; the Book of Mormon; or the Tao Te Ching, a scripture written by Lao Tsu. Some, frankly, are screeds — there's an "Atheist Manifesto," which in my opinion relies too much on ad hominem arguments and generalizations to convey the reasons for atheist belief effectively.

All are accessible to eWorld users, especially because some are supplied in the popular Macintosh HyperCard format, which makes them easier to read on a Mac. I particularly like the King James text and search tools files, which work together to offer an inexpensive — and interactive — Mac version of the scriptures.

Internet Browser

Users of eWorld's version 1.1 software can download a free browser that will display pages from the World Wide Web (see Figure 6-6). It's based on the same proprietary technology used by AOL for its Mac Web browser, so don't expect Netscape here. It is a good introduction to the subject, though.

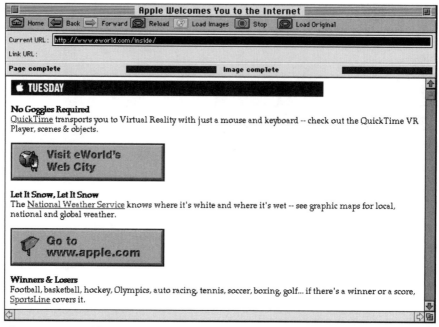

Figure 6-6: eWorld Internet browser.

You will likely want to start with the eWorld "inside" home page (http://www.eworld.com/inside), which will offer you several ways to access the Internet. This home page will also offer a link to the WebCity page and details on the Apple Internet Connection Kit.

The kit, which is sold in stores for around $50, offers a Web browser and other software that will bring you online and keep you there. It's going to be the primary delivery vehicle for Internet access for Apple users — at least that's what Apple Computer hopes — and it's worth checking out. We'll discuss it in the section on software tools for Internet access.

Prodigy: The Oldest and Newest Online Service

One of the Oldest Online Services, Now "Reinvented"

Prodigy was established in 1987 as a joint venture of IBM and Sears, with CBS first joining and then dropping out along the way. It is one of the oldest online services, granted that *old* is a relative term in this burgeoning new world.

The idea was somewhat radical: convince people to pay for an online service that offers news, sports, weather, electronic mail, what-have-you, but also provide advertisements that would appear at the bottom of the screen. The hope was that you would click on the bottom of the screen in order to, well, order . . . shoes, fashions, books, records, and so on. This would be the first electronic mall, or so it was hoped when Prodigy turned up its service nationally in September 1990.

Part of Prodigy's allure was its promise of a graphical presentation of online information back at a time when much of the computing world — and just about all of the online world — was character-based. You could access CompuServe, but all you'd see is a bunch of text. Prodigy promised pictures — crude ones maybe — but pictures nonetheless. The medium was officially called "videotex," which offered this intriguing combination. Well, it *was* intriguing back in the days before the World Wide Web was *invented*, let alone popularized.

Indeed, the pedigree of the founders was impeccable. IBM was the traditional leader of the computer business, producing machines that moved a generation into the digital age. OK, they sort of missed the boat when their original PCs were undercut by an unpopular expansion system (remember the Micro Channel Architecture?) and by less-expensive clones, but at the end of the 1980s, IBM was still a force to be reckoned with — and it remains so in many cases.

Sears? At the time Prodigy launched, it was still "The Place Where America Shops," the central retailer in hundreds of communities across the land. The Sears catalog — the wish book of generations — was a fixture in homes of almost every station. But by the beginning of the 1990s, Sears' fortune had begun to change, thanks in part to changing tastes in the marketplace and also in part to a fellow from Bentonville, Arkansas, named Sam Walton. You might have heard of his little Wal-Mart chain.

Of the three Prodigy partners, CBS brought the most interesting background to the mix. The "Cadillac" of broadcasting networks, the home of Edward R. Murrow and Walter Cronkite, CBS's patrimony included a rich legacy of media savvy and world-wide reach. If anyone could polish what was originally a digital diamond in the rough, it would be CBS, which should have had the graphics down pat.

But "Life," John Lennon once observed, "is what happens while you are making other plans." In the case of Prodigy, its life didn't turn out quite as planned. The service got its members, to be sure, but it wasn't the overwhelming success its backers had hoped. CBS pulled out early in Prodigy's life. Advertisers stayed, by and large, but the rush to online shopping didn't exactly happen as hoped. By 1993, even though Prodigy claimed more members than any other online service, it didn't claim much in the way of profits: the firm laid off 23 percent of its workforce that year.

Today, Prodigy claims more than two million subscribers, and it is gearing up for a new expansion which, the firm hopes, will ride the wave of enthusiasm for "surfing the Net" into profit and presence in the electronic marketplace. In July 1995, Prodigy rolled out a new look (see Figure 7-1)that blends the Hypertext Markup Language (HTML) appearance of the World Wide Web with its formerly graphical appearance.

"This new interface represents the most sweeping and important change in [our] history," explained Ed Bennett, president of Prodigy Services Company, the IBM-Sears joint venture. "Members told us they wanted someone to make sense of the Web and give the Internet a much-needed context. They wanted a new, clean, interface that was Web-centric."

Sometime in 1996, a Macintosh edition will follow on the heels of the Windows version of the new Prodigy software. (From its start, Prodigy has been more oriented toward PC and Windows systems than toward Macs, doubtlessly due to IBM's favoring of DOS and Windows from its early days.) The illustrations are from the Windows version, as new users will find when they use their Windows-based PCs to log on to the service.

Figure 7-1: The Prodigy welcome screen, sporting a new look, circa 1995.

Many Religious Areas/Features

In part thanks to its longevity and in part thanks to a substantial subscriber base — and in one instance, thanks to having the right person in the right place at the right time — the spiritual seeker traveling the Prodigy road will have little trouble finding the major religion areas and features of the service.

Part of this is just numbers: when you assemble two million people, albeit online, you are bound to find several thousand with a common interest. Another part apparently comes from a Prodigy commitment to offer more family-oriented content.

As you'll see, too, serendipity had something to do with it. Thanks to someone with connections in the office of a prominent leader, Prodigy became the first online service to play host to a Cardinal of the Roman Catholic Church in a discussion forum. This blending of a 2,000-year-old church with late twentieth-century technology caught the imagination of many. It was front page news in New York newspapers and drew every television station in town to watch John Cardinal O'Connor, New York's eighth Archbishop, take questions — and some tough ones at that — from a national cyber-audience.

For a variety of reasons, then, Prodigy has had an inside track on the religion beat. Its bulletin boards have often been cutting-edge forums, and I've witnessed some life-changing experiences take place. Particularly notable was a young woman who was fearful about leaving what she called a "cult" and who found immediate reassurance and acceptance from people online.

As seen in Figure 7-2, Prodigy's religion concourse is a bulletin board area of many parts. This is the more "traditional" of Prodigy's services: the firm's original videotex look still dominates. Now, in its move toward the Internet, Prodigy is adding a host of Web-based services, which are illustrated in part in Figure 7-3.

This Web page, moderated by Sharon Gotkin, takes visitors all over the spiritual map, as you shall see. It is a unique presentation because it not only blends commentary with Web links but it also covers all aspects of religion. Also notable is the little window nestled into the Web page reference. This "Interact" screen takes people to Prodigy's chat areas and to Internet's newsgroups related to religion.

Finding your way around Prodigy is basically keyword-based; you select a topic, click on the Jump button, and presto! You're transported there. The Web-based approach of Prodigy's religion Web page makes it easy to find related information; you can also search Prodigy's news wires for items of interest using the Search options on the main menu. A Quick Search permits you to specify date ranges and other qualifiers.

Figure 7-2: Religion Concourse 1 bulletin board.

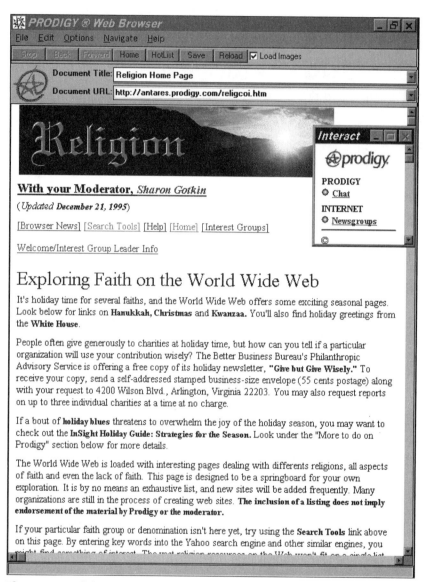

Figure 7-3: Religion resources via Prodigy.

Libraries and E-mail Features

Prodigy contains many libraries of items for use by subscribers. Some of these touch directly on religion, others will enhance your computing enjoyment. Among these is a religion section of "The Software Labs," as seen in Figure 7-4, which offers Christian and Islamic software. Prodigy members have access to an Astrology/New Age software section, as well as the shareware collection of ZD Labs, the software unit of Ziff-Davis, the large computer magazine publisher.

Figure 7-4: The Software Labs religion section offers shareware downloads.

E-mail on Prodigy is another useful area for members. Initially, Prodigy was a closed system where members could only exchange e-mail with each other. Again, in a neighborhood that has numbered as high as two million, that's not necessarily all that bad. Then users could exchange mail with other services via the first major public component of the Internet, which is X.400-based e-mail. (The X.400 standard is one under which users can exchange messages by utilizing a common addressing standard. Much of the work "translates" proprietary addresses such as TVCE42A, my Prodigy address, into something that can be understood across the Net.)

Originally, Prodigy's e-mail format was an extension of its videotex display. Users found that saving messages to disk was difficult, and while the typeface was larger than that used by other services, it was not necessarily easier for writing messages.

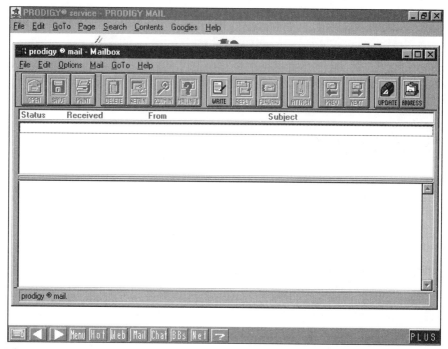

Figure 7-5: Prodigy mail display screen.

Now, however, Prodigy's mail adheres to Internet standards in every respect (see Figure 7-5). Using the graphical interface of Windows, Prodigy is freed from having to use a non-standard display for its e-mail. Combined with Internet addressing capabilities, anyone can easily send an e-mail message to just about anyone else connected to another online service or the Internet.

Also, like some other services, Prodigy will generate faxes and paper mail for you. The faxes are sent via phone lines from a Prodigy server; the paper mail is printed for delivery via the U.S. Postal Service.

Web Browser

Prodigy's Web browser (see Figure 7-6) is now integrated with the rest of the service, as discussed previously. It is straightforward and easy to use, particularly in conjunction with the religious resource list shown in Figure 7-3. You can jump from place to place easily, and you see both the document's title *and* its Universal Resource Locator, or URL. You can save these locations in a "hotlist" for future reference, as you can with other browsers.

Cardinal O'Connor Goes Online

John Cardinal O'Connor is the eighth Archbishop of the Roman Catholic Church's Diocese of New York, which covers the boroughs of Manhattan and the Bronx. In that respect, he is no different from any other Catholic archbishop in the United States, a pastoral overseer who shepherds the churches, schools, and institutions under his purview.

But in part because of the history behind the New York diocese and in part because O'Connor himself has been a provocative figure in the religious "scene" of New York and even the nation, the Archbishop has been an outspoken commentator on the subjects of abortion, homosexuality, and social spending. As a vicar of the Catholic chaplaincy corps in the U.S. armed forces, his views extend beyond the pulpit of St. Patrick's Cathedral.

At the start of 1993, Cardinal O'Connor was the guest in a Prodigy online session, and as mentioned before, it drew national attention, including a front-page story in *The New York Times*.

"I believe the Church can use anything that helps us talk to the people," Cardinal O'Connor said when asked by an audience member about a possible "marriage" between the Catholic Church and technology. "We're not talking to the machines, they're helping us talk to the people."

During the hour-long session, O'Connor answered questions on a variety of topics, ranging from his personal entertainment preferences (no Broadway shows, so far, but the occasional old movie on late night TV) to whether a non-Catholic can receive communion at a Catholic church (only under extraordinary circumstances) to his view on why Pope John Paul II is so popular ("When he looks at you, you are the only person in the world").

One of the most poignant moments came from a person who might have been perceived as a hostile questioner. "As a gay man and one with AIDS, I feel the [Catholic] Church is persecuting me. Can you tell me why I should not convert to a *kinder* and gentler faith such as Episcopalian?"

Cardinal O'Connor's answer was direct and compassionate: "Clearly, you should belong to the church that you think God wants you to belong to. I regret it if you feel the Catholic Church is persecuting you. We have tried to provide enormous facilities for persons with AIDS. I have met with many gay men and women. I believe that the church teaches what Christ taught. If I tried to change that teaching, I would be lacking integrity and lying about what I believe. Give me a call."

The session ended with Cardinal O'Connor saying, "I love doing what I do. . . . This has been a wonderful experience!"

With his online dialogue, Cardinal O'Connor didn't bring about world peace, cooperation between the nations, or even a Mets pennant. But he did open up an important dialogue, showing a pastoral concern — as seen in the last exchange — which was of comfort to many. It's something one hopes that O'Connor's brothers in leadership will undertake, and something other religious leaders should contemplate as well.

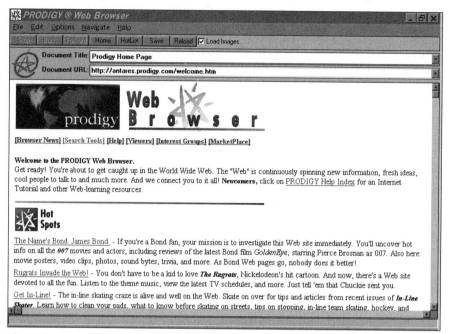

Figure 7-6: Prodigy Internet browser.

One of the interesting things about the Prodigy browser is how it displays those pages composed for Netscape, which at this writing is the dominant Web browser. The short answer is that it does a fairly good job; you can see the graphics and text, although occasionally the words will run together.

The links from one page to another work well with the Prodigy browser, although some tabular displays fall flat. Part of this is likely because of the way a given page is composed, and not totally the fault of the Prodigy browser. At times it can be frustrating, whereas at other times it can be exasperating.

The bottom line is that you may well want to consider the Prodigy browser a good start for getting acquainted with the Internet. Ultimately, you may wish to move on to another browser, and it is very likely that Prodigy will allow that; otherwise, you may need to gain another Internet account.

A New Look and Feel for Prodigy: Expanded Content

The changes that Prodigy is undertaking even as I write this book appear positioned to keep Prodigy astride both the content-provision basis and the burgeoning Internet services race. These changes will ultimately lead to a service that integrates both into a seamless presentation, much as CompuServe has done in its latest release.

This stops a bit short of eWorld's essential "surrender" to the Internet, where the service is going to metamorphose into an Internet service. Whereas eWorld's content may or may not stay as that service changes, Prodigy seems determined to master and expand its content while building a solid bridge to the World Wide Web. It makes sense: it preserves the experience of two million members, and it allows users to venture beyond Prodigy into the Net.

In short, my feeling is that Prodigy has a good plan and is worth a good look by any newcomer to cyberspace.

Two Newcomers: The Microsoft Network and AT&T Interchange

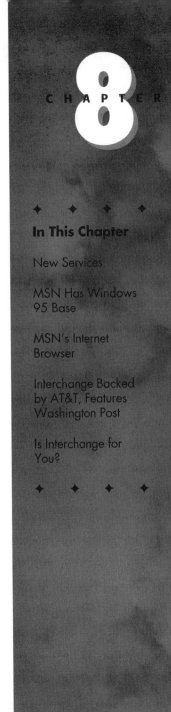

New Services

By this point in time, you might reasonably think that only a fool — or a very, very rich organization — would launch an online service today. After all, we have America Online, CompuServe, eWorld, and Prodigy, not to mention GEnie and Delphi (both of which I will discuss separately). Not every service has succeeded beyond its backers' wildest dreams. Witness the so-far less-than-stellar performances of eWorld, Delphi, and GEnie, which have led Apple Computer to metamorphose eWorld into an Internet service and Delphi to pursue the Internet market separately with differing content and capabilities.

Yet, within the past couple of years, two contenders for online customers have arisen. One is the Microsoft Network, possibly the most controversial online launch in history. The other is Interchange, which Ziff-Davis (a computer publisher) originally started but then sold to AT&T (a long distance communications firm of which you may have heard) when the Ziff family decided it didn't want to be in the online business.

Neither operation seems foolish. The Microsoft Network has achieved modest success: nearly half a million members signed on in the first six months, thanks to the phenomenal launch of Windows 95, which users currently need to run the MSN software. (A Mac client is being planned, Microsoft promises.) Interchange is growing, too, although its growth seems to be tied to the strength of local content providers. In the Washington, D.C., area, for example, Interchange is subtly advertised every day when *The Washington Post* promotes its "Digital Ink" online service, which appears exclusively on Interchange.

An interesting part of these developments is that *both* services are heavily invested in the Internet. Microsoft, as you'll see, is moving toward the Internet at record speed. In December 1995, the company announced that it will support the Java language, that it had released the Beta version of its Internet Browser (although you can use Netscape with MSN just as well), and that the firm will make all of its applications Web-savvy.

Interchange, on the other hand, has always been based on the main aspect of Internet connectivity: TCP/IP. You can acquire an Internet browser to use with Interchange, and the service is touted by its promoters, such as the *Post*, as a "point-and-click" means to the Infobahn.

So perhaps the online services glass really *is* half empty, and not four-fifths full. The nascent success of Interchange and MSN indicates that room may still be left for newcomers in the online services field. Now, let's see what each offers.

MSN Has Windows 95 Base, Internet Browser

The Microsoft Network (Figure 8-1) is perhaps the more interesting of the two new services, mainly because it is not only limited to an operating system platform (as eWorld currently is limited to the Macintosh) but to a specific *version* of an operating environment. Right now if you want to run MSN client software, it's Windows 95 or bust.

This basis in Windows 95 made it relatively easy for Microsoft to roll out and support the service. The company could be sure everyone was singing from the same operating system page, and it could integrate the MSN e-mail system with Microsoft Exchange, the messaging component of Windows 95. And, oh, yes, the nice-looking Windows 95 graphical environment would let users maximize the network's design.

The debut of the Microsoft Network was marked by a fair amount of hoopla and suspense, not only because it was linked with Windows 95 — you might even say intertwined with the new operating software — but because the United States Department of Justice had wondered aloud, via its Antitrust Division, whether Microsoft was unfairly blocking its rivals in the online industry to access of its customer base.

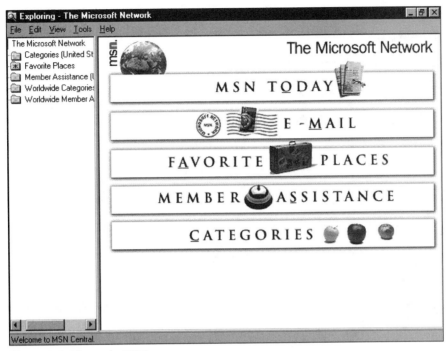

Figure 8-1: The main MSN menu screen.

Firms such as America Online and CompuServe maintained that the MSN software, bundled with Windows 95, would tempt people to sign up for *that* service before they thought about signing up for others. Microsoft countered that users were not obligated to opt for MSN, and, besides, personal computer makers had bundled software for AOL, CompuServe, and Prodigy with their machines for years.

Tensions ran high for a few weeks. The Feds hinted at a probe, or maybe an injunction against the distribution of MSN software. Microsoft averred that it would sign up no more than 500,000 members in its first year, an amount that would equal just about 12 percent of America Online's year-end 1995 total of 4.5 million members. The Justice Department decided not to intervene. MSN bowed, but the rush to sign on wasn't overwhelming.

Built on Windows 95, the Microsoft Network shares the same sleek lines of the operating environment. The main screen offers several key areas: e-mail, news, member services, and "MSN Today," a digest of highlights on the service. From here, you can go to key areas in news and entertainment (see Figure 8-2).

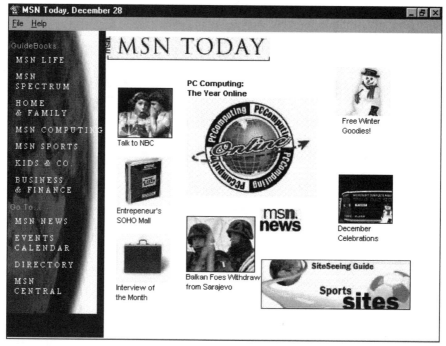

Figure 8-2: MSN Today screen: where do *you* want to go today?

I should mention that the MSN Today screen changes every day, and from it you can determine where in the service you want to visit.

You'll find the Religion section in the "People and Communities" area of MSN (see Figure 8-3). "This area … is devoted to faith(s), denominations, religious communities, news of religion in the modern world, texts, philosophies, religious events, and all related areas of the world's religious beliefs," says the introduction, found in the Religion "information kiosk."

Under the "Religion" message folder, you can find message sections for Afro-Caribbean religions, Baha'i, Hindu, Islam, Orthodox/Eastern Christian Churches, Protestant, Roman Catholic, Latter-Day Saints, and Pagan/Wiccan interests (see Figure 8-4). A message from Lynne Bundesen, who manages the religion area for MSN, invites those who haven't found a category for their faith to send her an e-mail and investigate the possibility of establishing one.

Figure 8-3: "People and Communities" categories include religion.

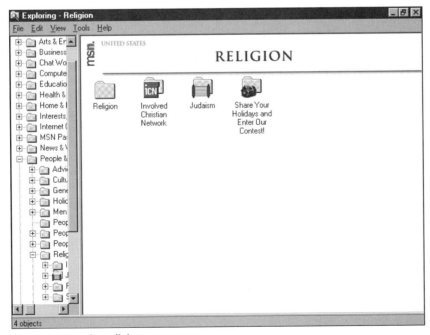

Figure 8-4: Main Religion screen.

The amount of message traffic in a given category depends, naturally, on the number of people involved in that category. Protestant messages account for a fair amount, for example, whereas the Afro-Caribbean section usually contains only about a dozen messages. The sections, I should note, are *unmoderated*, which allows just about anyone to say just about anything. Obviously, obscene, harassing and/or threatening messages are removed, as I've discussed elsewhere, but an unmoderated forum is more freewheeling than some may be used to, so be warned.

A separate folder contains messages of interest to Jews and those interested in Judaism. Two main subfolders exist. One is for messages relating to Chabad Lubavitch, the external outreach of the Lubavitch Hasidic movement, which is one of the more orthodox varieties of Judaism. Among the Lubavitch offerings is a weekly discussion of the key thoughts of the late spiritual leader of the movement, Rebbe Mendel Menachem Schneerson, in "What the Rebbe Says." (See Figure 8-5.)

Yet another feature of the MSN Religion section is the "Involved Christian Network" (see Figure 8-6), which its operators describe as "a place for seekers of fellowship, truth, and other things that really matter in life, like spiritual growth, helping the needy, strengthening your family, and more."

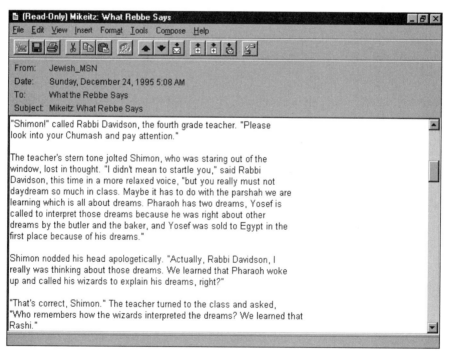

Figure 8-5: A look at "What the Rebbe Says."

Figure 8-6: The Involved Christian Network.

As you can see from Figure 8-6, ICN offers a wide variety of features, including an electronic "Good Newsstand," a "Coffee House," and a guide to various charities to which you may want to contribute.

While I was writing this chapter, I noticed that the ICN's coverage varied in its depth. Improvements are being planned: the group intends to add news from Prison Fellowship, which is one of the most active ministries involved with those who are incarcerated and their families. The group was started by Charles W. Colson, former counsel to the late President Richard Nixon. Colson's conversion experience during the Watergate crisis won worldwide attention.

For now, though, the ICN's offerings — like those of MSN's religion offerings in general — are a bit thin. This doesn't mean that you should avoid MSN, but you will want to investigate it carefully before committing to a long-term relationship.

The MSN Internet Browser

One of the promising features of the Microsoft Network is the Internet Browser provided by the firm to its subscribers. Based on Mosaic, the MSN browser (see Figure 8-7) is certainly adequate for most purposes, and it displays pages designed for Netscape better than some other non-Netscape browsers.

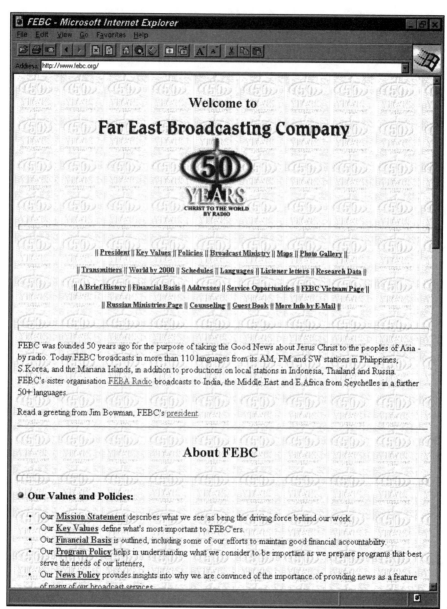

Figure 8-7: The MSN Internet browser, displaying the 50th anniversary home page of the Far East Broadcasting Company (`http://www.febc.org/`), which has provided religious programming to the peoples of Asia for half a century.

At the end of 1995, Microsoft said that it would integrate the Internet even more tightly into its online service. This could involve refinements to its browser but will also likely involve the integration of Java and other technologies into the service.

 For now, though, the Microsoft browser is a good way to begin exploring the Internet, and it can be integrated with the main MSN service to make switching between the two a mouse-click away.

 Another key factor of the Microsoft Network is not just how it can help you with spiritual matters, but how you can use it to keep in touch with Microsoft (and fellow users) about its software products. If you are, particularly, using a product such as Encarta (a CD-ROM-based encyclopedia) or Bookshelf (a collection of reference works on CD-ROM), you'll want to take advantage of the update opportunities that MSN provides.

Just as this book went to press, Microsoft began testing a Macintosh client for its Internet browser. This could provide a gateway into MSN for Mac users, so keep your eyes open for a Microsoft Network for Macintosh announcement!

Interchange Backed by AT&T, Features *Washington Post*

The AT&T-backed Interchange service aims a little higher, perhaps, than some others in the online game. Not backed by a computer maker nor created from the downtime of a mainframe network, Interchange is designed to key in on the interests of readers based on a specific content supplier. In this sense, it is going for class, not necessarily mass, in its subscriber base by appealing to communities of interest, instead of seeking all takers *en masse*.

For example, if you reside in the Washington, D.C., area, as noted before, you'll probably encounter Interchange via the *Washington Post* and its Digital Ink service. Is your home in the twin cities of Minneapolis and St. Paul, Minnesota? Your entree will likely come via the *Star & Tribune*, Minneapolis' leading daily newspaper. And if New Haven, Connecticut, is your home, the *New Haven Register* may invite you to join "Register Online." It's fair to expect that other media will be invited to join as partners in the venture, each time adding a local "spin" to the project.

All of these services, plus the Ziff-Davis ZDNet, tie into Interchange, which is the backbone network. You can switch between these services with a few mouse clicks on the appropriate buttons in the main Interchange screen (see Figure 8-8).

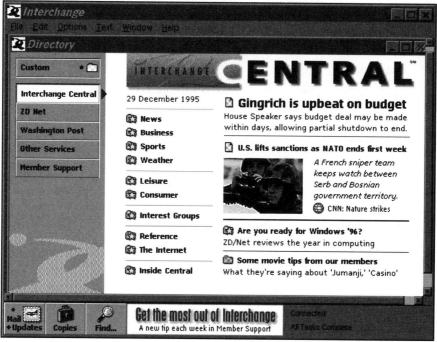

Figure 8-8: The main Interchange screen.

In the case of Digital Ink, for example, presentation is designed to resemble the front page of a conventional newspaper, albeit much more graphical and far less crowded than today's *Washington Post* front page (see Figure 8-9). (Unlike its printed version, the "electronic" *Post* makes liberal use of color in its news "pages." By contrast, readers of a printed newspaper in the Nation's Capital must turn to the *Washington Times* for color on their front page and in their sports section!)

You'll find the Religion section of Interchange (see Figure 8-10) under the "Interest Group" listing of the main Interchange service. Under the Religion banner are 20 different items, including explanatory notes from R. Michael Wilkinson, who manages the section.

"This is an area where you can share your beliefs with people like yourself," Mr. Wilkinson writes in the notes "About Religion" that introduce the forum. "This is also the place to exchange thoughts and ideas with people of different faiths. At the core of it all, you may find that these people are all striving for the same goals that you are: [they're] just using a different path to get there."

Figure 8-9: The *Washington Post*'s Digital Ink "front page."

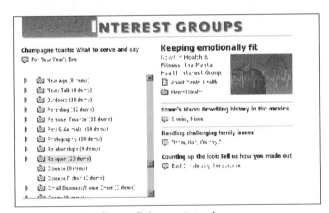

Figure 8-10: Finding Religion on Interchange.

In Figure 8-11, you see some of the 20 different items that fall under the Religion banner. Each of these categories has subgroups. As you might expect, a larger number of items are found in the Christianity section than that for Baha'i, for example, but there's a wealth of material to be found throughout.

Charles Haddon Spurgeon is a widely celebrated evangelical minister, even though more than a century has passed since the height of his popularity. This "Prince of Preachers" was based in London in the nineteenth century, but one of his works lives on, digitally, as shown in Figure 8-12. You can download it from Interchange.

Figure 8-11: Religion Section selections.

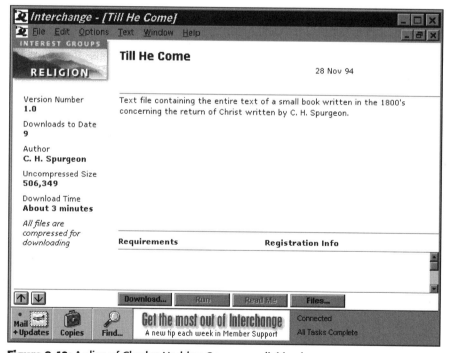

Figure 8-12: A slice of Charles Haddon Spurgeon, digitized.

From the Interchange menu, you can select a keyword search and look up your desired item in any of the main Interchange areas. A quick search on the word *religion* revealed 23 items, just with the click of a mouse button. It's a great way to begin your hunt for spiritual information.

Is Interchange for You?

Interchange is an up-and-coming service, there's no doubt about that. Not as broad as CompuServe or America Online, its elite group of information suppliers represents a powerful source of information nonetheless.

But like MSN, some of its discussion groups are a bit thin. One searching for a great deal of message traffic would do better with Internet newsgroups or one of the larger online services, such as CompuServe or AOL.

That said, I believe Interchange has promise. Like MSN, it is integrating Web access with its basic service. And even though I currently write for the competition, I must acknowledge that the *Washington Post*'s electronic product is interesting and informative, even for those who don't reside in the Washington area. Interchange deserves a look-see, at least.

Ready for the Internet

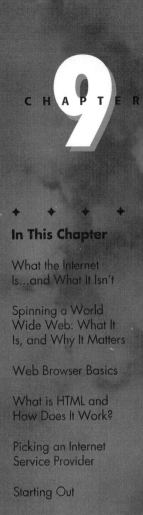
What the Internet Is... and What It Isn't

It's a funny thing about the Internet: that old line about "there's nothing permanent except change" really applies here. When I first outlined this book, about nine months before its first publication, I had a rather clear demarcation between the major online services and the Internet. I knew what CompuServe was, and I knew what an Internet service was.

Back then, in mid-1995, the situation was not quite as stratified as Kipling's famous line, "East is East, and West is West, and never the twain shall meet," but it was relatively close.

Then, everything changed. Perhaps George Eliot was right: "Life is measured by the rapidity of change, the succession of influences that modify the being," and perhaps not, but the fact is the Internet is merging with the online services. As noted in the chapters on the various services, you now have either one click switching between the main service and a Web browser or an integration of the two services. Look at CompuServe, America Online, Prodigy, or eWorld, and you'll see the tight integration of Web browsing with the core services.

So to say — as I would have nine or more months ago — that the Internet is not a traditional online service and vice versa is no longer entirely correct. Instead, I should more correctly say that while the Internet *remains* a "network of networks" where you can hook up with other computer sites all over the planet, it is *becoming* a component of many online services, if not taking on the characteristics of one in and of itself.

What you see in Figure 9-1 is *not* a menu for a traditional online service...or is it? It's the main menu screen for Pipeline USA, part of the PSInet family of Internet services, as seen in Windows 95. Though it looks very similar to menus for CompuServe, *et al*, it does not point toward specially reserved sections but rather toward various areas *on the Internet* where you can find these items.

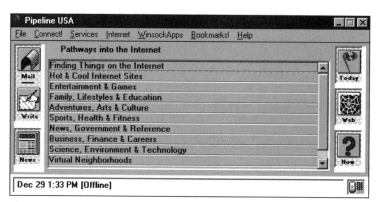

Figure 9-1: The Pipeline Internet Service Menu, as seen in Windows.

This is at once the beauty and challenge of the Internet. The beauty is that you can find so much out there, from the Vatican (`http://www.vatican.va/`) to Chabad Lubavitch (`http://www.chabad.org/`) to the Dalai Lama (`http://www.manymedia.com/tibet/DalaiLama.html`), but you need help in finding it. You have many tools for this, one of which is this book. But the Internet itself, or, more properly, Internet Service Providers, are helping too, and that's a good thing.

So what is the Internet, and what *isn't* it? The definitions are changing, but as a general rule of thumb, Internet services are those available to customers of more than one Service Provider, albeit if they know the *location* of the given item. Conversely, if you *must* sign up with a given network to access a given item — say the religion forums on CompuServe — that's *not* an Internet service.

Perhaps the most interesting thing will be what happens in the next two years. By that time, who knows what will and won't be available on the Net. Your guess is as good as mine at this point — and perhaps we'll meet in a new edition of this book to discuss the results.

Meanwhile, what is this thing called the Web?

Spinning a World Wide Web: What It Is, and Why It Matters

Earlier in this book, I discussed the origin of the World Wide Web and how it was created in Europe as a way to display related "pages" of information easily. That information included graphics, and as a result, paved the way for the kind of Web displays we see today. The following examples show the diversity of the displays available, as well as the diversity of the organizations behind those displays.

The simple design of the introductory page for the Vatican's home page (Figure 9-2) is a lead-in to other pages featuring (at this writing) a handwritten greeting by Pope John Paul II, the text of his Christmas message, and greetings in dozens of languages. In itself, these items aren't much different from those available in Vatican City publications, on sale at a bookstand there, or perhaps by mail.

Figure 9-2: The Vatican's Web page.

The big difference, however, is that you can instantly access these items from your home. Indeed, in the 48 hours after the Christmas Day launch of the Vatican site, the Holy See reported 307,786 visits to the Vatican site. The Vatican press office read close to 1,000 e-mail messages that were sent in (the Pope is not known to use a personal computer).

This is the beauty of the World Wide Web. We can all "visit" St. Peter's Square without jet lag. This is also the importance of the World Wide Web: religious organizations can put their messages out with relatively little effort and expense, and they can reach astonishingly far.

With roughly 1.4 million congregates worldwide, the Salvation Army is about 1/1000th the size of the billion-strong Roman Catholic Church. Yet its World Wide Web site (`http://www.SalvationArmy.org`) (Figure 9-3) has attracted thousands of visitors, people inquiring about the organization's services, asking for help in finding lost relatives (an Army specialty), or offering assistance. Leaders of the movement have pronounced the WWW venture a success, and why not? It has given this "Army without guns" exposure that it might not have gained otherwise.

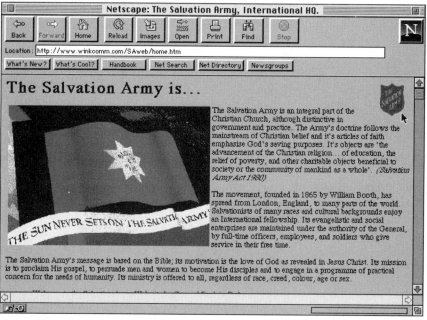

Figure 9-3: The Salvation Army's home page.

Neither the Salvation Army nor the Roman Catholic Church would say they are directly competitive, nor is this comparison meant to suggest that. In the marketplace of ideas, which the Web has certainly become, these two organizations are on a roughly equal footing, Web-wise. *That*, I would submit, is the great secret of the Web: you can be as large as the Roman Catholic Church or as small as a storefront congregation. On the Web, you can be equals.

Why does the Web matter? I'd like to suggest a lesson from history. In one of the greatest misunderstandings of reality, Communist leader Josef Stalin once asked, derisively, "How many divisions does the Pope have?" Today, Stalin, who commanded a vast military, is reviled, whereas Pope John Paul II, who saw Stalinist oppression invade his native Poland, is loved around the world, even by non-Catholics. Perhaps the question to ask today is, "How many Web pages does the Pope have?"

No, I'm sad to report that the Web will not likely replace the field of battle for settling human conflict, but it is emerging as perhaps the leading forum for ideas and their expression as the twentieth century winds down. In this sense, the Web is extremely important, and it's why *you* need to become involved with it.

Web Browser Basics

The pages illustrated in Figures 9-2 and 9-3 were first displayed on my computer screen using a piece of software called a *Web browser*. A browser translates the raw coding of documents created for the Web into something graphical. That's because a Web page is created in *Hypertext Markup Language* or *HTML*, a series of codes that tell a Web browser that the picture goes here, the text goes there, and a graphic goes over here.

Look at Figure 9-4, which shows the HTML-coded text of the "World Wide Web First Ward," a site for members of the Church of Jesus Christ of Latter-Day Saints, also known as the Mormons. The codes and characters you see are great for a Web browser to read: it will translate them into the proper display. For you and me, however, trying to extract the salient information could be a challenge without a browser.

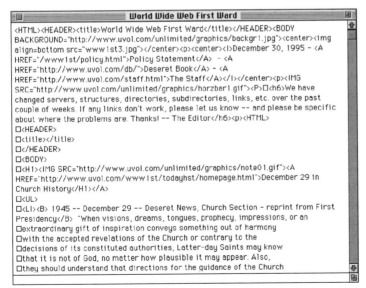

Figure 9-4: The HTML coding of the "World Wide Web First Ward," a page for Mormons. In its raw form, this is not very appealing or easy to read.

Now, take that text and view it with Netscape. The jumble of codes becomes an eye-catching display that informs the viewer and draws him or her in. As you can see, a Web browser makes looking at information much easier. But that's not all. A Web page, unlike even the printed page of this book, can contain not only words and pictures, but *hotlinks* to other sites on the Web. Somewhat like a never-ending chain, these links can lead you from a general subject (let's say it's the home page shown in Figure 9-5) to various other resources of interest for those who follow Mormon topics.

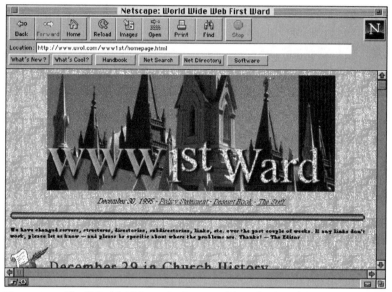

Figure 9-5: The "World Wide Web First Ward," as displayed by version 2.0 of the Netscape browser.

The beauty of a Web browser is that it lets you see and explore all these things. At this writing, Netscape is the most popular Internet browser, but NCSA Mosaic and browsers supplied by America Online, Prodigy, CompuServe, and eWorld each have their devoted followers. No doubt the popularity of Web browsers is having an effect beyond the Web. Shares in Netscape Communications, which hadn't really posted a profit as of this writing, opened at $28 apiece, within 10 minutes the price went to $78, and at the end of 1995, Netscape traded in the $130 range. Whether this will continue is anyone's guess, but the impact of the Web on Wall Street is a good measure of its impact on society at large.

What is HTML and How Does It Work?

Hypertext Markup Language, or HTML, is a system for coding text so that it shows up in the proper fashion on the Web. The nuts and bolts behind HTML were created by the now-famous Tim Berners-Lee, who worked with the Swiss research facility known as CERN and is now affiliated with MIT, along with Daniel Connolly of Atrium.

HTML is an application that conforms to the *Standard Generalized Markup Language*, or *SGML*, which the International Standards Organization classified as ISO 8879. This may sound like gibberish, but it means that HTML conforms to certain standards for computer text display. In turn, documents that conform to HTML can be displayed on the Web and will, more or less, look the same regardless of the browser used.

One way to think of this is to transfer the model from ISO standards to operating systems and applications. These days you can share files between Macs and PCs with relative ease, but not too long ago you needed to have either the same program on two different machines or a *file translator* to handle the job. Ultimately, these applications grew up, so a PC running Windows 95 can read a Microsoft Word or WordPerfect file created on a Mac (albeit one saved to a PC-format disk), whereas a Macintosh running WordPerfect, Nisus Writer, or Microsoft Word can read just about any word processing file you throw at it from a PC, although you may need extra translators.

Have I lost you yet? I hope not. What HTML does is act as a "super" word processor for the Web. Create your Web page on whatever computer you want to use (PC, Macintosh, UNIX, Amiga, whatever) but *code* the final product with HTML (and save it all as a *text* or *ASCII* file) and post it to the Web. I can then *view* your page regardless of which computer I am using, so long as I have a good Web browser.

The really *neat* part of this is that I can save your Web page with Netscape as an HTML file, import it into my word processor, and edit it or use elements from it.

As you will read in a moment, this capability does not dissolve the meaning of copyright, or the protection of copyright law. If you are going to use copyrighted material for any purpose other than "personal use," which is loosely defined as being for your own education and enjoyment, then *don't even think* of doing that *without* getting the permission of the copyright holder, preferably in writing.

Copyright aside, this means that HTML is a "universal" document language. You and I could share documents across the Web and collaborate on creating pages, so long as we both use HTML and compatible editors on either end. It would matter little whether we used the same computer or even the same editor/word processor.

As to the nuts and bolts of HTML editing, that's beyond the scope of this book. In fact, a quick glance around my office revealed four different books on HTML editing, and I know several more are out there. One book that I can recommend is *HTML For Dummies*, written by Ed Tittel and Steve James. It's an IDG book, yes, and it's very thorough while being very easy to use. Windows users will appreciate the included diskette of templates.

Then again, you may decide that you don't want to delve that deeply into HTML, and that's OK, I guess. After all, I'm not an auto mechanic, yet I drive a car; you don't have to be an expert in HTML in order to either benefit from its creation or even create pages for the Web.

How so? By using software that will help code documents into HTML for you. If you're a devotee of Microsoft Word for Windows, a program called Quarterdeck Web Author (`http://www.quarterdeck.com`) will be of interest. It works with Word 6 for Windows and lets you design pages for the Web based on Word documents. Users of WordPerfect for Windows can download a free add-on from the company that allows you to translate WP files into HTML files (`http://www.novell.com` will point you there).

On the Macintosh, you have a couple of options. One is PageMill, a program from Adobe, Inc. (`http://www.adobe.com`) that you can use to generate Web pages. The other — and one I particularly like — is WordPerfect 3.5 for Macintosh. It is supplied with HTML editing tools built right in and a free Netscape browser, so you can preview your pages before you upload them to the Internet. You can, by the way, find out more about this truly excellent program in an exciting, humorous, and informative book called *WordPerfect 3.5 For Macs For Dummies*, published by IDG Books and written by — aw, shucks, me! Yes, I'm a bit biased (and proud), but I had a lot of fun with WordPerfect and I gained a great deal of appreciation for the included HTML features in this software.

If you are neither a WordPerfect or Microsoft Word fan — and many users are neither — don't fret. ClarisWorks, available on both Macintosh and Windows 95 platforms, includes HTML support (`http://www.claris.com`). So does Nisus Software, Inc. (`http://www.nisus-soft.com/~nisus`), and its Web page will also direct you to Sandra Silcot's Nisus HTML Janus Macros Home Page (`http://www.unimelb.edu.au/~ssilcot/SilcotsHTMLMacrosReadMe.html`), where you can find a bunch of macros that you can use with Nisus Writer 4.1 to create HTML documents.

Another interesting resource, from the University of Melbourne in Australia, is an "Introduction to HTML Course," which supports the HTML 2.0 standard. Point your browser to `http://www.unimelb.edu.au:801/courses/publish/HTML/IntroHTML.html` and begin your adventure. Isn't this neat? You can *use* the Web to learn how to *write* for the Web, and there's no extra charge beyond your Internet service fee. Bravo to David Morton of the University of Melbourne for providing the course, and a tip of the hat to the aforementioned Nisus aficionado Sandra Silcot for including a pointer to the course on the Nisus HTML Janus Macros Home Page.

Here's the bottom line: HTML is part of the wave of the future. You should be aware of its importance, at least, and perhaps will want to gain some proficiency with it.

As a final note, new enhancements and authoring tools for the Net are emerging all the time. One of the newest is Java, which is being supported by Netscape, Sun Microsystems, and even Microsoft. Though I have no practical experience with Java to share with you — at this writing, it's just too new — I can offer a couple of locations where you can aim your Web browser for more information: `http://www.acm.org/ ~ops/java.html`, which is maintained by Omar Patiño Siliceo and the Association for Computing Machinery. It's unofficial but loaded with resources for would-be Java programmers/authors. The official Java home page is `http://java.sun.com/` and it contains a wealth of information straight from Sun Microsystems.

Picking an Internet Service Provider

Finding an Internet Service Provider may be as easy as clicking a mouse button on your computer, or it may be a long, arduous search that involves numerous phone calls, e-mails, and a night or two of comparisons.

Part of it depends on you. No, that's not right — *all* of it depends on you. On your location, your budget, your computer, your need for support, your preferences, your budget (did I mention that one?), and the like. Therefore, the pointers in this section are just that: pointers. You will need to do some research, run some numbers through a spreadsheet or calculator, and perhaps experiment.

If you are a student or teacher at a university, an engineer in a technology-savvy corporation (or an employee in one), in government, or in the military, you may have free access to the Net through your employer or institution. Indeed, if you're one of the growing legion of telecommuters, you might have that access from your home. I knew a young lady who once worked at a major West Coast university. OK, it was Stanford University in Palo Alto, California. The school gave her a special modem and contracted with Pacific Bell to run an ISDN line to her home. The result? She had super-fast Internet access, 24 hours a day, seven days a week.

If you plan to be an occasional visitor to the Internet, you may be satisfied with the access provided by America Online, CompuServe, or Prodigy, especially because the latter two now offer (or soon will) support for the Netscape browser. Apple's eWorld, as noted earlier, is evolving into an Internet-based service, and Mac owners may want to find some solace there. The plusses may seem obvious: you may have all the software you need, or the service will let you download and install some easily. You have one number to call, one bill to pay, and in the case of all of the services named earlier, you will see Web service integrated with their main service offerings.

In my opinion, the major negative feature of using one of the major online services as an Internet access provider can be cost. Take it from me, it's easy to get lost in Internet searching and spend many more hours there than you may want to otherwise. You may want to use certain features of the Internet, such as Internet Relay Chat, or you may want to have some storage space for your own Web pages. Not all of these are available through the online services.

Therefore, you may want to pick an Internet Service Provider apart from your online service. You can find a list of those providers through the famous Yahoo search engine. Use the reference `http://www.yahoo.com/Business/Corporations/Internet_Access_Providers/` and you will locate a life raft of sources. The list currently includes links to 16 other listings of ISPs, listings of close to 1,700 regional providers, 10 international providers, and 76 national U.S. providers. Yahoo is a great search engine for the Internet and this area is a good sample of what you can find there. Another good source for ISP information is maintained by UNIX-fanatic Matthew James Marnell at `http://www.portia.com/matt/ISP/menu.html`.

If you need to find a provider and you don't have access to a computer yet, many public libraries offer free Internet connections. And if you need to find a provider the old-fashioned way (without a computer), try the Yellow Pages under "Internet Service Providers" or "Information Services."

Your criteria for picking an Internet provider will vary. You may want a national service if you travel frequently or plan to move around a bit. If you know you're going to stay put in a given area, a regional or local provider might be your best buy, dollar-wise.

In investigating ISPs, you should be aware of the kinds of computers they support, the type of access they provide (in my opinion, a good provider will offer dial-up access to 28.8 kilobits per second as well as ISDN access and even higher speed service if need be), and the level of support they offer. If you're a computer novice, you'll want the ISP to either install and configure your Internet software for you or give you serious hand-holding on how to do this. If you're ordering a high-speed service, you'll want them to coordinate the installation of the special phone line and perhaps provide any other equipment you need.

Pricing for Internet services is fluid. Most local and regional providers are offering an "unlimited" access account for $12.95 to $25 per month, with the amount dependent upon the kind of Internet connection you desire. If you want to dial up the Net with a SLIP or PPP connection, many services will price access toward the higher end of the scale. If you can content yourself with text-only Internet access you can pay toward the lower end of that range.

SLIP and PPP are what are known as *transfer protocols* — in other words, a way of translating and sending data over a network to your phone line, to your modem, and finally to your computer. They are higher demand services than some other Internet connections, which is why some providers charge a premium price for SLIP and PPP connectivity. You can use pseudo-SLIP and TIA-like services to get around the high cost, but with the advent of ISDN access to the home (another story beyond the scope of this book), it should become cheaper and easier to get full, unfettered Internet access.

You *can* make a lower-priced Internet account behave like the SLIP/PPP service account that costs more. Many Internet hands affirm The Internet Adapter, or TIA, as a great pseudo-SLIP option. It works with most Internet host computer platforms, and allows your computer to display graphical information from the Internet using a Web browser. I have not had personal experience with TIA, but you can use an online service browser to point to `http://marketplace.com/tia/tiahome.html` and find an abundance of information about TIA.

Starting Out

Once you've picked a provider, the time has come to set up your software, dial up the provider, and log on. As you do, you will either go to a home menu similar to that in Figure 9-1 or to a Web home page. From there, you should be able to negotiate around the Internet either by clicking on links from the home page or by entering locations, typing in the *Uniform Resource Locator* or *URL*.

You've seen URLs throughout this book and, starting in the next chapter, you'll see more of them. The idea is to find the ones that most interest you, enter them, and explore.

Don't worry about making mistakes as you surf the Net. It's very difficult to do anything seriously wrong, and around almost every corner of the Net is a new adventure worth taking.

Are You Netsurfing with Me, God?

The Top Ten Religious Web Sites

Just about any Top Ten selection you can think of is, of course, subjective in one form or another. Even if done by a ballot, the subjectivity comes from those who do the voting. Therefore, this list of the Top Ten religion sites is subjective. It's based on my own perspective, searches on the Net, and information I've gleaned from a variety of sources. Therefore, my Top Ten isn't necessarily your Top Ten.

I would be remiss if I didn't mention one important reference source, whose listings inspired me to do some searching of my own. That's Point Communications, a New York City-based organization that rates Web sites and dishes out a seal of approval, if you will, by designating a site among the Top 5 Percent of available Web sites. Point can be found at http://www.pointcom.com and it's well worth your inspection.

A caveat before you dive in: As the good people at Point will tell you, the Internet is a constantly changing place. It is possible that some of these sites will have changed either in terms of content or location. Some may no longer be in existence for various reasons. They are presented as a snapshot of what's out there.

Consider this chapter, then, as an introduction to the rich diversity of religious topics available on the Net, a starting place for your own investigations and discoveries. And remember, the Internet is not necessarily a scary place filled with bad things. You can find a great deal that is worthwhile, but only if you look.

Number One: Facets of Religion

http://marvin.biologie.uni-freiburg.de/~amueller/religion/

Part of the World Wide Web Virtual Library, the Religion index (see Figure 10-1) is maintained by Armin Müller of the University of Freiburg in Germany. It offers a wide range of links to other religious sites all over the planet and does so in a straight-forward manner.

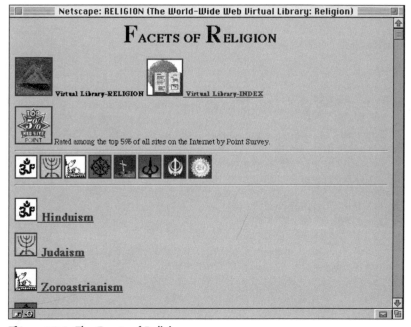

Figure 10-1: The Facets of Religion page.

Müller offers little in the way of commentary, other than to categorize his main religion listings (from Hinduism to Baha'i, arranged, he says, by the age of the religion). You can click on each of these categories to find a great number of listings on each topic, or you can search across the lists for a keyword.

If this were all Müller offered on this page, it would easily qualify for top flight status, but there's more. He includes links to sites featuring relics of ancient religion, interreligious resources, religious newsgroups, and six more religion indexes on the Web.

Behind the individual categories lies a fair amount of depth. That's one of the reasons why this is such a good site: It personifies the Web concept of links leading to other links. For the person wanting an overview of religious resources available on the Internet, this is an ideal starting place.

Number Two: Fides Quaerens Internetum (The Christian Theology Page)

http://apu.edu:80/~bstone/theology/theology.html

Bryan Stone of Azusa Pacific University is the creator and maintainer of this page (see Figure 10-2), which is aimed at presenting "serious Christian theological activity" for Internet users. Though accessed only 3,400 times in its first 10 weeks, the site was rated in the Top 5 Percent by the Point survey, in large measure because of its comprehensiveness.

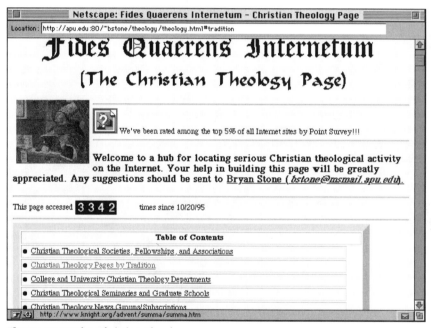

Figure 10-2: The Christian Theology page.

This is not a home page for the faint of heart, theologically speaking. This is, mostly, a roll-up-your-sleeves-and-get-to-work page, aimed chiefly at theological students and professors, and those who follow theology from an educational perspective. Its links run the gamut from Christian theological associations to pages with links to colleges and universities.

Those looking for publications in the theological field or for jobs in this arena will find resources here. If the going gets too difficult, you can click on a link to what is advertised as theological humor, although the jokes (which are rather abstruse) center more on philosophy and academics than on theology *per se*.

Overall, this is a good site worth looking at, particularly if Christian theology is a special interest of yours.

Number Three: The Judaica Web World

http://www.nauticom.net/users/rafie/judaica-world.html

Jews — or people who are interested in Judaism — will want to check out this site. (See Figure 10-3.) From daily Torah readings to a multitude of links to Jewish Web sites, you will be able to examine the broad range of culture and religious beliefs that fall under the broad banner of Judaica. The site provides links to major cultural and religious sites of just about every stripe of Judaism.

Figure 10-3: The Judaica Web World home page.

As you will see in a later section, to be a Jew is not merely to embrace a religion. It involves, in large part, ethnic identity and a way of life that transcends an hour or two each week in a synagogue. For the observant Jew, one who seeks to uphold the basic laws and commandments, this involves an emphasis on Torah study, on educating one's children, and on what one eats, among other things.

One of the interesting aspects of this site, therefore, is a link to Kosher recipes for Asian-style meals. For those who envision that a Kosher lifestyle means a diet of boring foods because things such as pork, lard, shrimp, and the like are forbidden, this link alone is worth a look. You'll be surprised at the good things you find there.

Number Four: Adventist Information Ministry

http://www.andrews.edu/homes/Staff/aim/shared/www/aim.org/index.html

According to the latest available figures, nearly 8 million people around the world are baptized adult members of the Seventh-Day Adventist Church, which began in the United States roughly 150 years ago when William Miller, a preacher, created quite a stir with predictions of the end of the world and of the return of Jesus Christ in 1844. When this did not happen, some "Millerites," as his followers were known, formed their own church, incorporating seventh-day Sabbath worship as part of their distinguishing beliefs.

Adventist Information Ministry (see Figure 10-4), or AIM, is a part of the North American division of the SDA church and fulfills requests for information and literature. With its Web site, visitors can find information about the SDA Church and its beliefs, and they can read basic literature by Ellen G. White, the movement's founder.

This site is interesting for several reasons:

◆ The SDA Church is one of the few founded and led (for several years) by a woman.

◆ The SDA Church is one of the most successful American-born religions.

◆ The Adventist's emphasis on health and vegetarianism has had a wide impact on society. The movement's Loma Linda University in California has been the site of many breakthroughs in medical research, and independent studies have shown that the Adventist lifestyle offers significant health benefits.

◆ Largely through the Adventists' influence, Battle Creek, Michigan, gave birth to two cereal empires (delightfully satirized by T. Coraghessan Boyle in his novel, *The Road to Wellville*), which brought the idea of cereal to America's breakfast tables and changed the eating habits of a nation.

Those who want to study Adventism seriously can find links to just about every SDA site in existence, including its universities and individual churches all over the world (those that have Web pages, that is). AIM is a terrific example of what can be done by a denomination to make itself more accessible to the masses.

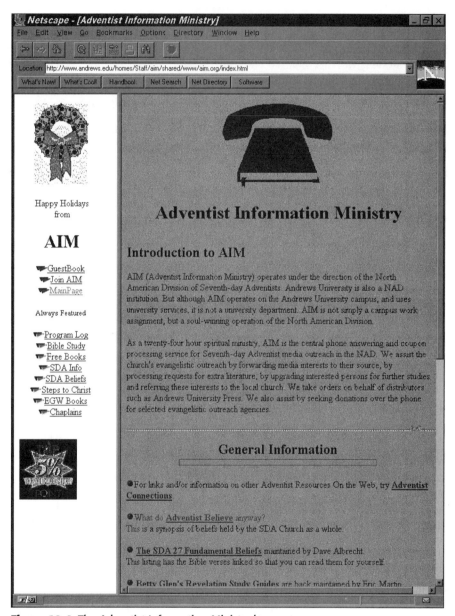

Figure 10-4: The Adventist Information Ministry home page.

Number Five: The Jerusalem Mosaic

http://www1.huji.ac.il/jeru/jerusalem.html

Benjamin Disraeli said it best: "The view of Jerusalem is the history of the world; it is more, it is the history of earth and of heaven." No single city has seen more controversy, engendered more passion, or birthed more religious views and traditions than Jerusalem. Today, perhaps no city on earth is more important, more newsworthy, and more interesting to more people than Jerusalem.

This site (see Figure 10-5) is not specifically religious in nature, in that it is not sponsored by a given movement or denomination. But to separate the city from its spiritual nature is, quite frankly, impossible. Jerusalem is a city suffused with spiritual import. In the older sections of this 3,000-year-old city especially, it seems as if every inch of ground has a religious significance to one or more of the three major religions that claim an interest in Jerusalem: Judaism, Christianity, and Islam.

You will find much of interest here in seeing sights in both the "old" city and today's Jerusalem. Whatever your belief and background, I challenge you to "visit" Jerusalem via this Web site and not be moved. Click on a button and see the Second Temple. Learn about the food and customs of the people. Learn the background of the early Muslim sites in Jerusalem. These items are found in the site's "mosaic" tours of the old and new cities, and are a great introduction to this city of the ages.

Number Six: The Taizé Community

http://www.almac.co.uk/taize/taize.html

Since the days of the Reformation more than 500 years ago, not to mention since the split between the Roman Catholic and Eastern Orthodox churches centuries earlier, many Christians of all persuasions have desired greater unity in the Church at large. One of the more recent efforts at ecumenism and reconciliation, which started on the Roman Catholic side, is Taizé, a monastic community in France whose outreach activities include much work among young people.

This site (see Figure 10-6) features news of the group's activities, devotional material, and recordings of music from the community. It's not for everyone, I suppose, but the concept of greater cooperation among the branches of Christianity is appealing on at least one level: when you consider the damage, human and emotional, that sectarian strife has caused, maybe reconciliation has something to offer us all.

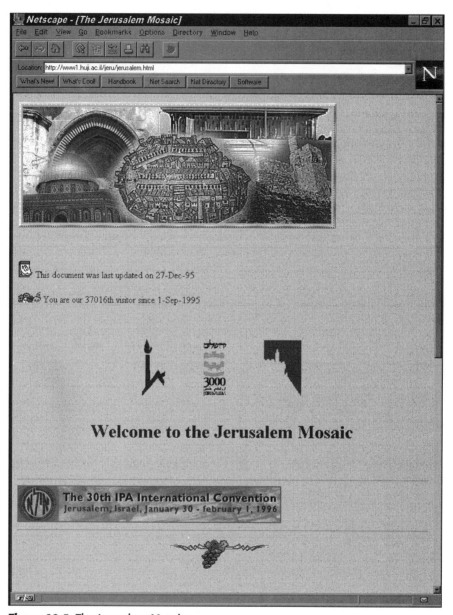

Figure 10-5: The Jerusalem Mosaic.

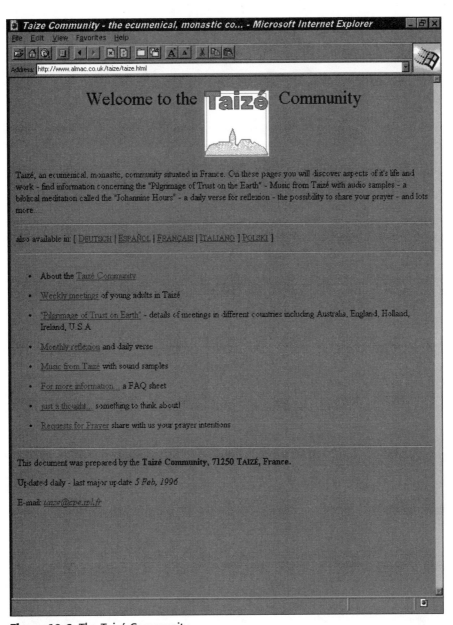

Figure 10-6: The Taizé Community.

Number Seven: Jews for Jesus

http://www.jews-for-jesus.org/

Perhaps no other group in the history of organized religion has at once created as much astonishment, anger, excitement, and resentment as this band of, well, Jews who believe that Jesus of Nazareth isn't merely for Christians, but *is* the Jewish Messiah. To many observant Jews, this belief is a most profound heresy. To many non-observant Jews, the movement rejects what they believe to be an essential part of Judaism, the idea that Jews don't believe in Jesus as the son of God.

But to those with a "more open mind," the Jews for Jesus movement has touched many lives, both Jewish and Gentile. Its work has helped Jews place Jesus of Nazareth, or *Yeshua ha-Notzee,* in a Jewish context, and it has helped thousands of Christians understand the very Jewish roots of their faith.

This home page (see Figure 10-7) offers an interactive link with the organization, a place to read testimonies of Jews who believe in Jesus, and one where a user can find out about the Liberated Wailing Wall, a musical group associated with Jews for Jesus. Though some may reject this concept out of hand, I believe this site — one of the first evangelical Web sites to appear on the Internet — is worth a look.

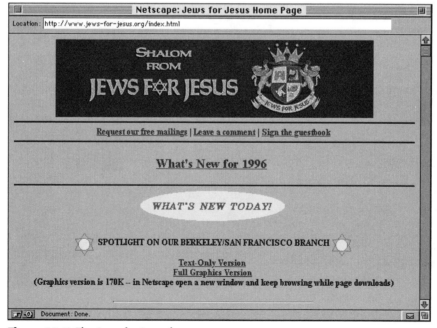

Figure 10-7: The Jews for Jesus home page.

Number Eight: Soka Gakkai

http://www.sgi-usa.org/

In 1995, when the subject of religion in Japan was mentioned in the West, it was most likely in connection with Aum Shin Rikyo, the cult whose leaders and members were accused of complicity in a nerve gas attack in Tokyo's subway system.

There is another native religious movement in Japan that has attracted global attention, however. It is the Soka Gakkai flavor of Buddhism, a group that grew exponentially in the 1980s and gained a reputation — deserved or not — as a "prosperity" religion. Soka Gakkai's disciples follow the teachings of the 13th century Japanese Buddhist monk Nichiren.

This home page (see Figure 10-8), maintained by the group's United States office in Santa Monica, California, seeks to introduce the movement to the West and to offer details about the benefits of its chant, *Nam-Myoho-Renge-Kyo*. Impressive are not only the details of its belief but the breadth of the movement: you'll find Soka Gakkai disciples just about everywhere on the planet.

Figure 10-8: The Soka Gakkai home page.

Number Nine: Global Hindu Electronic Network

http://rbhatnagar.csm.uc.edu:8080/hindu_universe.html

Armin Müller's religion site (see Figure 10-1) lists Hinduism as the oldest religion in the world. Scholars can debate that point, perhaps, but there's no denying that the religions based on the Vedic scriptures have had a tremendous influence both in India and, during the last 100 years, in the West.

Since the British colonization of India (which ended in 1947) and especially since the introduction of Hinduism to the United States during the nineteenth century's Parliament of World Religions in Chicago, Hindus have found a receptive audience among those who were not born in India. The Hindu Universe home page site (see Figure 10-9) offers a good introduction to the basics of Hindu belief and practice, as well as links to the Vedic texts, including the *Bhagavad Gita*.

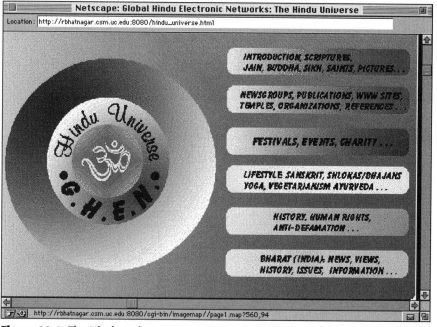

Figure 10-9: The Hindu Universe.

Number Ten: CyberMuslim

http://www.uoknor.edu/cybermuslim/

The rise of Islam in recent years, both in the West (it's the fastest-growing faith in Britain, for example) and in the resurgence of Islamic belief and practice in the more "secular" of the Middle Eastern states, has given some cause for concern and others cause for rejoicing.

The majority of Muslims, claims former Egyptian Chief Justice Sai'd Al-Ashmawy in a *Reader's Digest* article, are people who "pray, give to the poor, [and] make the pilgrimage to Mecca." They are not warring fanatics and militants bent on destroying Western civilization.

Indeed, there are similarities between Islam and Judaism and between Islam and Christianity. Like Jews, Muslims eschew "unclean" foods, emphasize study of scripture, and honor Abraham as a prophet. Like Christians, Muslims revere Jesus, whom they believe was a prophet sent from God. Although clear theological differences exist among Islam, Judaism, and Christianity, reasonable people on all sides can find common ground and areas of mutual respect.

The CyberMuslim (see Figure 10-10) archive is a good step toward that goal. Using it, you'll get a good introduction to Islam, the Holy Koran, and Islamic practice.

Figure 10-10: The CyberMuslim site.

Using What You Find

As you'll see in your wanderings across the World Wide
Web — and as you'll discover in the remaining chapters
of this book — a *lot* of information is out there for you to find.
What can you do with it once you find it? You can read it on the
screen of your computer, yes, but you may not be able to carry
that screen onto a commuter bus or bring it to class that day.
You can make a "bookmark" of a given location, telling your
browser to point to that spot again whenever you select that
notation.

But the good news about the Web is that you can do more than
just visit a given site. You can interact with many sites in many
ways. You can send e-mail (the Vatican received more than 1,000
pieces of e-mail in a 48-hour period after its Christmas Day 1995
Web-site debut, for example), or you can call a given organization. You can also print out a given Web page, send the page (or
its address, called a URL) to a friend, or even download the page
and edit it with a text editor.

Why would you want to do any of these things? For the same
reason that you might want to tear an article out of the daily
newspaper and send it to Aunt Gertrude or to Bill over in
Accounting: you find something of interest and want to share it.
You may want to refer to that site later on for research. You also
may want to direct a study group to that site for joint exploration.

One of the beautiful — and, in my opinion, currently under-
appreciated — facets of the Internet is that this is really a global
classroom, a world-spanning U.S. Library of Congress, if you will.
I well remember my first visit to the Library of Congress, one of
the most impressive repositories of knowledge in the world.

I looked in a card catalog, filled out a form and waited. Presto! (or so it seemed to my teenage eyes)—a library worker brought me the items requested, from deep within the bowels of the institution.

Now fast-forward to this Internet age. You're part of a study group that is trying to understand more about the Vedic scriptures of Hindu belief. You type in a few characters, a search engine finds what you're looking for, and your group moves to a higher level of understanding.

This chapter will discuss how to make the most of what you find online. I hope it will give you some ideas — and, yes, some cautions — about how to move forward.

Understanding Web Links to Other Sites and References

One thing you'll notice soon after your arrival on the Web is that almost every site you visit offers you information on *other* places to visit. These are generally referred to as *links,* and if you click on a given link, your browser will move from its present location to another site. Sometimes, as in Figure 11-1, a Web page contains links to other Internet sites.

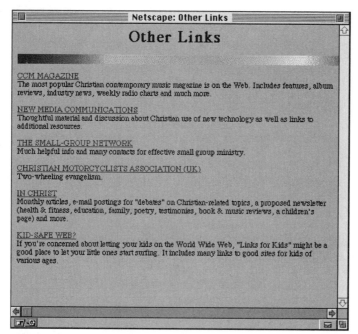

Figure 11-1: A Web page offering links from one site to another site.

Using these links is an easy way to continue your search for a specific bit of information or to explore a different path from the one you've begun. This is another nicety of the Web: you can travel many divergent roads by clicking on the links in a given page.

In Figure 11-2, you see a specific link, as highlighted on a Web page. By clicking on that link and holding the mouse button, the Netscape browser offers the opportunity to go there instantly, as seen in the figure. Using other browsers, a click or two on the link will issue the command, "Hey, Charlie, let's go there!"

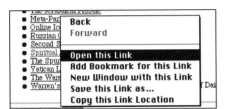

Figure 11-2: A specific link, with the option to go there, courtesy of the Netscape browser, version 2.0.

Here's the bottom line on links: they're the Internet's equal of a magic carpet. Click on one and you can go places. (But don't worry, every Web browser I've seen also allows you the opportunity to go *back* to the page that you were previously visiting, either by a command on a pull-down menu or by a button on the toolbar.)

Saving a Web Page

Say you want to keep a Web page on your computer's hard disk. The best thing to do is to save it onto your disk drive. How to do this?

Generally, you have two options: you can save it as an HTML file or you can save it as text. Saving it as an HTML file will save all the codes used in creating the page, but, generally, it won't save the graphics associated with that page.

This is a good method if you are planning to

- ✦ Edit the text or rework it for posting in another place
- ✦ Reprint it in a compact form for others to see

Remember that you should be concerned with copyright laws. See the section on "Fair Use" for details.

If you use a word processor that directly imports HTML files (such as ClarisWorks on both Macs and PCs, or WordPerfect 3.5 on Macs), you can bring these captured files in and edit them easily.

Saving a page as text will give you an ASCII file that you can open with any word processor. It's certainly adequate, but if you want a nice presentation, you will probably have to format the file a fair amount before printing.

For myself, I save pages in HTML, bring them into WordPerfect 3.5 for Macintosh, and go from there. Your mileage may vary.

Sending Pages to Friends

You may want to share a given Web page with friends, so send it to them. More properly, send them the page and the URL.

If you're using Netscape, this task is very simple:

1. Click on File.
2. Select Mail Document.
3. Fill in the mail form and click send.

See? I told you it was simple.

Mailing a page to someone is the electronic equivalent of the sticky note. It's a great way to spread the word about a site of interest.

If your browser doesn't support this option, you may have the option to send a given URL. That is also found under the File menu, in many cases, and brings up a similar e-mail message.

Printing Web Documents

Most browsers make it easy for you to print a given page while online with your Internet Service Provider. However, you will want to be sure that your printer can handle the layout of a given page before you print it. Check your page layout settings before printing.

Again, using Netscape or most other browsers, you can print directly from the Net. You'll usually find this option under the File menu.

Even though I talk about printing a Web page, what you're normally doing is printing a Web document, which can run over several pages of printed text. Be sure you count the number of pages before you start printing and make sure that your printer has sufficient paper. My personal preference is to download a document and print it from a word processor. But there are times when you want to print directly from the Net, and this is how to do it.

If you have a color ink-jet printer, check your printer's manual about higher-resolution printing and see if special paper is needed to achieve this result. In such cases, your printer can faithfully reproduce the on-screen images for your own use or sharing.

Fair Use: What You Can and Cannot Do with Copyrighted Information

*The Congress shall have power…to promote the progress of science and useful arts, by securing for limited times to authors and inventors the **exclusive** right to their respective writings and discoveries.*

Article I, Section 8, Constitution of the United States *(emphasis added)*

Going back more than 200 years, the United States has looked after the rights of creators of what is called *intellectual property*. These rights are now a source of contention in cyberspace.

As mentioned in Chapter 9, rules govern the use of material that has been protected by copyright. Basically, you cannot republish, distribute, or sell something whose copyright belongs to another person or organization *unless* you have the express written permission of the copyright holder. Moreover, you cannot post copyrighted material on the Net without permission from the copyright owner.

The consequences of not respecting the copyrights of others can be rather serious. You can be sued for tens of thousands of dollars, and courts will almost always side with the copyright owner.

In 1978, a series of reforms called the Copyright Law of 1976 (17 U.S.C. 302) changed the length of copyrights. In most cases, for works created after January 1, 1978, copyright extends to 50 years after the death of the author, or after the death of the last surviving author if more than one individual wrote an item. A"work for hire"—or something written anonymously or under a pseudonym — lasts for either 100 years from the date of creation or 75 years from the date of first publication.

Because the rules are strict concerning copyright protection, quoting copyrighted material without permission can lead to trouble. Businesses that have illegally duplicated newsletters and other items for internal distribution (making one subscription do the work of, say, 20 or 30) have been sued successfully for hundreds of thousands of dollars. Publishers are very proactive in protecting their intellectual property rights, and this will extend to cyberspace.

Therefore, it's best *not* to reproduce copyrighted material — either in your Web page or by printing a Web page, copying it, and passing around copies. When in doubt, don't do it.

You can point people to a given Web site and invite them to look at it, however. You can generally make a copy of something for your own reading offline. However, you can't redistribute the material, and you'll find copyright notices to that effect on many Web sites and online services.

You should not construe the previous paragraphs as legal advice, nor is any representation made as to their veracity. Also, other rules and restrictions may apply outside the United States. You will want to obtain definitive information on copyright, and perhaps consult an intellectual property lawyer if you are thinking about using copyrighted material in your Web site.

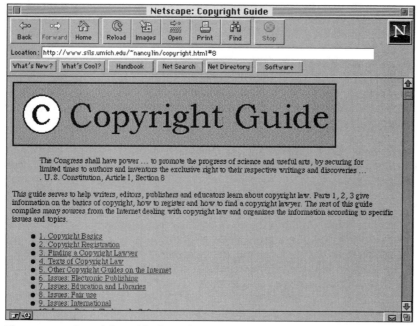

Figure 11-3: Copyright Guide, from the University of Michigan and MLS graduate Nancy Lin.

To acquire the most information about copyrights, point your browser to Nancy Lin's Copyright Guide (see Figure 11-3), which the Masters of Library Science graduate maintains at the University of Michigan's computer system. The URL is `http://www.sils.umich.edu/~nancylin/copyright.html#8`, which is a good starting place for research on copyright law. The many links in these pages will guide you to a wealth of information on copyright, but the basic rule stated previously still applies: when in doubt, don't.

E-Mailing a Webmaster

Generally, the first line of contact between a user and the creator of a Web page is e-mail to the *webmaster*, or the individual who manages a given site. Webmasters range from highly technical computer people to those of us who know "just enough to get by." In the case of personal Web pages, of course, the webmaster is usually the individual involved.

Many browsers support e-mail, either directly or via the main component of the online service. Figure 11-4 shows a sample form, waiting to be filled in.

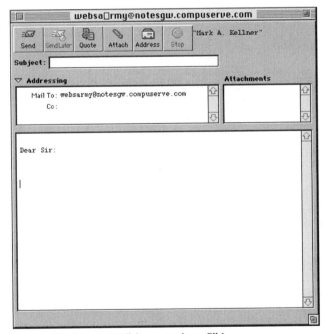

Figure 11-4: An e-mail form ready to fill in.

I should add some thought on e-mail etiquette. Keep your message brief and friendly, and be sure to say "thank you for your time" somewhere. Popular Web sites receive hundreds, sometimes thousands, of messages every day, so be patient in waiting for a response. Also, avoid statements such as "Dear Mush-for-brains" if you want to gain the cooperation of the webmaster.

In general, I've found those individuals who run Web sites to be extremely helpful and cordial, and a brief note will elicit a useful response. In addition, sending e-mail to people all over the world is a digital-age throwback to the pen pals many of us had as youngsters. Except, of course, you don't have to buy stamps, and the response time can be much faster.

Digging Deeper for More Information (Yahoo, Lycos Searches)

Sending e-mail to a webmaster can lead to your finding additional information about a given topic, but few Web site administrators have the time or resources to assist individuals in detailed searches. Fortunately, they don't have to.

Yahoo is not only what you'll exclaim after finding it, but the term also stands for *Yet Another Hierarchical Online Oracle* (http://www.yahoo.com). It's the creation of David Filo and Jerry Yang, scholars at Stanford University who dropped out three months shy of graduating from their Ph.D. programs.

Yahoo is one of the best search mechanisms for finding various sites on the Net. It is updated constantly and offers great pointers to a wide variety of sites. As you can see from Figure 11-5, Yahoo provides a mechanism to search by keyword *and* an index under specific subject categories. Each index in turn provides links to the sites found in the Yahoo database.

From the main Yahoo menu, you can go to the Society & Culture section's religion page (Figure 11-6). Here is a plethora of links that'll keep you busy for hours. Yahoo offers its services free, relying on advertising support. It's a great starting point for your exploration of the Web, and, oddly enough, it's detailed in a book called *Yahoo Unplugged*, which is published by IDG Books Worldwide.

As of last fall, Lycos' catalog (See Figure 11-7) covered 10,797,133 Web sites. Current calculations put the number of Web pages, or Uniform Resource Locators (URLs), at 11,745,521 hosted around the world on 103,059 Web servers. New Web servers are coming online at a rate of 6,000 per month, adding more than 1.1 million URLs every month.

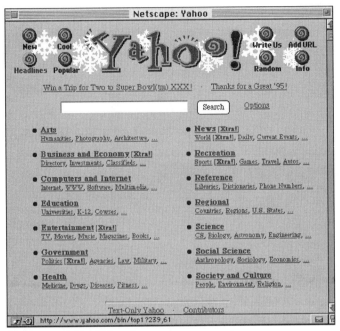

Figure 11-5: The Yahoo home page.

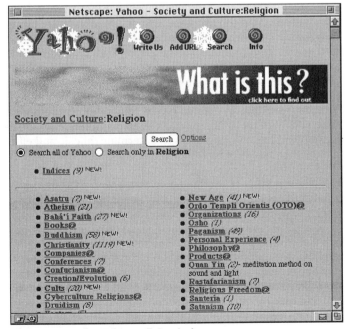

Figure 11-6: The Yahoo religion index page.

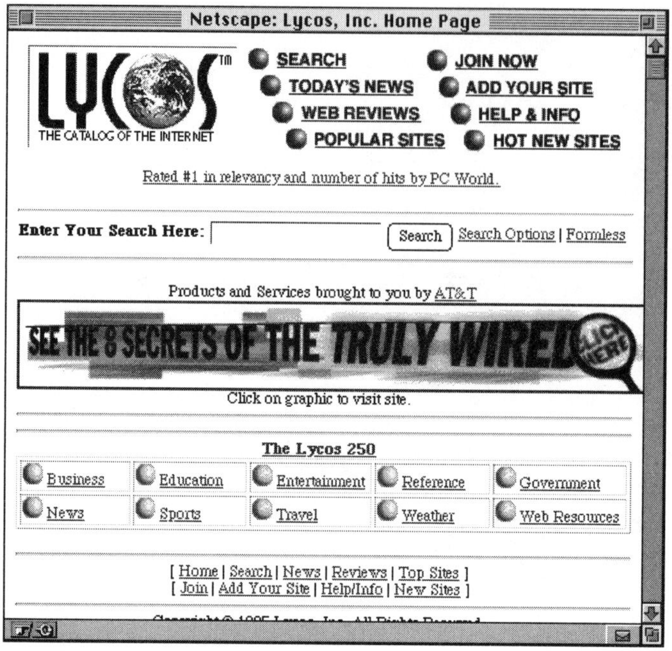

Figure 11-7: The Lycos home page.

Using patent pending technology, the Lycos *spider* samples the Web continuously and merges the results of its searches into the Lycos catalog on a weekly basis. Lycos searches not only the Web pages known as "http" sites, but also includes FTP and gopher addresses. Unlike other Web catalogs or directories, Lycos indexes non-text Internet resources, including graphics, sounds, full-motion video, and executable programs. Lycos provides a user with not only a list of all sites a search has found but also a ranking of the sites based on a popularity score for each of the sites. The popularity score for a particular site is calculated on the total number of other sites that contain links to that site. With its technology, Lycos also automatically creates abstracts of the most popular sites, allowing users to determine quickly and efficiently which sites are relevant to their searches.

The address is http://www.lycos.com and it's a site worth your examination. Lycos also owns Point Communications of New York City, discussed in Chapter 10. Point publishes an online review and rating guide for the Internet, known as the Point Survey. By offering thousands of reviews of Web sites, Point provides what it considers to be the largest and most timely collection of Web reviews available anywhere online and serves six million hits per month. In addition, the free Point Now service provides a real-time update of news and general interest stories from around the world, along with personalized updates on a variety of special interest subjects. The URL for Point is http://www.pointcom.com.

Interlude: The Network That Broke a Church

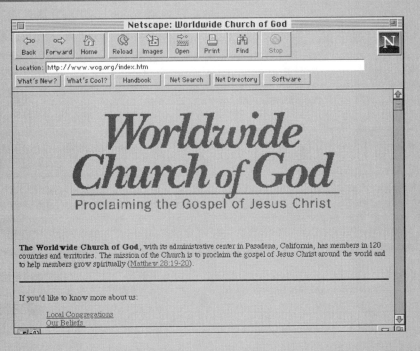

In January of 1995, the Worldwide Church of God (WCG), based in Pasadena, California, had approximately 100,000 members and 400 ministers in various places around the globe. By May of 1995, some 12,000 members had left its ranks, along with 100 ministers in the United States. Revenues had dropped precipitously and hundreds of employees at the group's headquarters were given buyout offers or pink slips. (The first figure shows the logo of the Worldwide Church of God, as shown at its Web site.)

Computer networks and the Internet played a part in this schism, insiders believe. But, first, some background and context.

The other major event of January 1995 was the announcement by WCG (http://www.wcg.org) that it was changing its doctrinal stance. No longer would various observances be enforced under penalty of excommunication; instead, some issues were left to members' consciences and others scrapped altogether. The figure at the top of the next page shows Joseph W. Tkach, Sr., as displayed at the WCG Web site.

(continued)

(continued)

WCG leaders, including then-Pastor General Joseph W. Tkach Sr., had intensively studied the Bible in the years since the death of WCG founder Herbert W. Armstrong, and determined that Armstrong had been wrong on several key doctrines. Known for a fire-and-brimstone broadcast style and for setting a date for the end of civilization, Armstrong's style won tens of thousands of followers on television and radio, as well as for the magazine he founded, *The Plain Truth*.

After Armstrong's death in 1986, the WCG began relaxing and reversing some doctrinal positions. Medical care — once scorned by Armstrong as "not offering a cure in a carload" — was permitted. You could wish family members "Happy Birthday" without fear of being kicked out. And the long-taught doctrine that the Anglo-Saxon peoples of the United States, Canada and Britain represented two of the "lost ten tribes" of Israel began to be downplayed. The church also revised its view of the nature of God: instead of a "God family" into which believers are born at the resurrection, the WCG embraced a Trinitarian view, lining up with the bulk of Christian churches.

On January 7, 1995, WCG members, in a videotaped sermon from Tkach Sr., heard more startling news: the seventh-day Sabbath, once enforced as strictly as any Orthodox Jewish sect would, was now optional, particularly if a member might lose his or her job over the matter. *Tithing*, the donation of 10 percent of one's income, was a "recommended standard" for giving, not a mandate. And the WCG's devotion to Levitical dietary laws — no ham, shrimp, or catfish — was dumped as part of the "ceremonial" law of the Old Testament. (The bottom figure shows Joseph Tkach, Jr., now Pastor General of the WCG.)

Church officials pleaded for tolerance, understanding, and patience, saying those who wanted to continue these observances could do so without worry. Underlying these moves was, Tkach Sr. said, a desire to conform more closely to an accurate understanding of the New Testament's view of Christian practice. He was backed up by son Joseph Tkach, Jr., and with articles explaining the changes in *The Plain Truth* (see fourth figure). (Incidentally, *The Plain Truth* is now available online as well as in print.)

Thousands of church members, however, were shaken. The distinctive beliefs preached by Herbert W. Armstrong were a source of pride for some, indicative that they had found the "true" church in a sea of apostasy. Besides, these members would later say, we've observed these teachings for 20 or 30 years, often at the cost of jobs (over Sabbath observance) or even marriages (over a no-remarriage-after-divorce policy abandoned 11 years before Armstrong's 1986 death) and family relationships (over charges that the WCG member was a "fanatic"). Was our sacrifice in vain, they asked.

Enter the Internet

This wasn't the first time the WCG had been thrown into a crisis, although some observers believed it might be

the final one for the 61-year-old church. Earlier upheavals focused on the telephone and mail as means for distributing information and staking out positions in the midst of a fracas, as occurred in 1974 when some ministers who wanted to "liberalize" the group (with far fewer radical changes than Tkach imposed) were kicked out.

Long distance calls were expensive back then, and despite lower costs, the telephone can only carry so much when it's used for voice. But hook up a modem, and members can cross time zones, continents, and oceans with aplomb. Moreover, members could examine material from "dissident" groups in the comfort of ther own homes, without fear of discovery. And they could get that information instantly.

As a result, WCG bulletin boards on Prodigy, American Online, CompuServe, and the Internet became hotbeds of discussion, debate, and information. Like the parent group, the boards soon splintered into various factions, pro- and anti-change, and into groups promoting the views of "dissident" organizations.

(continued)

(continued)

Some critics are anticipating the demise of the WCG. "Those of us who are not following Tkach [Sr.] know that when the WCG collapses, [we] who adhere to our former doctrines will re-form and continue," said one minister, who asked to remain unnamed, in an e-mail to me.

Most interesting were the postings of sermon notes, articles, and letters, either authorized or unauthorized, from various participants in the conflict. Those who opposed the changes were able to present "the real scoop" about the rapidly accelerating pace of reform; those who supported the moves were able to counter with their arguments.

It must have been somewhat frustrating for WCG leaders to see articles from their internal newsletter for ministers, called "Pastor General's Report," posted or summarized online before those ministers may have had a chance to digest them. And the dissidents didn't count on the forceful response from supporters of the new theology.

The bottom line? This section is being written about 12 months after the WCG changes hit its membership full force. The parent church survived the defections and the tragic passing of Joseph W. Tkach, Sr., from cancer, just before the group's fall "Festival of Faith," an eight-day convention patterned after the Biblical Feast of Tabernacles. His son is now leader of the WCG. Evangelical Christian circles are welcoming the WCG into the mainstream of Christian belief, as is evidenced by David Neff's excellent editorial in *Christianity Today* (which you can find in a search of Christianity Online on AOL).

The WCG's home page (http://www.wcg.org) presents the organization's views in a succinct fashion. It includes links to the online version of *The Plain Truth* and *The Worldwide News*, a bi-weekly newspaper for members. You will find clear links to the church's core of information, as well as to a home page for the WCG's accredited four-year post-secondary institution, Ambassador University. That page was under construction at this writing. Most mainstream Christians will find much to praise in today's WCG, and the quality of *The Plain Truth*'s articles, at this writing, is on a par with many other Christian magazines.

The main dissident group formed this year was the United Church of God, headed by former WCG spokesman David Hulme (http://www.ucg.org), and it reported an attendance of 17,000 at its fall convention. The group is starting a monthly magazine and many of its congregations have home pages on the Web as well. This site will likely appeal to those who are not fans of the "new and improved" WCG, and to scholars and others interested in new religious movements.

Some other sites will also appeal to those who want to watch the WCG and its spin-off groups. One is the Church of God International, which Garner Ted Armstrong started in 1978 after he was kicked out of the WCG by his father. The CGI basically carries forward Herbert Armstrong's doctrines, with some modifications, as can be seen from articles in the group's *Twentieth Century Watch* magazine (http://www.cgi.org). The organization was shaken somewhat in November 1995 when Garner Ted Armstrong resigned from his leadership positions in the wake of sexual abuse charges. Mr. Armstrong denied the allegations.

Another site worth a look by those interested is the Global Church of God's *World Ahead* magazine (`http://www.deltastar.nb.ca/worldahead/index.html`). This group was founded by Roderick C. Meredith, a longtime lieutenant of Herbert W. Armstrong who said he was fired from the WCG when he refused to go along with the doctrinal changes. Among the interesting aspects of this site are versions of their magazine and booklets in the .PDF format, which allows those documents to be viewed with the Adobe Acrobat reader.

For an overview of much of the action surrounding the Worldwide Church of God from a somewhat independent perspective, check out *In Transition: News of the Churches of God*, which is edited by John Robinson, founding editor of the WCG's *Worldwide News* and a longtime WCG observer (`http://www.io.com/~robinson/`). I say "somewhat independent" because Mr. Robinson is clearly a sabbatarian who does not appear to support many of the changes which have taken place in the WCG. He is a fair reporter, however, and *In Transition* reflects balance in its reporting.

Perhaps the most important conclusion which can be drawn from this episode is that the online services and the Internet not only played a role in helping people in the WCG communicate, but it also *collapsed the levels of leadership* within an organization. Things didn't have to flow from the top down — they moved laterally as people at all levels began communicating with each other. Therein lies a lesson for all of us who are involved with organizations. Once the people start talking, democracy can break out. While the WCG deeply regrets the loss of members it has suffered, the fact remains that when lines of communication are open, things happen!

Searching Usenet from the Web

If you've found one or more newsgroups that you frequently visit, that's terrific. But what if you want to jump into a discussion about a certain topic, but you don't know where to look? In the vast Usenet universe, finding people to talk to has never been a problem. Finding people who are interested in the exact same issues that you are, however, is a little more difficult.

The DejaNews Research Service (`http://www.dejanews.com`) is a giant online archive of Usenet postings (see Figure 11-8). This fantastic service takes every message posted to various newsgroups, catalogs it, and stores it for your own personal research. The DejaNews archives span at least the last month in the life of the newsgroup, and in many cases, the service stores an entire year's worth of messages. DejaNews' long-term goal is to archive an entire year's worth of messages for every appropriate newsgroup.

Although DejaNews contains an immense amount of information, the service has chosen not to archive postings from every newsgroup. DejaNews does not archive postings from newsgroups that begin with `alt`, `soc`, and `talk`, or newsgroups with `binaries` in the title (`binaries` groups contain dowloadable pictures). At first, you

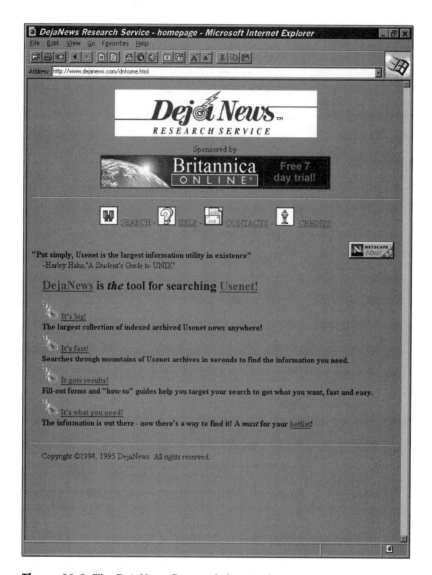

Figure 11-8: The DejaNews Research Service home page.

may think that this exclusion will limit your search, but don't be too sure. Even without these groups, you still have access to some of the most heavily traveled Usenet groups — including `biz` (business), `comp` (computers), and `sci` (science), as well as various religious groups such as `shamash.jewstudies` and `uk.religion.hindu`.

With DejaNews, you can take a topic of your choice and perform a keyword search through all of the DejaNews archives. The results come quickly, and you'll be surprised at the number of *hits*, or keyword matches, that you find. The results of your search include the posting date, the subject line of the post, the newsgroup in which the message occurred, and the sender (see Figure 11-9). The subject line is *hotlinked* to the actual post, which means that with one click, you can read the entire message. You can impose various restrictions on your searches as well, telling the search engine to include only those hits from a particular newsgroup, only those hits from a particular sender, recent posts instead of older posts, and so on.

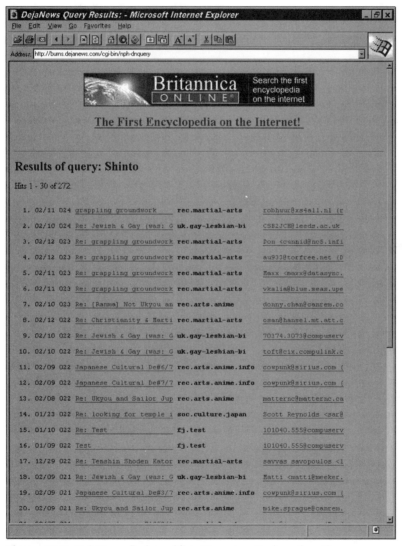

Figure 11-9: DejaNews finds and lists Usenet posts, based on the information that you provide.

DejaNews is a valuable tool for making online research fast and efficient. In fact, the DejaNews archives contain over 4GB of searchable data. If you can't find the discussion that you're looking for in that mass of data, that discussion may very well not exist.

Finding Your Faith on the Internet

PART

III

◆ ◆ ◆ ◆

In This Part

◆ ◆ ◆ ◆

Buddhism

A Brief Introduction to Buddhism

Possibly the dominant religion in much of southeast Asia,
Buddhism is also one of the world's oldest faiths. Though many
of Buddhism's adherents are found in China, Tibet, Japan, Korea,
Sri Lanka, and Thailand (where it is the official religion), the faith
began a bit further west, in what is today India.

According to the "frequently asked questions" file of the
`alt.zen` newsgroup:

> *Siddhartha Gautama was a prince in that region around 500
> B.C. At the age of 29, deeply troubled by the suffering he saw
> around him, he renounced his privileged life to seek understand-
> ing. After 6 years of struggling as an ascetic, he finally achieved
> what he termed* Enlightenment, *at age 35. After this he was
> known as the* Buddha, *which can be translated "one who is
> awake." He realized "everything is subject to change and that
> suffering and discontentment are the result of attachment to
> circumstances and things which, by their nature, are imperma-
> nent." Buddhist teaching avers that if you rid yourself of these
> attachments, including attachment to the false notion of self or
> "I," you can be free of suffering.*

> *The teachings of Gautama Buddha have, to this day, been
> passed down from teacher to student. Around 475 A.D. one of
> these teachers, Bodhidharma, traveled from India to China and
> introduced the teachings of the Buddha there. In China, Bud-
> dhism mingled with Taoism. The result of this mingling was the
> Ch'an School of Buddhism. Around 1200 A.D. Ch'an Buddhism
> spread from China to Japan where it is called (at least in
> translation) Zen Buddhism.*

In the United States, the consciousness-raising movements of the 1960s and 1970s drew many to the contemplative nature of Buddhism. The study of Buddhism by poet Allen Ginsberg, as well as lectures and books by Alan Watts (1915-1973) have had wide circulation in this country and have contributed to the promotion of Buddhist studies by many people. Celebrity followers of Buddhism have included singer Tina Turner and actor Richard Gere, who reportedly spends one or two months each year in the Far East studying with disciples of the Dalai Lama. In the 1990s, the explosive growth of New Age thinking brought many people to Buddhist texts and wisdom as they searched for keys to personal development.

Like many religious movements, Buddhism has spawned many disciplines and schools of thought within China, Korea, and Japan. In Chapter 10, we discussed briefly the Soka Gakkai sect of Nichiren Buddhism in Japan. Buddhist movements number in the dozens, each adding its own interpretation to the Gautama's teachings. As with Islam and Judaism, one can find a political aspect in Buddhism today, namely the struggle over Tibet, home to the Dalai Lama, who is the supreme authority over Tibetan Buddhism.

The Buddhist resources available on the Internet cover all these aspects of Buddhism. In terms of culture, art, and spirituality, they represent as wide a range of Buddhist practice as you are likely to find anywhere.

Buddhist Web Sites

Searching the Web for Buddhist sites yields a wide variety of locations. At this writing, for example, Yahoo has cataloged 58 major Buddhist sites, including 14 Buddhist organizations. As imagined, just about every flavor of Buddhism is available online. Along with the listings in this book, you will want to aim your Web browser at http://www.yahoo.com/Society_and_Culture/Buddhism/ to see the latest in Buddhist sites (Figure 12-1).

If you are looking for the basics of Buddhism, you may want to begin at the WWW Virtual Library's Buddhist Studies web site, http://coombs.anu.edu.au/WWWVL-Buddhism.html#TOC, a top-rated Internet site renowned for its comprehensiveness (see Figure 12-2). The site is maintained by Drs. T. Matthew Ciolek and John C. Powers, and currently provides links to 144 information facilities around the globe. The maintainers inspect and evaluate the links before posting them, so you have some assurance of quality, comprehensiveness, and independence. This site is favored because it represents links to so many branches of Buddhist teaching.

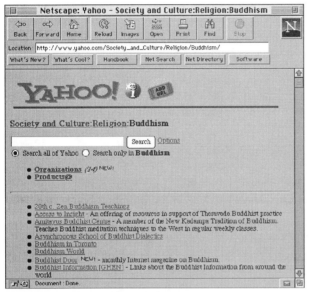

Figure 12-1: Yahoo's Buddhism Index.

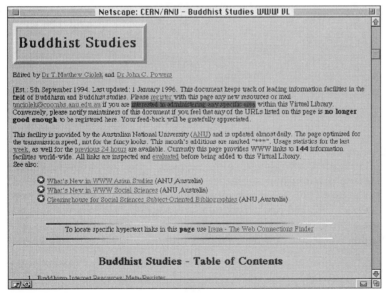

Figure 12-2: WWW Virtual Library: Buddhist Studies.

Those with an interest in Zen Buddhism as it is taught in Japan will want to visit *The Electronic Bodhidharma* (see Figure 12-3), `http://www.iijnet.or.jp/iriz/irizhtml/irizhome.htm/`, which is maintained by the International Research Institute for Zen Buddhism, located at Hanazono University in Kyoto, Japan. The organization maintains what it says is the "largest collection of Buddhist primary text materials on the Internet," which appear to be mostly in Chinese. It also offers a CD-ROM containing these documents for $10 (U.S.). The site includes links to other Zen sites and ways to contact the IRIZ organization for more information.

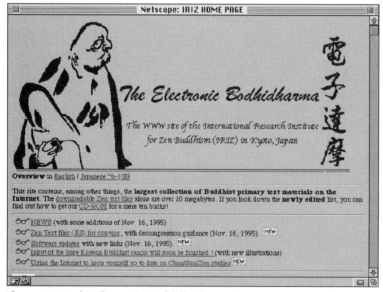

Figure 12-3: The Electronic Bodhidharma.

The Buddhist Publication Society, founded in Sri Lanka in 1958, represents the viewpoint of Theravada Buddhism, which it claims is "the oldest living Buddhist Tradition, where Pali Canon gives us the most authentic account of what the historical Buddha himself actually taught." Point your browser to `http://world.std.com/~metta/bps/home.html` and you'll find the home page for this group (see Figure 12-4), from which you can download certain texts; you can also see its international mail order catalog. You can order books directly from Sri Lanka or from a variety of bookstores in the United States.

Describing himself as "a simple monk," the Dalai Lama is the living embodiment of the aspirations for a free Tibet, liberated from the occupation it has suffered from the People's Republic of China since 1959. The Dalai Lama won the Nobel Peace Prize in 1989. The page shown in Figure 12-5 is one of several devoted to a Free Tibet and has links to several areas for the study of Tibetan Buddhism. It is impossible to divorce that study from the question of freedom for Tibet, a once-quiet, peaceful nation whose people have suffered cruelly at the hands of their invaders.

Figure 12-4: The Buddhist Publication Society.

Figure 12-5: H.H. the 14th Dalai Lama, Tenzin Gyatso.

Another major Buddhist Web site worth mentioning is BoW, Buddhism on the Web, which is maintained in Thailand, another major Buddhist nation. Point your browser to `http://www.inet.co.th/cyberclub/bow/main_contents.html`, and you'll find this interesting, multi-layered site (see Figure 12-6). It offers a range of links to sites promoting Thedavara Buddhism, as well as "Buddhist Perspective on Modern Issues."

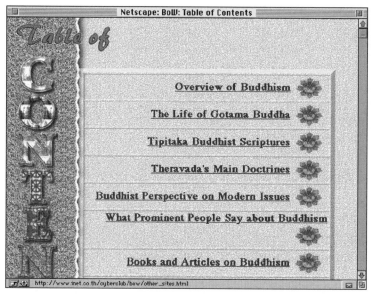

Figure 12-6: Buddhism on the Web.

The Tiger Team Buddhist Information Network (see Figure 12-7) has its humor and its instincts. The gentle humor comes with a picture of a Buddha sitting atop a 28.8 modem, which I found in good taste. This page (`http://www.newciv.org/TigerTeam/`) is run in the San Francisco/Oakland area and is in one sense more aggressive than the others. The operators want you to sign up as a member and send in money in order to receive maximum benefit from their site. In turn, they claim more frequent updating of their site than other operators, whom they say rely on volunteer efforts and the uneven nature thereof. The operators are entrepreneurial and creative, and the serious student of Buddhism will at least want to investigate the possibility of joining the Tiger Team.

These are but seven of the major Buddhist sites. You can find the others by starting with the Yahoo search described earlier and following the many and varied links that are available.

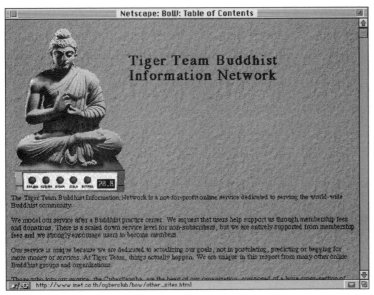

Figure 12-7: Tiger Team home page.

Buddhist Newsgroups

Several newsgroups contain messages of interest to those who want to know more about Buddhism. One of the most active is the previously mentioned alt.zen, which not only offers an ongoing series of messages about Zen Buddhism but, like another group, talk.religion.zen, shows no fear in veering into controversial areas. A recent thread involved the propriety of sexual relations between a Buddhist teacher and student, for example. Other newsgroups include talk.religion.buddhism (see Figure 12-8), uk.religion.buddhist, and alt.religion.buddhism.nichiren.

These newsgroups are *unmoderated.* As noted in earlier chapters, that means these groups are *not* censored by a maintainer, other than to remove the most offensive and/or threatening messages. Figure 12-9 shows some of the contents of alt.zen.

I would imagine that these groups are better suited to those who are either well established as Buddhists and want to find those of like mind, or those who like to be a little rowdy, albeit within limits.

Figure 12-8: A sample listing of the contents of `talk.religion.buddhism`, summarized by InfoSeek.

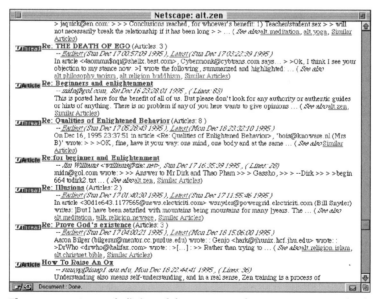

Figure 12-9: A sample listing of the contents of `alt.zen`, summarized by InfoSeek.

FTP Sites

Some of the nice things that you will find when starting with the WWW Virtual Library of Buddhism are links to numerous FTP sites where you can read, or download, many texts on Buddhism. Many of the pages listed earlier in this chapter also offer this capability. In your searchings, you'll be able to assemble a good basic library with just a few mouse clicks.

Be certain of the language of the document you are downloading. Some sites, such as those in Japan and Thailand, emphasize documents in languages other than English. No harm will come to your computer from downloading these pages, but they may be worth little if you don't have a command of the language involved. Of course, if you're seeking material for someone who *is* fluent in those languages, you'll have hit a gold mine. Be sure, also, to check whether you need to download any foreign-language fonts in order to display or print those documents. These fonts are often available from the same FTP sites.

Catholic Resources

The World's Largest Religion

In mid-1994, the latest period for which statistics were available
at this writing, the Roman Catholic Church claimed a worldwide
membership of 1,058,069,000, about 25 million people ahead of
Islam to be the world's largest single religion. It is also by far the
world's largest Christian community, approximately 2.7 times
the number of Protestant believers on the planet (who number
over 391 million, making them the second-largest Christian bloc).

The Church traces its history to Jesus Christ, who named Peter
the first vicar of the church, and to the proselytizing of Paul and
others in Rome after Jesus's death and resurrection. The
conversion of imperial Rome in the fourth century A.D. brought
the Roman Empire into the Catholic fold and established a basis
for the growth of the Roman church.

The Church is run in a hierarchical fashion by the Supreme
Pontiff, who is currently Pope John Paul II, born Karol Wojtyla in
Wadowice, near Kraków, Poland, in 1920, and elected as the
successor to Pope John Paul I on October 16, 1978. He was
installed six days later, survived an assassination attempt in
1981, and persevered through other health problems in recent
years. He has traveled more than any of the Popes, having made
numerous journeys that have drawn immense crowds. His most
recent visit to the United States was in 1995, and it was the first
to be "broadcast" on the Internet and on online services (see
sections that follow).

Supporting the Pope is the College of Cardinals, whose members both elect the Supreme Pontiff and assist in church governance. Most members of the College are also members of various councils within the Vatican, supplying counsel to the Pope on a variety of ecclesiastical and theological matters. But it is the Pope who speaks in the name of the Church, and it is the Pope who must approve the encyclicals issued by the church.

Many of the Catholic resources available on the Net are based in America, and as you can expect in a group this diverse, Catholics express rather diverse opinions. The Church is having its official say, both through the Vatican's home page (see Chapter 9) and through a multitude of supportive resources. But you'll also find dissident voices that campaign for reforms involving reproductive rights, celibacy, and other issues, including a restoration of the traditional Latin mass, the obligatory use of which was changed by the Second Vatican Council in 1965.

The non-Catholic visitor to these sites can also gain much from visiting the Vatican and related sites. You can learn about the Catholic church, research official doctrines and beliefs, and study texts favored by the Catholic church, such as the Vulgate Bible of St. Jerome, the Douay-Rheims Bible translation, and many early church writings. You can also tour the renowned Vatican library from your desktop.

Catholic Web Resources

You might imagine that a tour of Catholic resources on the World Wide Web would start with the Vatican. Not always. When I want to survey available Catholic resources across the Internet, I first point my browser to a site located at Carnegie Mellon University in Pittsburgh, Pennsylvania. This school — which by the way was one of the first to require all of its students to have a personal computer in their dorm rooms, way back in the early 1980s — has a page that offers a truly vast list of sites.

The site, found at `http://www.cs.cmu.edu/Web/People/spok/catholic.html`, is maintained by John Mark Ockerbloom and offers resources both at the school and elsewhere (see Figure 13-1). It provides 12 different subcategories ranging from Liturgy and Worship to Catholic Organizations and Related Resources. This page is, by the way, a bit ecumenical in its scope, offering links to some non-Catholic sites maintained by Protestant groups.

At this writing, the maintainer of the site says it is being reorganized. "Look for several revisions to this Web collection to develop in the near future." It's nice to know that this page — elegant in its simplicity and highly resourceful in its scope — will not remain static.

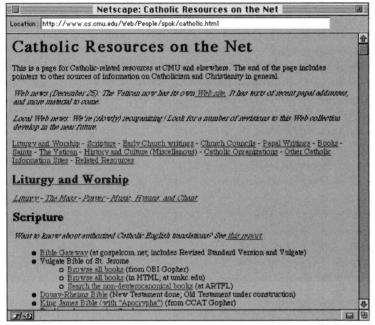

Figure 13-1: Catholic Resources on the Net offers a wide range of links.

From this page, I can zip over to the small city-state located within the city of Rome, Italy, known as Vatican City. I'd start with The Holy See, the home page for the Vatican (http://www.vatican.va), which was discussed and illustrated in Chapter 9. Initially, this page has not contained as much as some, but it does offer its text in several languages and a way to e-mail the top levels of the Catholic Church (or at least its press office).

Another useful Web site is the Catholic Files/Roman Catholic Resources page at American University in Washington, D.C., http://listserv.american.edu/ catholic, which is maintained by Jim McIntosh and has attracted more than 5,400 visitors since December 1, 1995. There's an immediate link to a whole library of Catholic documents (see the section on encyclicals that follows) and to numerous other Catholic Web sites. It's illustrated in Figure 13-2 and is well worth a visit.

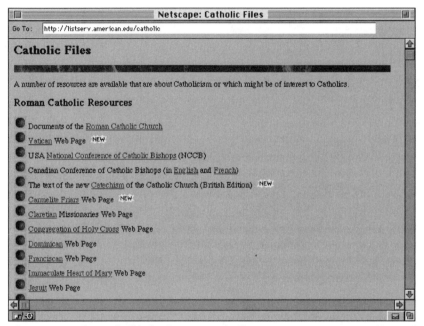

Figure 13-2: The Catholic Files/Roman Catholic Resources page at American University.

Vatican City Online

Vatican City is not just the center of a great world religion, it is an important repository of Catholic history, literature, and artworks. Those fortunate enough to visit Rome and Vatican City can examine many of these treasures in person. Those fortunate enough to have a computer, modem, and Internet access can visit this renowned institution without having to renew a passport.

One of the first sites that the cyber-tourist will want to visit is *Christus Rex et Redemptor Mundi* (http://www.christusrex.org), which is a labor of love for Michael Olteanu, a Romanian émigré to the United States who fled to this country in 1975. He is a lay member of the Marian Movement of Priests in the Roman Catholic Church and a data network engineer. His passion is church art, both that which explains and represents the Bible story and which shows off the Vatican and other churches. As shown in Figure 13-3, it is a popular site (according to *PC Magazine*, at least), and it offers links to all sorts of Vatican resources.

Among these are 255 images of Vatican City or, as it is known in Italian, *Città del Vaticano* (Figure 13-4), breathtaking in their comprehensiveness, and more than 350 views of the Sistine Chapel. You'll see historical commentary, links to the Vatican's home page, and links to texts of messages by Pope John Paul II.

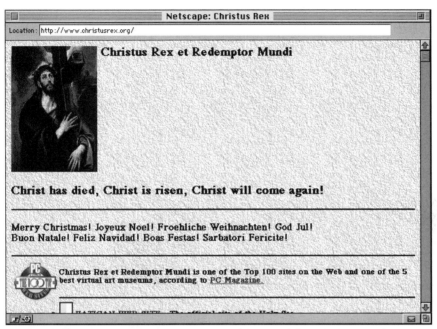

Figure 13-3: *Christus Rex et Redemptor Mundi* is one of the premier sites for a photographic tour of Vatican City.

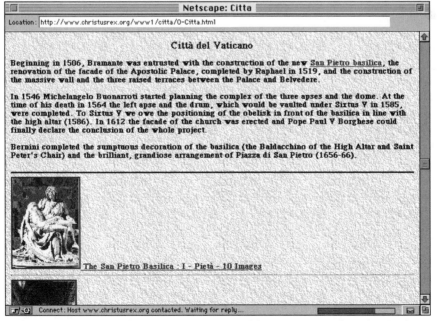

Figure 13-4: Visit *Città del Vaticano* for a tour of the Vatican — without leaving home.

Christus Rex is one of the most comprehensive, helpful, and unassuming religious sites I've seen. Olteanu deserves commendation for his efforts — and, in my opinion, his Web site deserves your visit. It's a tremendous gateway to Vatican City.

Virtual Parish — "Fired" Bishop Opens Shop in Cyberspace

"Partenia" is the name of a Roman Catholic diocese located in southern Algeria. It doesn't really exist today, because Partenia is in fact an ancient, destroyed city whose ruins have been covered by the sands of the Sahara for hundreds of years. It doesn't really exist, except on old Vatican maps, and on occasions when the Pope needs to reassign a troublesome cleric.

That reassignment occurred when Bishop Jacques Gaillot, 60, refused to back down from his support for homosexual rights, married priests, and condom distribution as a protection against AIDS. All of these are the antithesis of the current Pope's views, and when Gaillot wouldn't tone down his stance, he lost his parish of Evreux in Normandy last year and was transfered to a diocese that didn't really exist.

Until early 1996, that is, when Gaillot set up a Partenia page on the worldwide web, `http:/ /www.partenia.fr/`, which is illustrated here.

Partenia gives virtual parishioners the story of Gaillot's dismissal, the text of the Bishop's last sermon at Evreux, a letter from Gaillot to Pope John Paul II, and a display of pictures of the two men at the Vatican in a December 1995 meeting.

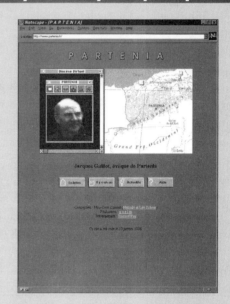

Gaillot's efforts have generated worldwide publicity and attention. If he expands his efforts into other languages, Partenia could be a rallying station for dissident Catholics worldwide.

Online Documents of the Roman Catholic Church

Finding the documents of the Roman Catholic Church online is a great benefit both for Catholics and non-Catholics alike. I was impressed with the range of these documents that is available from the American University site (referred to previously) and is introduced at http://listserv.american.edu/catholic/church/church.html. Here, you can find documents from the Council of Trent (which established basic Catholic doctrines, encyclicals, and other documents from the Popes), statements from the Vatican and the United States Catholic Bishops, the British edition of the new Catechism of the Catholic Church, and writings of early church fathers. Figure 13-5 illustrates this index.

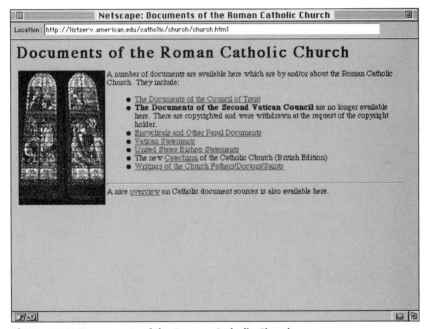

Figure 13-5: Documents of the Roman Catholic Church.

The messages of the Supreme Pontiff of the Universal Church (one of Pope John Paul II's official titles) are of interest not only to Roman Catholics but to many people around the world. Theological scholars of many backgrounds study them to chart the course of the Catholic church. Journalists examine them to determine what the Church is saying and the effect of those sayings on people around the world.

In technologically ancient times, say around 1991, the only way to pick up these writings was from a Catholic bookstore, from a diocesan office, or from the Vatican itself. Need instant access? You'd better have had one of those places handy.

Now it's much easier. The same *Christus Rex* website that links you to photographs of Vatican City and its artistic treasures will link you to many of the Pope's statements (Figure 13-4). These documents are now available with the click of a mouse button, ready for reading and downloading. You can also reach this page from the American University Catholic website.

Figure 13-6 shows the first Papal Encyclical to be distributed on the Web, shortly after publication. "On the Value and Inviolability of Human Life," known in Latin as *Evangelium Vitae,* was also the first encyclical to be published on diskette by the Vatican at the same time as the printed version. Many experts anticipate that future messages will be available online almost simultaneously with their printed release.

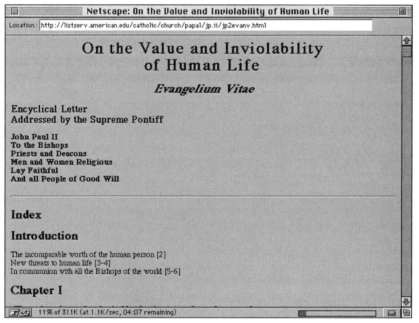

Figure 13-6: Papal encyclicals a la Web.

An example of simultaneous publication is the Christmas 1995 message of Pope John Paul II shown in Figure 13-7. The traditional "Urbi et Orbi" message ("To the City and the World") is delivered by the pontiff on Christmas Day. In 1995, the Pope had to cut short the greetings he dispenses in several dozen languages after feeling the effects of the flu. The Vatican Web site, however, has all the greetings and the text of this message. It also published the Pope's New Year's Day greeting for 1996.

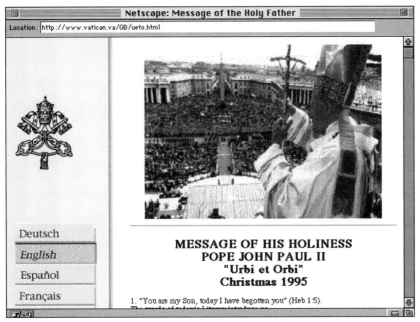

Figure 13-7: "Urbi et Orbi" ("To the City and the World"), online.

Finding Seminaries and Colleges

Catholic education is one of the hallmarks of the church; its universities are renowned as institutions of higher learning.

Finding these schools is not difficult, and online you can explore many of these institutions' resources. You can start with a list that is maintained on the Catholic Resources on the Net website, shown in Figure 13-8.

Along with many institutions in the United States, you'll find some surprising locations. The Pontifical Gregorian College in Rome has a home page for its theology department (http://www.leonet.it/culture/stf/), but, unfortunately for those who do not speak the language, its content is in Italian.

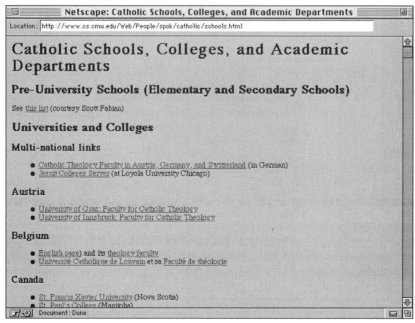

Figure 13-8: Catholic Schools, Colleges, and Academic Departments listed on the Web.

CyberPope: John Paul II's 1995 Visit

The 1995 visit of Pope John Paul II to the United States also touched cyberspace. America Online provided onsite coverage from his Mass at Camden Yards in Baltimore; the *Newark Star-Ledger* set up a special Web page for the visit, as did *The New York Times*.

It was also possible to hear, via special connections, papal addresses over the Internet. You needed either the RealAudio software (`http://www.realaudio.com`) or an MBONE (multicast backbone) setup, which requires users to have a high-bandwidth connection to the Internet. (The RealAudio service is becoming more widespread, and checking out that organization's home page and software might be a good idea.)

The Catholic University of America maintains a great page of information on the papal visit, including links to texts of the Pope's addresses

and related sites. For reporters, the CUA provides a list of experts at the university who can comment on the visit and its significance.

While it is unknown when the Pope will next visit the United States, I would not be at all surprised to see future papal trips undertaken with cyberspace coverage. The Vatican's own home page might be a good place to check for such details.

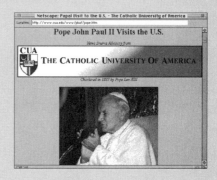

You can find some pleasant surprises among Catholic institutions on the Web. The Notre Dame Women's College in Kyoto, Japan, is a four-year institution run by a Catholic order. Its home page is illustrated in Figure 13-9 and shows several jumping-off points. One of these is POETS, a service designed to help non-English speakers learn English. Included is an Internet pen pal service that matches up those who want to engage in this age-old correspondence method via the Net.

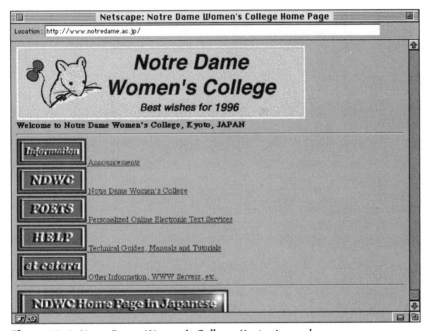

Figure 13-9: Notre Dame Women's College, Kyoto, Japan, home page.

Also accessible via the Internet is the premiere institution of Catholic higher education in the United States, the Catholic University of America, which is the only Catholic school to have its charter directly from the Vatican. Its elaborate, yet elegant, home page is illustrated in Figure 13-10. Those interested in pursuing a Catholic education in the Nation's Capital will want to pay a visit to `http://www.cua.edu/`.

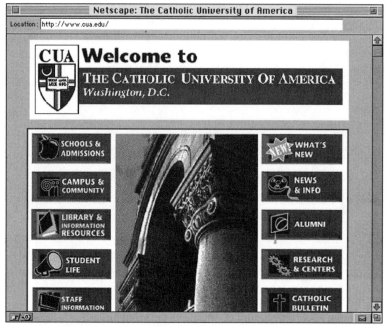

Figure 13-10: Catholic University of America home page.

Our all-too-brief tour of Catholic university home pages would not be complete — and I, your servant, would be barred from entry into the state of Indiana — were I not to include a brief stop at the University of Notre Dame in South Bend, Indiana (`http://www.nd.edu/`). The "Fighting Irish" are known for much more than football and this site shows off all of the school's advantages.

Catholic Discussions and Newsgroups

From what by now must clearly be my most favorite Catholic starting point, Catholic Resources on the Net, you can jump to the `bit.listserv.catholic` discussion group. On a recent visit, I found over 350 messages, most of which were sober-minded and on topic. (There are moments of humor, too, but little of the acrimony that is found in some other newsgroups.)

You can also find discussion forums on America Online, CompuServe, and Prodigy. The CompuServe package includes the Catholic Information Network, which is designed to bring Catholics together online.

Other Catholic discussion areas pop up on the Net, under the `tnn.religion.catholic` handle. As with other newsgroups, be aware that some messages posted to each of these groups may contain messages that are not germane to the subject at hand. But with discretion, you can find useful information.

Catholic Mailing Lists

DEACON-L is a list restricted solely for permanent deacons in good standing in Roman Catholic (arch)dioceses in the USA. Diocesan directors of deacons also may subscribe.

Those asking to subscribe will be asked to identify themselves, which information will be cross-checked in official ecclesiastical directories and lists. To subscribe, send the following command, and nothing else, in the *body* of an e-mail message (not the Subject line) to `listserv@ls.csbsju.edu`.

`SUBSCRIBE DEACON-L firstname lastname`

For example: `SUBSCRIBE DEACON-L John Smith`

Hindu Connections

The World's Oldest Religion?

According to *The World Almanac and Book of Facts* (1996 Edition), 764 million people worldwide embrace Hinduism as their religion. Founded perhaps around 500 B.C. (although some people date it 500 years earlier than that), Hinduism is a religion of many deities and traditions. From its base in what is now India, the religion is also found in Nepal, Malaysia, Guyana, Trinidad, Sri Lanka, and Suriname, among other places.

A growing number of Westerners are embracing Hindu beliefs as direct disciples; indirectly through the teachings of *Transcendental Meditation* (or *TM*), which was founded by the Maharishi Mahesh Yogi (who was a guru to Beatle George Harrison); or through other teachers, including Deepak Chopra, whose books *Quantum Healing* and *Ageless Body, Timeless Mind* have been bestsellers in the United States.

Hindu practices are both a way of life and a religion for many followers. For others, they are seen as an adjunct to religion, or, alternatively, a supplement to good health practices. In the case of meditation — something fervently practiced by many in the West — followers can achieve the state of higher consciousness evoked by TM within the context of religion. I remember a news conference at the American Association for the Advancement of Science convention 20 years ago, in Boston, where a researcher from Mormon-backed Brigham Young University in Utah advocated "Christian Meditation" using the same method as TM but focusing on the name of Jesus instead of saying a mantra.

On the health side, the growing interest in a vegetarian diet leads many to consider the Hindu basis for such practice, as well as the cultural aspect of recipes for vegetarian dishes prepared by people in India and elsewhere. Here, the Hare Krishna movement has had an advantage by sharing its higher taste on the Internet. Another aspect of Hinduism that has gained popularity in the West is *ayurvedic medicine*, which relies on theories of the nature of the body derived from Hindu belief. Deepak Chopra and others have reported some amazing results from ayurvedic medicine.

Hinduism came to the United States formally in 1893 when Swami Vivekananda addressed the Parliament of Religions in Chicago. He told the assembled participants that Hinduism was "the mother of all religions," which brought the concept of "universal tolerance" to sectarianism.

Unlike many faiths, there is no central Hindu "authority" to which all devotees report. Each branch of Hinduism is centered on a given authority, a *guru* or other priest who generally is a member of the Brahmin caste. There are three main Hindu traditions, devoted to the gods Vishnu and Shiva, and the goddess Shakti. Lord Krishna, from whom the Hare Krishna movement takes its name, is found in relationship to Vishnu, for example.

As a result, the seeker after Hindu traditions and information will find many sources for such information and many viewpoints. This is somewhat a case of *caveat lector:* "Let the reader beware." You will want to examine as many sources as possible if you are seeking to determine an aspect of Hindu belief because there are divergent opinions on some subjects. But, then, isn't that the case in many traditions?

Finding Classic Hindu Sites

There is, as mentioned, no equivalent of the Vatican for Hinduism, hence there is no central authority to which readers can be directed. However, there *is* something close, and that is Global Hindu Electronic Networks: The Hindu Universe, which is located at the University of Cincinnati, in Ohio, and sponsored by the Hindu Students Council. The URL is `http://rbhatnagar.csm.uc.edu:8080/hindu_universe.html`, and it offers both a graphical index (see Figure 14-1) and a textual one. It is truly a Hindu "universe," as you shall see, because it offers so much to explore.

G.H.E.N., as the organization calls itself, is a great central resource for classic Hindu sites: those that are directly linked to basic Hindu practices and not necessarily "spin-off" philosophical movements. It offers links to repositories of classical Hindu texts, links to other sites, and a general wealth of resources for the seeker of Hindu wisdom and lore.

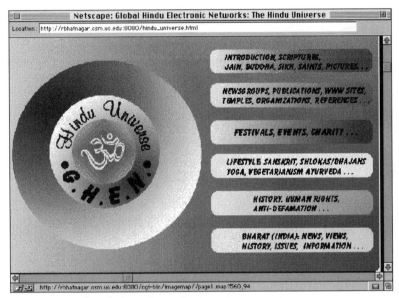

Figure 14-1: The Hindu Universe home page.

What particularly impresses me about G.H.E.N. is that it has such a wide variety of links within its Web site, in large part because Hinduism is a religion of books, texts, and learning passed down from prior generations. Because, as Swami Vivekananda said a century ago, Hinduism sees itself as both the mother of all religions *and* as being fulfilled in Buddhism, you'll see many links on the G.H.E.N. site to other Indian and Asian traditions and texts.

The first stop for the new visitor to G.H.E.N., after the home page, could easily be the page containing an introduction to Hinduism and links to several *dharmas,* or traditions, including those of Jainism, Sikhism, and Buddhism (Figure 14-2). The introduction is taken from the 1965 *Gazetteer of India* and is a somewhat scholarly discussion of the Hindu faith and its impact upon India. The scriptures include the *Mahabarata,* the epic story of Vedic history, and the *Bhagavad Gita,* the latter in several translations along with commentaries by Swami Chinmayananda and His Divine Grace A.C. Bhativedanta Swami Prabhupada, founder of the Hare Krishna movement.

Finding additional "classic" Hindu sites is made somewhat easier through the G.H.E.N.'s listings of "interesting links" (Figure 14-3). It includes gateways to many organizations, lists of Hindu temples, and other useful bits of information. One of the interesting links among Hindu temples is the Hindu Center of Western New York, which is building a temple (Figure 14-4) and would appreciate your donation.

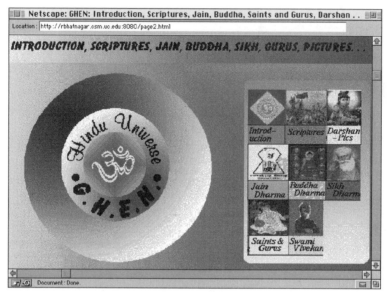

Figure 14-2: An introduction to Hinduism and other dharmas.

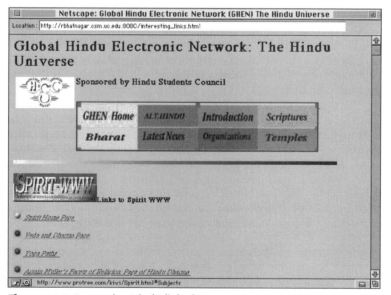

Figure 14-3: Interesting Hindu links from G.H.E.N.

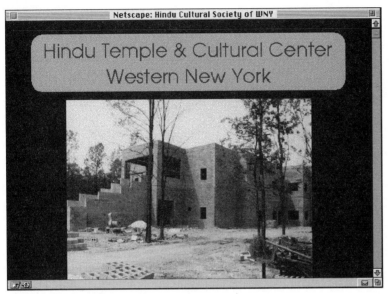

Figure 14-4: The Hindu Center of Western New York.

The "links" available from this page in the G.H.E.N. site don't stop with Web pages, though. There's a full archive of the `alt.hindu` and `soc.religion.hindu` mailing lists, as well as links to other Hindu-related lists and newsgroups.

In my explorations of religion and spirituality on the Internet, I have rarely found a site that offers as much in one location as does the Global Hindu Electronic Network. It not only points you toward a great range of locations, but it is a great site in itself.

The Hare Krishna Movement and Other Spin-offs

One of the most visible extensions of Hinduism in the United States arrived on these shores about 31 years ago. His Divine Grace A.C. Bhativedanta Swami Prabhupada had earlier separated himself from his wife and family and became a disciple of Srila Bhaktisiddhanta Sarasvati Gosvami, who had founded 64 religious institutes in India. Today, Prabhupada's disciples are staking their claim in cyberspace, with plans to create 108 Web pages in 1995-1996 to honor Prabhupada's birth centennial. Figure 14-5 shows an example of a Hare Krishna home page.

Prabhupada's work spread from a small storefront in Greenwich Village to encompass more than 100 ashrams and other locations around the globe. The International Society for Krishna Consciousness became known for its devoted followers who stood on street corners in orange robes, playing drums and chanting "Hare Krishna." The founder is well known for his translation of the *Bhagavad Gita*, "As It Is," which includes a verse-by-verse commentary.

Figure 14-5: A Hare Krishna home page.

The aggressive witnessing of these devotees — and equally aggressive fund-raising in airports and bus stations — made the Krishnas the butt of many jokes. Over the years, the movement has changed, maturing into a somewhat less confrontational organization, forsaking the orange robes for Western garb. The movement's latest forays (into Russia after the collapse of the Soviet Union and now into cyberspace) have continued Prabhupada's mission, that of bringing "Krishna Consciousness" to people everywhere (see Figure 14-6).

The Krishnas have been very aggressive in promoting aspects of their lifestyle as well as their faith. Many Krishna-related sites on the Net deal with vegetarian lifestyles and animal welfare. In addition, a good number of Krishna temples also have home pages.

Many people have objected to the Hare Krishna movement in years past, and some in the Hindu community have objected to the high profile accorded Srila Prabhupada (who died in 1977) as well as to some of their interpretations of Vedic scriptures, but the Krishna movement has had a definite effect on the spread of Hindu thought in the West. For that reason alone, these sites — and their associated links — are worth a look.

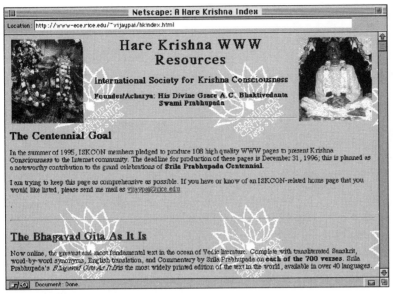

Figure 14-6: The Krishna Web page.

Hindu Academic Resources

Along with the Florida Vedic College, other academic resources are available for those interested in Hinduism. The Hindu Students Council site lists 48 chapters in the United States and Canada, for example, providing an active link for Hindu students on campuses.

One of the more interesting academic pursuits is a movement to reintroduce Sanskrit, an ancient language that is the tongue used for the Vedic scriptures. Figure 14-7 shows the Sanskrit home page, which hosts the "Speak Sanskrit" movement. According to Krishna Shastry, who is behind the effort, a knowledge of Sanskrit will open up a vast store of ancient literature to today's students.

Finding the Bhagavad Gita and other Yogic classics online

Although learning Sanskrit might be a good idea for the serious student of Hinduism, those of us with a more casual interest in Vedic literature can find a great deal of treasures in English, online.

The Bhaktivedanta Book Trust, a publishing company set up by Krishna founder Prabhupada, offers the *Bhagavad Gita As It Is* online, accessible through the G.H.E.N. site. You can also link from G.H.E.N. to other Vedic texts and commentaries, including "Gita Guidance" by Swami Chinmayanada.

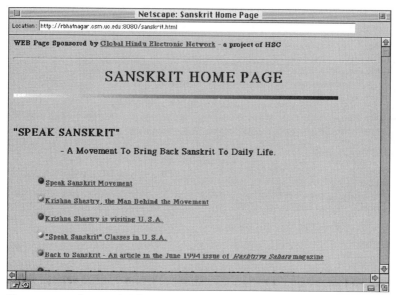

Figure 14-7: The Sanskrit home page.

Interestingly enough, some of these pages display the verses in their original Sanskrit, along with an English translation and commentary. One of these is the *Devanagari Versio*, which is available as a series of PostScript files that can be read offline with a PostScript file viewer. You can see selected verses online in the "Gita Guidance" version, whereas *Bhagavad Gita As It Is* offers an English transliteration of the Sanskrit version. Figure 14-8 shows the home page for the *Devanagari* version.

Along with a PostScript file viewer, such as Ghostview (which is necessary to display PostScript files), you will want to find out about a reader for *ixi/t*-coded files, which is how the *Devanagari* version of the *Gita* is supplied. No pointers to such a reader were found at the G.H.E.N. site, but a little searching should locate one.

Beyond the sacred Hindu texts, the G.H.E.N. site points readers toward books and Web pages about yoga practice and other aspects of a Hindu lifestyle. As mentioned, it's a truly valuable resource and a good starting place.

Hindu newsgroups

Several Hindu resources reside on the Usenet side of the tracks as well. Among those that see the most traffic are soc.religion.hindu, alt.hindu, alt.fan. jai-maharaj, uk.religion.hindu, and alt.religion.vaisnava. These newsgroups provide a great deal of interaction with those interested in Hindu pholosophies, and they will, in turn, point you to other Hindu sites around the Net for further research and enjoyment.

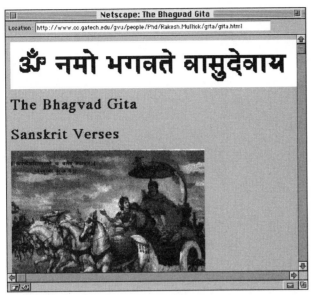

Figure 14-8: The *Devanagari* version of the *Bhagavad Gita* home page.

Jewish Life Online

Introduction

"I will always be grateful to the Jews for coming up with mono-theism," Larry Moffitt once wrote in *The Washington Times*. "Most people never give it a thought, but before there was one God, there were lots of gods. River gods, tree gods, Zeus, Aphrodite. . . . Judaism gave humankind some much-needed relief."

Indeed, way back in my Hebrew-school youth, one of the first stories I learned (later echoed by William Barclay, a Gentile, in his commentary on *Genesis*) was of Avram (his Hebrew name, which God later changed to Avraham, or Abraham) destroying all the idols in his father's shop, save one. When his father, Terah, came upon the site, the young Avram said that it was the lone standing idol that did the evil deed. When the father protested that the idols were not really gods, but statues, Avram asked why his father worshipped them.

Although Abraham is regarded as the patriarch of the Jewish people, the Torah (written by Moses after the Exodus from Egypt) goes back before Abraham to the creation of the world. The prophetic writings, Psalms, Proverbs, and other poetic writings compose the *Tanach*, or what non-Jews refer to as the *Old Testament*. Jews refer to these books as the *Holy Scriptures*.

Once a theocracy (the Torah is replete with stories about the way the faith should be organized and administered by those who follow it, under the administration of the priests, or Levites, who were the descendants of Moses' brother Aaron), Judaism has fragmented and decentralized since the Diaspora, when the land of Israel fell into Roman hands and the Jews left. The three main branches of Judaism familiar to Americans and Israelis are Orthodox, Conservative, and Reform, and there are many subgroups within those branches. In recent years, a new branch has arisen, Reconstructionism, which attempts to blend a respect for commitment to Jewish tradition with an evolving sense of Judaism.

Jews have been identified with two things: their scriptures and their land. Today, Jews are found in almost every country of the world, despite nearly two millennia of anti-Semitism and persecution. Most notable and tragic was the Holocaust, which was perpetrated by Nazi Germany and its sympathizers before and during World War II and resulted in the deaths of more than six million Jewish men, women, and children.

In the more than 50 years since the end of that war and the liberation of the survivors from Auschwitz, Buchenwald, Treblinka, and the other Nazi death camps, Judaism has faced challenges of assimilation and continuing attack from political and personal foes. Following the 1948 founding of the State of Israel, the surrounding Arab nations vowed to drive the Jews "into the sea" and reclaim what they had known as Palestine for their people. After four major wars and numerous terrorist attacks, Egypt was the first Arab League country to recognize Israel and conclude a peace treaty with the Jewish state in 1979. For that, Egypt's president Anwar el-Sadat paid with his life in 1981. Fourteen years later, with Israel having concluded a peace treaty with Jordan and the Palestine Liberation Organization — and being on the verge of a peace with Syria — Israeli Prime Minister and war hero Yitzhak Rabin was also assassinated, in this case the victim of a Jewish extremist who opposed the peace process.

No study of Judaism, ancient or modern, can be divorced from the Jewish people, their culture, and their land. This is why you will find that many Internet sites linked to Judaism are also tied in to Israel and what Jews call *Yiddishkeit* or Jewish culture. It is a joyous, optimistic, and persevering way of life, which has endured centuries of persecution and opposition and which gave birth to two other monotheistic religions, Christianity and Islam (the latter through Abraham's son Ishmael's descendants).

This brief overview of Judaism touches on only the main points. For greater depth and understanding, you will need to visit the Web sites and other resources you'll find in this chapter. If you are searching for your own Jewish roots or merely want to better understand Judaism, you are about to embark on a remarkable journey through a history of faith and hope.

In the Beginning: Project Genesis and Shamash

To commence that journey, I have two Web sites to recommend to you. One is called Project Genesis (http://www.torah.org/info/genesis.html) and the other is Shamash (http://shamash.nysernet.org/). These sites are excellent introductions to Judaism and the Torah, whose writings are read weekly in synagogues around the world.

Project Genesis is an independent organization based in the northern suburbs of New York City and is devoted to spreading Torah information over the Internet (see Figure15–1). Its maintainers are Orthodox Jews, but all Jews are welcome. The goal of Project Genesis is to "further Jewish education about our Jewish roots, as represented in Jewish sources."

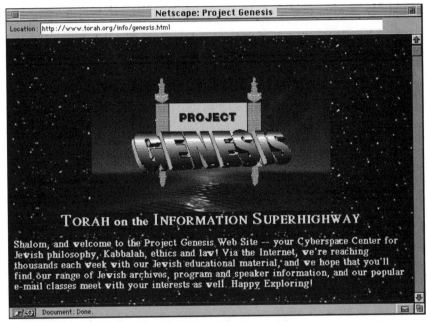

Figure 15-1: The Project Genesis home page.

As a result, Project Genesis' emphasis is on Jewish education, aimed at both Jews who are college students and those who are unaffiliated with a given synagogue or congregation. The "Global Learning Network" (Figure 15-2) offers a range of mailing list subscriptions to receive lessons based on the Torah, Jewish ethics, and Jewish law. It also contains a moderated discussion list of traditional Jewish perspectives, where participants can discuss just about any Jewish topic or text.

If you are *not* Jewish, please be respectful of the discussion participants and their views. You are certainly permitted to subscribe to these discussion lists and to raise questions that are germane to the matter being discussed. But non-Jews are *not* permitted to advocate their personal beliefs, especially if those beliefs are different from Judaism, for this would be a breach of good manners. One of the most important things to remember in interfaith dialog online is the need for mutual respect, and that includes honoring the "space" of the participants in the Project Genesis discussion groups.

Project Genesis' broad range of mailing lists is complimented by links to other Web sites and organizations promoting Jewish knowledge. It truly is a genesis point for the individual interested in exploring Judaism.

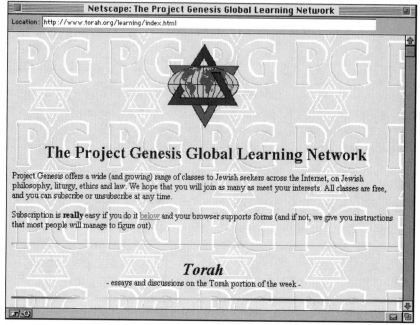

Figure 15-2: The Global Learning Network.

Shamash, on the other hand (Figure 15-3), bills itself as "The Jewish Internet Consortium," and as such features an even wider range of connections to all branches of Judaism (Orthodox, Conservative, Reform, and Reconstructionist) and a myriad of Jewish organizations and some businesses, such as the 1-800-JUDAISM bookstore. Along with links to major Jewish religious groups and traditions, the Shamash home page offers links to Jewish social welfare agencies: the B'nai B'rith, which offers a variety of services to the Jewish community, the World Zionist Organization, and others. Shamash is maintained by the Board of Jewish Education of New York, an agency of the United Jewish Appeal/Federation of Jewish Philanthropies that advocates and supports Jewish education in New York, now via the Internet.

As you'll see, the Shamash site offers several links to other Jewish sites. It's the home of Andrew Tannenbaum's Judaism and Jewish Resources Web page, which contains a vast number of links to other Jewish and Judaic Web sites. Tannenbaum created this in 1993 because, he said, it seemed like a logical thing to do. Although Shamash provides the Web space for him, Tannenbaum says he is independent of that organization (or any other), thus giving him the freedom to list a wide variety of organizations and sites.

Figure 15-3: The Shamash home page.

No doubt Tannenbaum's site is attracting interest from users: more than 16,000 people checked it out during December 1995 alone. He goes all over the map, literally, starting with a list of Web sites in Israel and continuing through references for Jewish organizations, books, Jewish singles, archaeology, travels, and miscellaneous links.

Before beginning to explore the sites relative to the three major Jewish traditions, those who are unfamiliar with the basic tenets of Judaism will want to visit a page maintained by A. Engler Anderson of Philadelphia, which is called Documents of Jewish Belief (`http://www.netaxs.com/~expweb/jewish_belief.html`) and is shown in Figure 15-4. It is an excellent resource for those who want to know the basics of Jewish doctrine as expressed by those traditions, culled from articles by leading Jewish intellectuals and theologians such as Solomon Schechter and Moses Maimonides, among others.

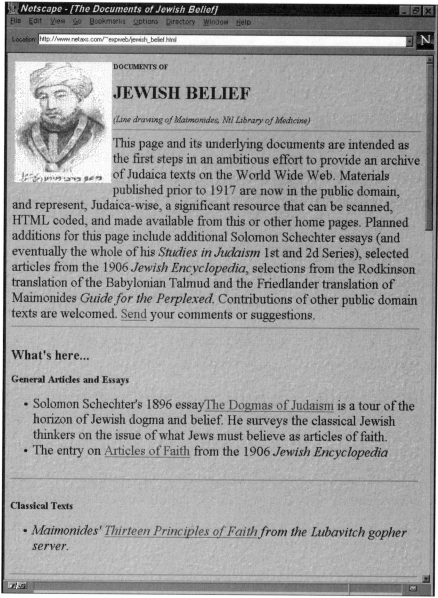

Figure 15-4: Documents of Jewish Belief, maintained by A. Engler Anderson of Philadelphia, contains many key statements relating to the basic tenets of Judaism.

Orthodox, Conservative, and Reform Web Sites

As mentioned, Judaism is represented principally by three major traditions: Orthodox, Conservative, and Reform. Therefore, you should not be surprised to learn that these traditions are also represented on the Internet. I'll begin with the Union of Orthodox Jewish Congregations of America, whose somewhat unassuming site is found at `gopher://shamash.nysernet.org/hh/ou`, and is pictured in Figure 15-5. The site is primarily a repository of texts and databases relating to Orthodoxy and *kashruth,* or "keeping kosher," as it is often referred to by Jews. You can read and/or download these texts, as well as access a Kosher for Passover database, which adds details about the proper observance of Passover, during which leavened products are not eaten.

For the observant, kashruth involves more than what many non-Jewish people imagine to be simply the avoidance of pork and shellfish or even the mixing of milk and meat, both of which are prohibited under Jewish law. But beyond these basic observances, kashruth requires the keeping of separate dishes for meat and dairy meals, and some extremely observant Jews will keep two sinks in their homes to avoid *any* mixing of the two kinds of foods. The strictures behind kashruth are of great importance to observant Jews, and the Orthodox Union, whose "OU" symbol is a seal of approval for products, is an arbiter of kashruth.

The Orthodox Union is much more than merely a body that helps oversee the proper observance of kashruth, as important as that is to Orthodox Jewish observance. It also features a youth organization, the National Council of Synagogue Youth, whose home page (`http://shamash.nysernet.org/ou/ncsy/`) is shown in Figure 15-6 and which sponsors educational programs throughout North America, Europe, and Israel.

The NCSY offers links to information about its programs, an online Torah project that provides daily and weekly readings, and a listing of leadership programs available from the NCSY national office. Though these resources are directed primarily at those who are already members of Orthodox congregations and youth organizations, the e-mail link supplied with these pages can allow inquirers to make a first step toward contacting an Orthodox congregation.

At this writing, the United Synagogue of Conservative Judaism (`http://shamash.nysernet.org/uscj`), which represents some 800 Conservative Jewish congregations in North America, offers more in the way of Internet resources than its Orthodox cousins. Along with 14 home pages for associated synagogues, the page (Figure 15-7) includes links to home pages for departments within the USCJ as well as to various mailing lists and Web pages, including one for the Jewish Theological Seminary of America, which includes a family education home page.

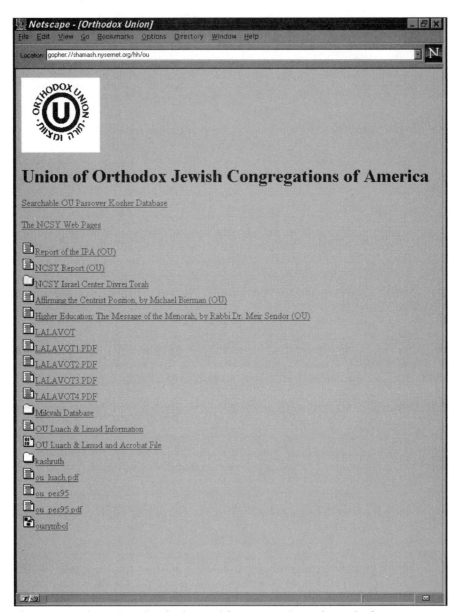

Figure 15-5: The Union of Orthodox Jewish Congregations of America home page.

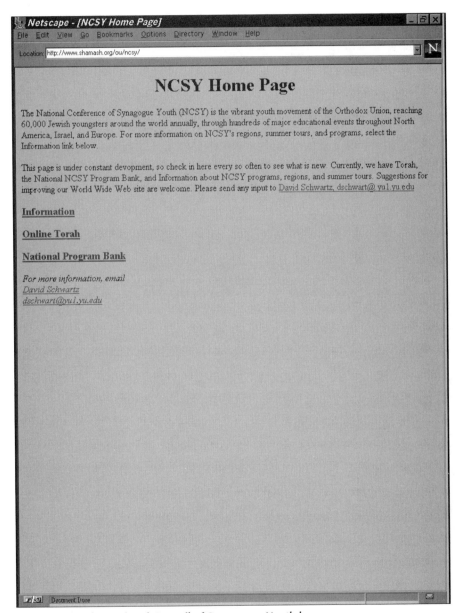

Figure 15-6: The National Council of Synagogue Youth home page.

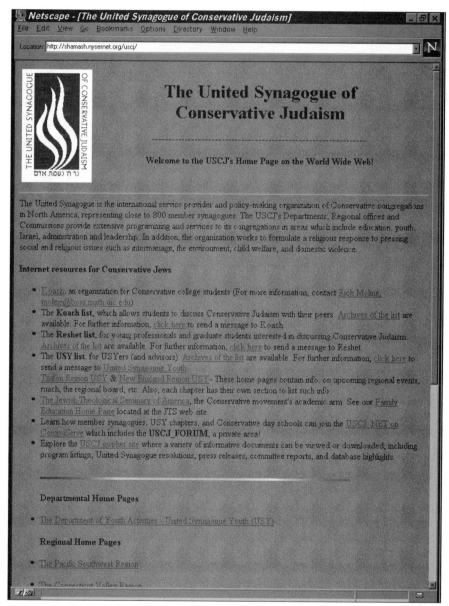

Figure 15-7: The United Synagogue of Conservative Judaism home page.

Though the USCJ is planning to expand its list of services, including a list of Hebrew day schools, many Conservative congregations are already maintaining home pages of their own, which are linked from the USCJ home page. One of these, for the Tifereth Israel Synagogue, is shown in Figure 15-8.

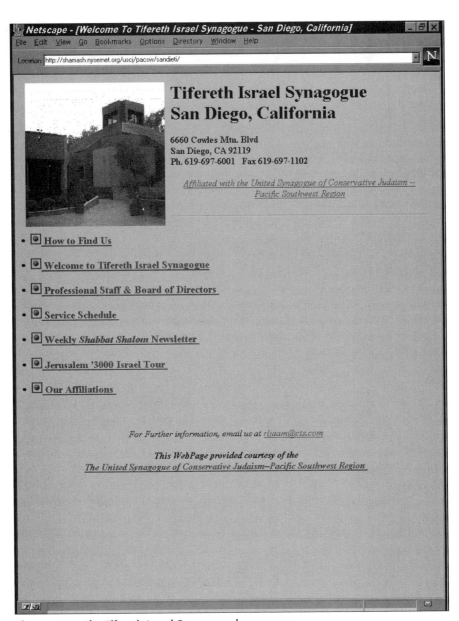

Figure 15-8: The Tifereth Israel Synagogue home page.

Rabbi Isaac Mayer Wise brought Reform Judaism (http://shamash.nysernet.org/reform) to North America more than 150 years ago. According to the Reform Judaism home page (Figure 15-9), "The word *reform* in our new name is a recognition that reform is part of our way of life, as it has been for Jews throughout the centuries."

In practice, this means that Reform Judaism's practices are more liberal than its Conservative and Orthodox brethren. Most importantly, Reform Judaism believes that although the Torah was written with divine inspiration, it was written in the language of the times and that the "process of reinterpretation" of the scriptures is an ongoing process in which every Jew has a role. The denomination stresses egalitarianism, or equal treatment of the sexes, which is why Reform congregations may have women serve as *rabbis* and *cantors,* the principal leaders of worship services, as well as allow them to make up a *minyan,* the requisite number of Jews (10) necessary to assemble for a worship service. By contrast, Conservative and Orthodox synagogues restrict all these roles to men.

Today, some 853 congregations in North America are affiliated with the Union of American Hebrew Congregations (http://shamash.nysernet.org/reform/uahc/index.html), which is the umbrella organization for Reform congregations. Its home page (Figure 15-10) offers a wide variety of links to its congregations and affiliated organizations and to *Reform Judaism* magazine and other published resources. Especially useful is a link to frequently asked questions about Reform Judaism, which offers insight into what the movement believes.

Also significant from the UAHC home page is a link to the home pages of many congregations, as well as a directory of all UAHC congregations. Typical of the active home pages (and kudos to UAHC for providing online instruction for its congregations desiring to post a page) is that for Temple Kol Emeth in Marietta, Georgia (http://www.shamash.org/reform/uahc/congs/ga/ga001/), which utilizes scanned photos and the frame elements of Netscape 2.0 to create an interesting and informative display.

Figure 15-9: The Reform Judaism home page.

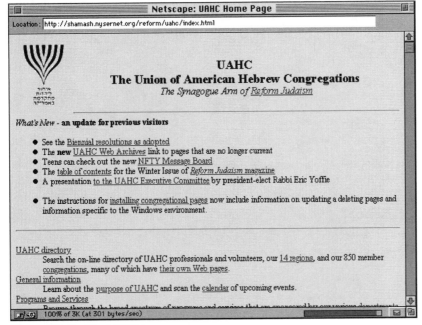

Figure 15-10: The UAHC home page.

Chabad-Lubavitch Online

One of the most interesting developments in Judaism in recent years has been the exponential growth of various Chasidic movements. Sometimes referred to as "ultra-Orthodox," the Chasidim (often descended from their forebears in eastern Europe) adhere to what they call a "Torah-true" lifestyle in observance of Jewish law and customs.

Chasidic leaders have interpreted and expanded upon these traditions through many years of study. One of the most vibrant movements is *Chabad-Lubavitch* (`http://www.chabad.org`), which is headquartered in Brooklyn, New York, but has spread around the world. Its leader for many years was Rabbi Menachem Mendel Schneerson, known as the *Rebbe* to his followers. The Rebbe's commentaries on the scriptures and Jewish law have extended the reach of the Chabad-Lubavitch and have been transmitted via cable television and satellite. Now, the movement has extended into cyberspace (Figure 15-11).

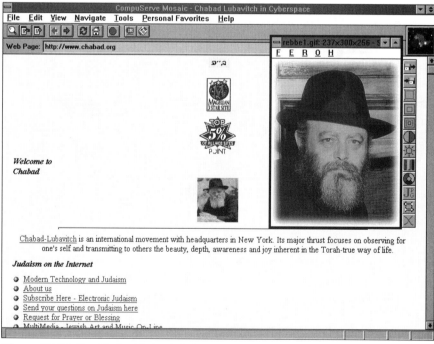

Figure 15-11: The Chabad-Lubavitch home page.

Writing in the *Village Voice*, an alternative weekly in New York City, Donna Gaines stated that the presence of Chabad-Lubavitch brought her back to her Jewish roots. That is the primary reason for the online work of the movement, according to Rabbi Yoel Yitzchak (or "Rabbi YY") Kazen, who maintains the site. Ministering to unaffiliated or geographically isolated Jews is a specialty of Rabbi YY, who recently received a letter from David Hornstein, a worker at the New Zealand Antarctic Program, who was spending a year away from his family and synagogue as part of his occupation.

"In the winter (May to August), I will be one in 10 people at Scott base at the dark end of the world where the sun doesn't rise for 4 months," Mr. Hornstein wrote in an e-mail to Rabbi YY, expressing his thanks for the assistance that Chabad-Lubavitch provides. "I want to thank you very much for the wise words from your 'resource Rabbi,'" he added.

For those who are interested in learning more about this movement and its impact on people's lives, this Web site is a very good place to start.

Jewish Discussion Groups and Mailing Lists

In addition to the Web pages that I have previously noted, you'll find over 100 mailing lists on the Internet that address Jewish topics and issues. You can find a good listing of these through Jewishnet (`http://www.jewishnet.net/lis.html`), with topics broken down into categories covering Israel, Zionism, Talmud and Torah studies, and special interests. Figure 15-12 illustrates the page that lists these.

The most popular Jewish newsgroup is `soc.culture.jewish`, which is a freewheeling discussion of Jewish issues between Orthodox, Conservative, Reform, and non-affiliated Jews. Susan Zakar, a Jewish woman from suburban Washington, D.C., credits the friendships that she made on the mailing list with steering her and her husband back toward Orthodoxy and greater fulfillment in her life.

"The resources for learning are mind-boggling," Zakar wrote in an article posted on the Chabad-Lubavitch site. She praised the opportunities for Jews to hold discussions on areas of common interest and over points where they might disagree. Zakar noted the many friendships formed as a result of her meeting people online that have helped in her spiritual journey.

You can learn a great deal from these mailing lists, if that is your desire. But, as noted before, these lists are *not* the place for "evangelization" or proselytizing, if you are of a different belief than the majority on that list. Respect for others is a keystone of the Internet, and it's something you won't find emphasized enough in this book. I believe fully in the free expression of ideas, but I would not be so presumptuous as to walk into your home, uninvited, and start preaching. By subscribing to a mailing list such as `soc.culture.jewish`, non-Jews are, essentially, inviting themselves into someone else's neighborhood. As such, respect is essential — unless you want to receive a raft of flames and possibly be banned from the mailing list.

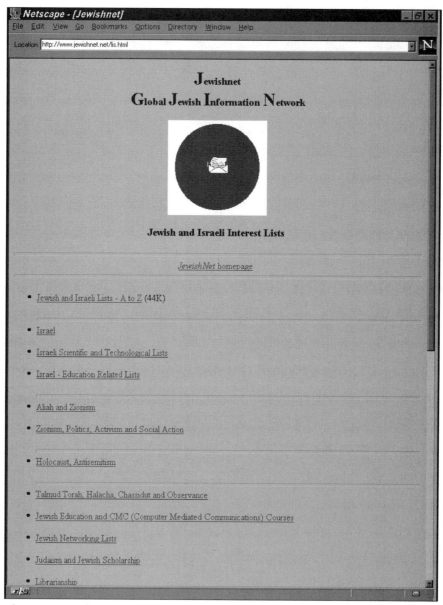

Figure 15-12: The Jewishnet listing of Jewish and Israeli interest lists.

Jewish Museums and the Dead Sea Scrolls

Finding Jewish museums and the Dead Sea Scrolls involves visiting sites in Israel, and the place to start looking is Andrew Tannenbaum's Judaism and Jewish Resources page, referenced earlier in the chapter. From this, you can find cultural, historical, and artistic resources on the Net. You can find a description of — but no exhibits from — the Jewish Museum in New York City (`http://www.jtsa.edu:80/jm/`).

Other museums offer more in the way of information and access. The Nahum Goldman Museum of the Jewish Diaspora (`http://www.ort.org/ort/museum/start.htm`) offers an interactive tour of the museum, which chronicles the dispersal of the Jews from Israel throughout the world (Figure 15-13).

Those wishing to examine the worst event in the history of the Jewish people, the Nazi-led persecution that has come to be known as the Holocaust, can investigate several sites online. One is the United States Holocaust Memorial Museum (`http://www.ushmm.org/`), which was established a few years ago in Washington, D.C. (Figure 15-14). The site offers information on planning a visit as well as access to several symposia and other museum resources.

Those looking for information on the famous Dead Sea Scrolls can point their browsers to a great online exhibit housed at the University of North Carolina (`http://sunsite.unc.edu/expo/deadsea.scrolls.exhibit/intro.html`), which offers the background and an introduction to these ancient manuscripts, which were found nearly 2,000 years after their storage near the ancient caves of Qumran. The online exhibit includes images of 12 scroll fragments and 29 other objects loaned by the Israel Antiquities Authority. Figure 15-15 displays the home page for the exhibit.

Of the many other Jewish and Israel-related exhibits cataloged on the Web, one other is worthy of immediate attention here. The Chagall Windows at the Synagogue of the Hadassah-Hebrew University Medical Center have attracted worldwide attention for their depiction of the 12 sons of Jacob, from whom the legendary 12 tribes of Israel are descended. Point your browser to `http://www1.huji.ac.il/md/chagall/chagall.html`, and you'll learn the story behind this fascinating work of art. Figure 15-16 shows this page.

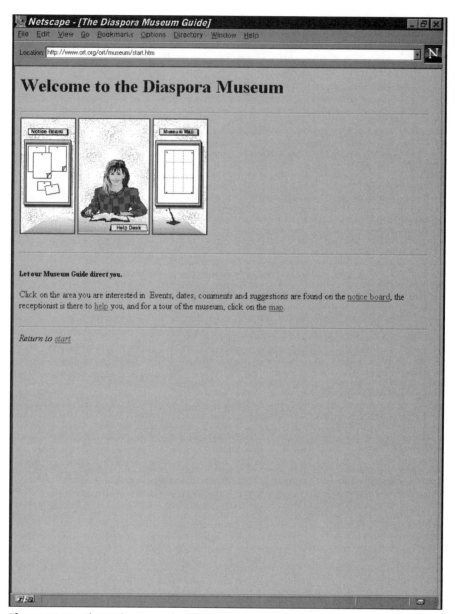

Figure 15-13: The Welcome to the Diaspora Museum page.

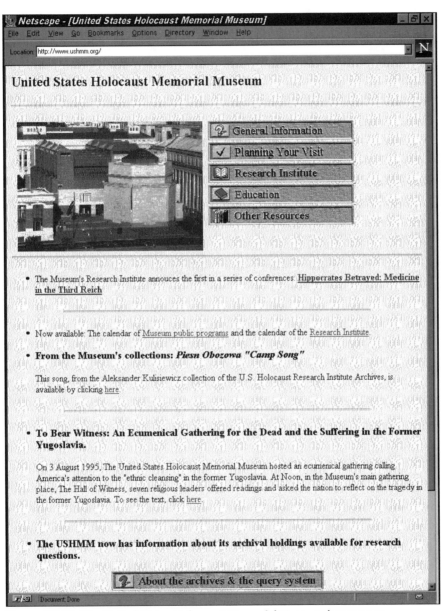

Figure 15-14: The United States Holocaust Memorial Museum home page.

Figure 15-15: The Dead Sea Scrolls exhibit home page.

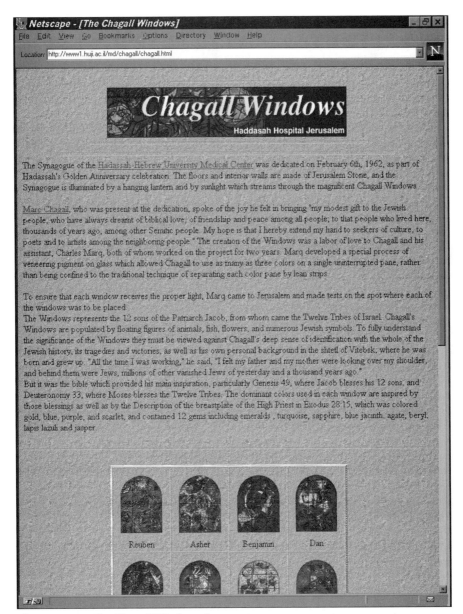

Figure 15-16: The Chagall Windows home page.

Hebrew-Language Resources

Hebrew, the language of the people of Israel and the language of the Tanach, is a living language today in the State of Israel. It also lives on in Jewish liturgy and worship because many Jewish congregations conduct their services partially or totally in Hebrew.

Learning Hebrew is something of interest to Jews and to many non-Jews as well. Starting with the Israel-based Macom Networking Hebrew language home page (`http://www.macom.co.il/hebrew`) (illustrated in Figure 15-17), you can begin to pick up basic words and phrases, and you can hear audio clips in Hebrew as well.

Figure 15-17: The Hebrew: A Living Language home page.

Those wishing to study in an organized way can start with the Organization for Rehabilitation and Training (ORT), a Jewish social service agency, and its Discovering Hebrew series, found at `http://www.ort.org/ort/hebrew/start.htm`. Ultimately, the course consists of 60 units that will lead students through Hebrew reading, listening, and speaking skills, including the use of Internet e-mail and Internet Relay Chat. Figure 15-18 shows this page.

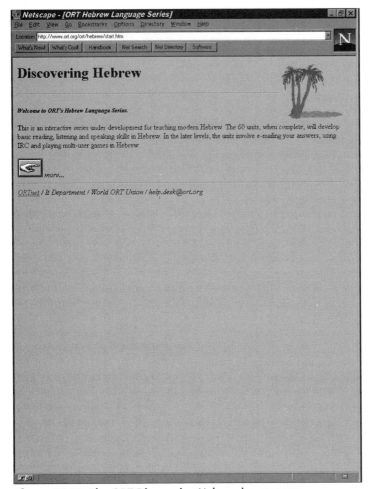

Figure 15-18: The ORT Discovering Hebrew home page.

Once you have developed or brushed up on your Hebrew skills, you can utilize the resources of the Internet. A helpful page maintained by the Society Hill Synagogue, an independent Conservative congregation in Philadelphia, Pennsylvania, offers instructions on how to read Hebrew on the Web, including pointers to the necessary Mac and Windows software. You can find it at `http://www-leland.stanford.edu/ ~nadav/hebrew.html`. I really appreciate how this page provides extremely clear and explicit instructions on how to download and install the software. This is a prime example of how to construct a really helpful Web page, and it's illustrated in Figure 15-19.

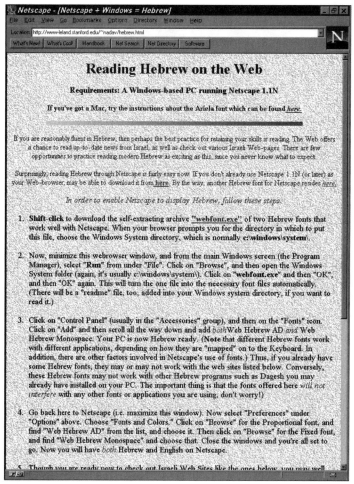

Figure 15-19: The Reading Hebrew on the Web page from Society Hill Synagogue.

The Yamada Language Center of the University of Oregon's Web Guide to Hebrew (`http://babel.uoregon.edu/yamada/guides/hebrew.html`) is also extremely useful, as it offers software for DOS, Windows, and Mac users. The comprehensiveness of offerings here commends this page (Figure 15-20) to all serious students of Hebrew.

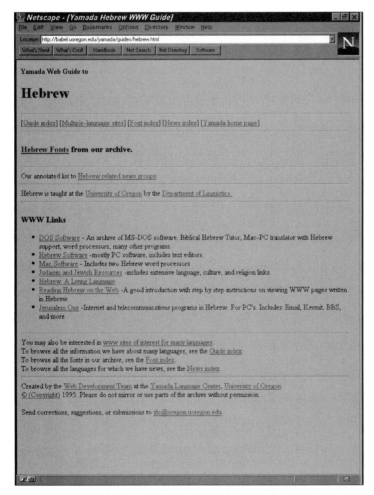

Figure 15-20: The Yamada Hebrew Web page.

After you've worked with these resources, you should be able to display Hebrew characters on your PC or Mac.

Jewish Culture: Drama, Music, and Food Online

I could probably devote an entire book to the subject of Jewish culture and still probably not cover it all. Because of the Diaspora, Jewish culture has taken on aspects of every nation where it has landed. For us in the United States, much of that originates in eastern Europe, for that is the source of many of America's Jewish emigrants.

Before I go to the subsections of this subject, let me direct you to the National Foundation for Jewish Culture home page (`gopher://shamash.org/hh/nfjc`), which archives documents and directories concerning the expression of Jewish culture in America. You'll find a complete range of information here, including the means to apply for doctoral fellowships and for commissions to write plays with Jewish themes. It's a comprehensive resource that will serve as a good starting point (Figure 15-21).

The short story

One of the most interesting aspects of Jewish culture has been the short story, the medium through which authors as diverse as Isaac Bashevis Singer, Grace Paley, and Philip Roth have expressed themselves. The National Yiddish Book Center has joined with public radio station KCRW-FM in Santa Monica, California, to produce a series of these stories read by actors including Rhea Perlman (Carla from *Cheers*), Elliot Gould, Carol Kane, and Alan Alda. Leonard Nimoy introduces each story. Click over to the Jewish Short Stories home page (`http://www.kcrw.org/b/jss.html`), and you'll see full details of the series and, if you have a Real Audio player, you can hear Rhea Perlman read Grace Paley's short story "Goodbye and Goodluck." (See Figure 15-22.)

Music

Jewish music is equally varied in its expression, ranging from traditional cantorial performances of liturgical music to modern Israeli songs and the recent revival of *klezmer* music, which is a form created in eastern Europe that has become wildly popular in America in recent years.

I found two major sites of potential interest in my Web wanderings. Of these, Radio Hazak is the Internet's answer to Kol Yisrael, the national radio network in Israel. It features detailed discussions of Israeli pop music, although it seems to be a bit short on audio content. Nonetheless, you'll find it a good starting point for exploring and discussing Israeli topics (Figure 15-23).

The klezmer revival is well documented on Ari Davidow's Klez Picks page (`http://www.well.com/user/ari/klez`), which he stores on the Well Internet service in San Francisco (Figure 15-24). Davidow's selections are personal and contain some admitted biases, but he offers a valuable resource for fans of this new/old musical style.

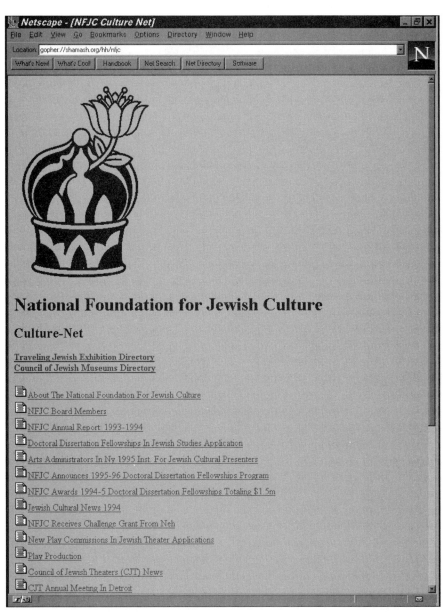

Figure 15-21: The home page of the National Foundation for Jewish Culture.

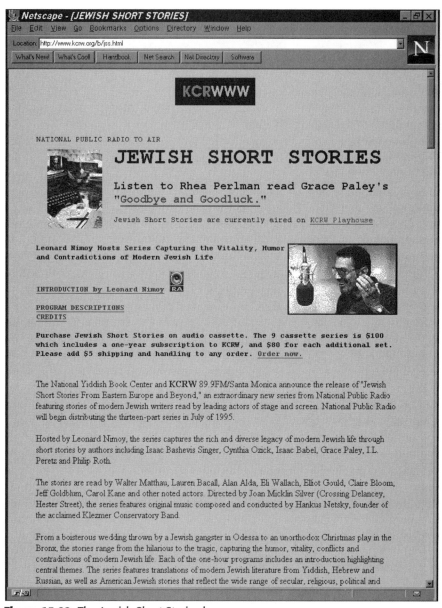

Figure 15-22: The Jewish Short Stories home page.

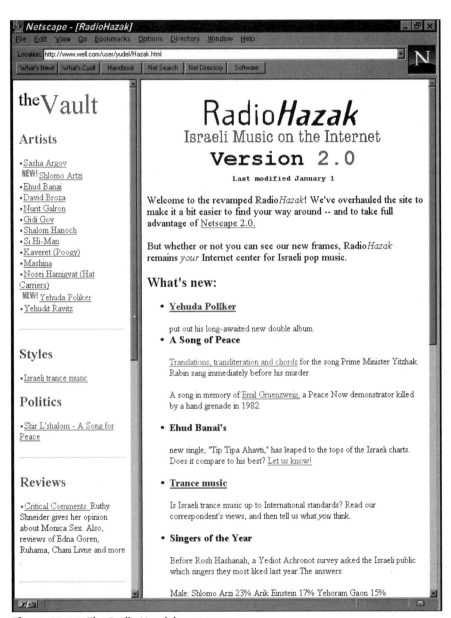

Figure 15-23: The Radio Hazak home page.

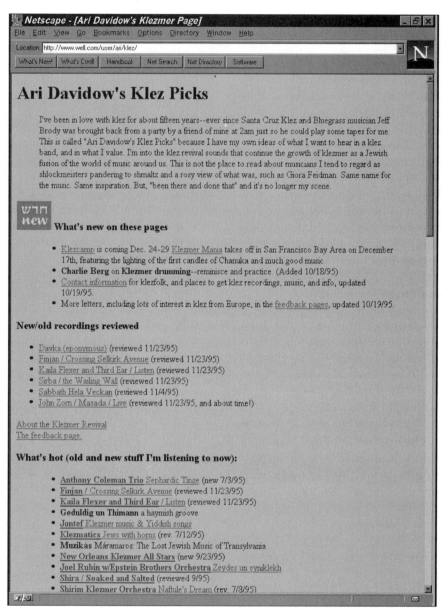

Figure 15-24: Ari Davidow's Klez Picks page.

Cooking

Of Jewish food, those who know it know how varied, and how good, it can be. Those who believe that keeping kashruth condemns one to a life of bland pot roasts and chicken soup with matzo balls are just not with it. It seems that virtually every cuisine known to humankind has had the kosher treatment.

If you don't believe me, point your browser over to `http://www.kashrus.org` and look at the Asian-American Kashrus Services Web page (Figure 15-25). This site, maintained by Rabbi Raphael Meyer, offers information about keeping kosher and provides a host of kosher Asian recipes. You won't find — as I did at the old Moshe Peking restaurant in New York City — analogue replacements for non-kosher dishes, but you will find Chinese, Indian, Thai, Vietnamese, and other recipes that adhere to the rules of kashruth.

Figure 15-25: The Asian-American Kashrus Services home page.

Other resources for kosher recipes include `http://www.epicurious.com/epicurious/recipes/recipes.html`, which takes you to *Epicurious*, a net-based magazine from Condé Nast magazines, publishers of *Bon Appétit* and *Gourmet*. At the Epicurious recipes page, you can perform a keyword search for terms such as *jewish* or *kosher,* or you can enter the name of a specific ingredient, which will search the Epicurious libraries for any dish that contains that ingredient. *Kosher Express* (`http://www.marketnet.com/mktnet/kosher/recipes.html`) also includes various recipes for use during the holidays and an archive of Passover recipes as well.

You can also find kosher recipes and discussion on the Internet in newsgroups such as `soc.culture.jewish`, `rec.food.recipes`, and `rec.food.cooking`. Be warned that searching these newsgroups by keyword can sometimes yield unintended results: a search for *kosher recipes* brought up one for a definitely non-kosher dish, Cantonese Shrimp with Lobster Sauce, whose only connection to the topic came when the recipe called for kosher salt. Oddly enough, that recipe came from Mimi's Cyber Kitchen, hosted by Mimi and J.B. Hiller, which does have some *real* kosher recipes (`http://www.smartlink.net/~hiller/food/`).

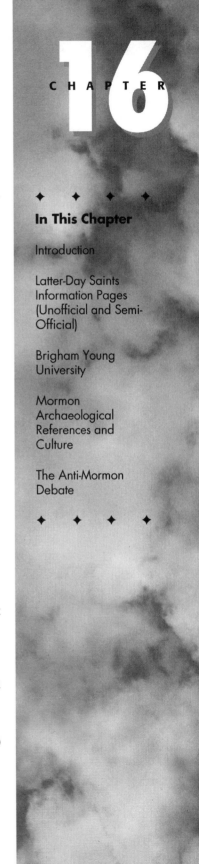

Mormons in Cyberspace

Introduction

Of all the major religious movements born in the United States
(Christian Science, Jehovah's Witnesses, and the Church of Jesus
Christ of Latter-Day Saints), the Mormons (as the Latter-Day
Saints are known) have arguably been the most successful. The
LDS church was founded primarily on revelations to church
leaders, starting with the 1830 discovery of the *Book of Mormon*.
LDS church founder Joseph Smith, Jr., testified that he translated
this book, held by Mormons to be "Another Testament of Jesus
Christ," from golden plates hidden in the "Hill Cumorah" in
upstate New York by Moroni, a prophet from ancient times. The
Book of Mormon details appearances of Jesus Christ on the
North American continent after his death and resurrection, to
people from ancient Israel who migrated in an early Diaspora.

Proclaimed by enthusiastic disciples throughout the Northeast
and then in England, Mormon faith took root but also garnered
opposition. Smith and his followers had to relocate from New
York to Ohio, then to Missouri, and then to Illinois, where Smith
died, after which the Mormons had to move once again. After
leaving their community of Nauvoo, Illinois, the Saints — as they
often refer to themselves — arrived in the Valley of the Great Salt
Lake in 1847.

Over the course of 150 years, the Mormon Church has grown
from a curious sect in upstate New York to a global church of 9.4
million members in 150 countries and territories. Young Mormon
men and women spend up to 24 months on a "mission" in a
distant city or country, allied with another young person in
door-to-door preaching. In the middle of 1994, the LDS church
reported that it had 49,000 missionaries serving in more than 300
missions worldwide. Since 1829, when it was first printed, more
than 76 million copies of the *Book of Mormon* have been placed
by LDS Church missionaries, of which 43 million were distributed in the past decade, according to the *LDS Church News.*

More than 40 temples stand around the world today as testimony to the faith of this native American religion and its acceptance by millions who believe it is what Joseph Smith Jr. said it was: a restoration of "primitive Christianity."

The accomplishments of the Latter-Day Saints are particularly visible in the state of Utah, which in 1996 celebrates its centennial as one of the United States. "The State of Deseret" took nearly 50 years to be admitted to the Union, in part because of controversy over the Mormon's belief in polygamy, or plural marriage, which the church dropped in 1890.

To think of the Mormons as merely colonizers of a Western wilderness is to seriously undervalue their contributions to American culture and to religion in general. Principles of industry, thrift, and caring for others in their community are hallmarks of Mormon tradition. In homes around the world every Monday, Mormon families celebrate "Family Home Evening," during which the cares of the world are set aside for a time of sharing. The Mormon commitment to genealogy has helped create an intense interest in genealogy among many Americans, as well as one of the largest networks of research centers in the world. Educationally, Mormonism has led to the establishment of Brigham Young University, one of the finest schools in the western United States, and other schools as well. The Mormons' interest in the ancient peoples of the Americas has led to many archaeological expeditions.

The leap from the pre-history of this continent to the information superhighway may not seem as great as it might at first. Utah also happens to be one of the key centers of the information technology industry, with software leaders such as Novell and WordPerfect calling the Beehive State home. That the Latter-Day Saints would find their place on the World Wide Web is only fitting.

At this writing, however, no *official* home page exists for the Church of Jesus Christ of Latter-Day Saints. Extracts from the weekly *Church News* are available online, however. My sources within the LDS church tell me that "deliberate" consideration of a home page for the church is being given, and one may well be up even as this book first appears in print in the Spring of 1996. Updates will be given both in future editions and at the God on the Internet Web site, `http://www.reston.com/kellner/kellner.html`.

For now, the church seems content to allow its members and institutions to do the "missionary" work online. This is being done, and with verve, by Mormons in Utah and elsewhere. Also, some groups that have spun off from the LDS church, such as the Reorganized Church of Jesus Christ of Latter-Day Saints in Independence, Missouri, (`http://www.rlds.org`) do have their own home pages.

From its start, the Mormons have met with opposition from other churches that have attacked their doctrines and beliefs and questioned the veracity of Joseph Smith Jr. and the *Book of Mormon*. Therefore, Mormon cyber-netters more than others are used to answering inquiries (both hostile and friendly), and unlike some other cybernauts, they'll likely be more willing to engage in online debate. I would, however, counsel extreme respectfulness in any contact, especially if you are attempting to dispute someone on a tenet of his or her faith.

Overall, even if one does not accept every tenet of Mormon theology, I believe that Mormonism presents much that people of other faiths could stand to learn: the emphasis on family values and industry, the doggedness and determination of their door-to-door workers, and the zeal with which Mormons hold and proclaim their views, to name just a few. Through the sites and mailing lists mentioned here, you can begin your journey.

LDS Information Pages (Unofficial and Semi-Official)

Barring the advent of an official home page for the Church of Jesus Christ of Latter-Day Saints, those curious about Mormonism will need to start with semi-official and unofficial information sites. For the purposes of this book, a semi-official page is defined as one maintained either by a Mormon-backed institution such as the *Deseret News* daily newspaper or Brigham Young University. Unofficial pages are defined here as those maintained by commercial organizations and individual LDS church members. A very good example of an unofficial page is shown in Figure 16-1; it's the Mormon.Net page (`http://www.mormon.net`), maintained by John D. Hays.

This home page advertises itself as "pro-Mormon" and features material from the LDS church and others. Hays has links to various sites featuring Mormon information and activities. One of these is what I would call a semi-official page, that for the *LDS Church News* Web site (`http://www.desnews.com/cn/`), which contains articles from this weekly newsmagazine put out by the church's *Deseret News* daily newspaper, which is published in Salt Lake City (Figure 16-2).

The *LDS Church News* is the place to go for current information about the church that bears the imprimatur of the LDS church. If also features articles about Mormon faith and doctrine, including study materials for the week. The paper, which is also available by subscription, represents the official viewpoint of the church.

That's not to say that the *LDS Church News* is dull reading, however. Along with official statements from church leaders (such as LDS President Gordon B. Hinckley's affirmation that the *Book of Mormon* is true), there are features about LDS members and how the church has affected their lives.

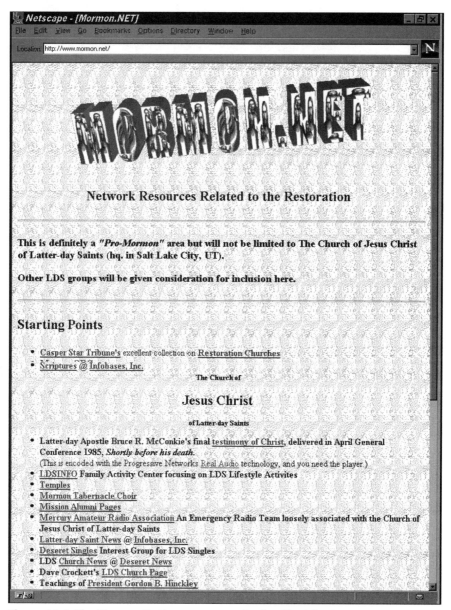

Figure 16-1: The Mormon.Net home page, maintained by John D. Hays.

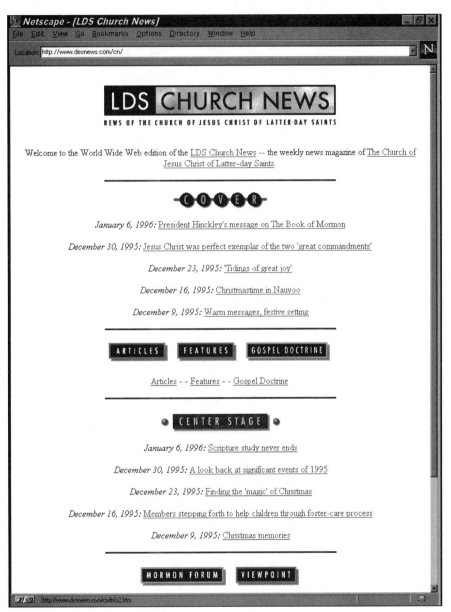

Figure 16-2: The *LDS Church News* home page, a semi-official LDS Web site.

From the Mormon.Net page, you can also go to an archive maintained at the *Casper Tribune* in Wyoming, which offers a wide range of information about the LDS church and other so-called "Restoration" churches, defined as churches which trace their origins back to Joseph Smith Jr., including the Reorganized Church of Jesus Christ of Latter-Day Saints and smaller groups. These groups range from the giant LDS Church to a tiny group called the Restored Church of Jesus Christ. Many of these spin-off groups claim to be lineal or spiritual heirs to Joseph Smith Jr., and many support the concept and practice of plural marriage. The historical information about these groups will be of interest to students of Mormon history.

One of the links from the *Casper Tribune* site is to a page maintained by Brandon Plewe of the University of Buffalo. Called LDS Info on the Internet (`http://wings.buffalo.edu/~plewe/lds.html`), this page brings together textual information about President Gordon B. Hinckley and his aides, called First and Second Counselors, as well as other unofficial documents detailing basic Mormon beliefs. You can also jump to Mormon scriptures and online versions of the Bible from this site, which is illustrated in Figure 16-3.

As with many of the other LDS pages that I've visited in the course of this journey, I found many links to other LDS-related sites while browsing Mr. Plewe's page. He keeps this page very well updated, and it's a good place to troll for Mormon-related information.

Mormons organize their congregations into *wards,* which are grouped regionally into *stakes*. Therefore, employees of Deseret Book, a retail operation in Salt Lake City, appropriately set up the WWW 1st Ward site (`http://www.uvol.com/www1st/`), which is illustrated in Figure 16-4. This site is very well designed, includes a virtual tour of Temple Square in Salt Lake City, and offers links to other Web sites related to Mormonism. The attitude here is somewhat casual but reverential of the tenets of the LDS church, and Saints will find much to enjoy here. One of the most useful aspects will probably be links to books available from Deseret Book, especially for those in areas without an LDS bookstore nearby.

I enjoyed my visit to the WWW 1st Ward site and not just because I normally don't hang out in LDS haunts. It was informative and enjoyable, particularly the feature columns of Donna Harlow Gelter, a 1976 graduate of Brigham Young University who may well qualify as the Mormon's Erma Bombeck, writing with wit and humor — and a good dash of LDS culture — about her family of seven children and seven pets. Leaving this site, I was again impressed with the well-rounded nature of the package and recommend it to readers wanting more than a surface glimpse of Mormon life.

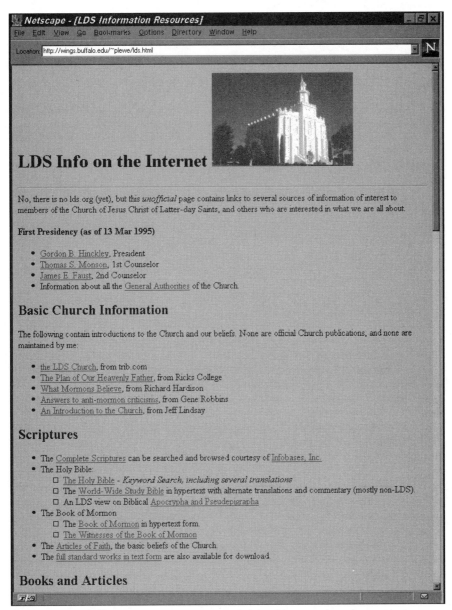

Figure 16-3: LDS Info on the Internet, as maintained by Brandon Plewe.

Figure 16-4: The WWW 1st Ward home page.

Brigham Young University

Known colloquially as "the Y," after the surname of its founder and namesake Mormon President Brigham Young, Brigham Young University is sponsored by the Church of Jesus Christ of Latter-Day Saints and is part of the LDS Church Educational System. At this writing, the BYU home pages represent a gateway to the school and to elements of Mormon teaching (http://www.byu.edu/). Figure 16-5 shows the home page.

Figure 16-5: The Brigham Young University home page.

From this page, you can take a virtual tour of the campus, examine admissions information and courses available, and, if you're a BYU alumnus, join the Alumni Association. You can also download devotional talks by Mormon leaders — known as *firesides* — in order to gain a greater understanding of Mormon belief.

The Religious Education department of BYU has its own pages, which offer access to two LDS religion texts online, *Teachings of the Prophet Joseph Smith* and *The Articles of Faith* by James E. Talmage, and also an online reconstruction of the first Temple in Jerusalem, after which the LDS church says its temples are patterned. You can also check exhibits on LDS church history and doctrine, including an exhibit tracing the migration of the LDS church from Nauvoo, Illinois, to points west, as shown in Figure 16-6.

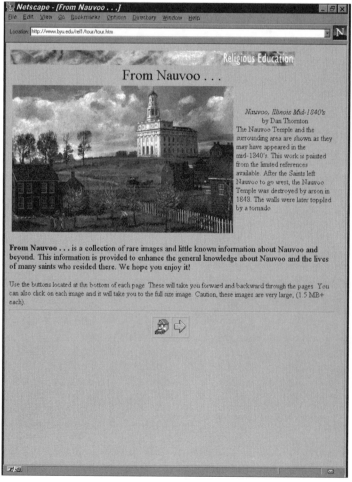

Figure 16-6: From Nauvoo…, an exhibit at Brigham Young University, via the Internet.

The BYU Web site is an excellent resource for insights into Mormon history and knowledge. If that is what you seek, it will be a rewarding stop on your journeys.

Mormon Archaeological References and Culture

Because the *Book of Mormon* deals heavily with ancient peoples whom the LDS church believes populated the Americas centuries before Columbus discovered the so-called "New World," you probably won't be surprised that the Mormons are keenly interested in archaeology, nor that you can find sites that link both on the Web.

At the Brigham Young University site, you'll usually find an online excerpt from a campus archaeological exhibit touching on ancient history. One centers on the ancient Egyptian pharaohs, whereas another deals with emperors of Imperial China.

The Foundation for Ancient Research and Mormon Studies (FARMS) has Web pages maintained by Walter C. Reade, currently a doctoral student at Penn State University. Mr. Reade includes information about the group, transcripts of various research papers, and publications. You may download the materials for personal use but not for republication.

Along with FARMS, you can find other links to Mormon archaeology and culture from Mormon.Net and other sites. You'll find a mailing list on the Internet that discusses *Studies in Antiquities and Mormonism,* to which you can subscribe by sending the request `Subscribe SAMU-L firstname lastname` (where you've substituted your actual name), to `listserv@bingvmb.cc.binghamton.edu`.

Many, many more Mormon links abound on the Net. A recent search with Yahoo (`http://www.yahoo.com/`) revealed more than 67 such links, so happy hunting.

The anti-Mormon debate

As noted before, the Mormons have encountered — and continue to encounter — opposition from those who disagree with church teachings and doctrines. From the start, critics have attacked Joseph Smith Jr. as a fraud or false prophet and have knocked the *Book of Mormon* as untrue.

Although some in the LDS church try to ignore their critics, others both inside and outside the church want to understand the critics or at least know what the arguments are. The Mormon Research Ministry, located in El Cajon, California, maintains a Web site that details the groups concerns about Mormonism, at `http://orion.adnc.com/~websites/mrm/`, which is illustrated in the following figure. It contains links to other apologetics ministries that deal with Mormonism as well as testimonies from those who have rejected the LDS church and its teachings.

(continued)

(continued)

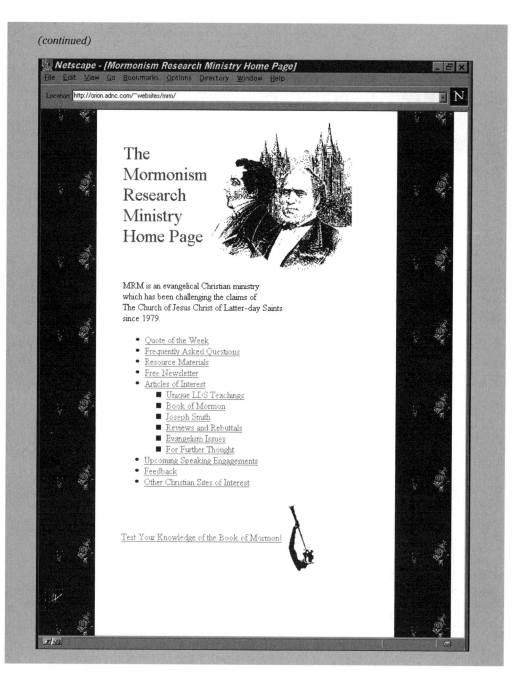

Seeing such arguments often leaves the faithful of a given movement with questions about the motives of those attacking their church's doctrines. "If these people are Christians," as they say, "why are they beating up on us?" The answer that you will hear from the "anti" groups is that they believe their message to be important enough that a direct challenge is required. My suggestion is that if you are insecure about your faith, don't visit a site challenging your beliefs. If, on the other hand, you are a member of the LDS church and want to be ready to answer your critics, the sites linked to the Mormon Research Ministries home page will provide you with much to research.

Protestant, Evangelical, and Pentecostal Pathways

What Hath Luther Wrought?

Tired of what he viewed as corruption within the Church of
Rome, Martin Luther, a young Catholic priest in Germany, in
1517 wrote up 95 statements of belief, many of which greatly
diverged from those understood by the Holy See. He posted
those theses on the cathedral door in Wittenberg, Germany, and
sparked a church trial that led to his expulsion from the Roman
Catholic Church. Luther married, started his own church, and
thus became the father of *Protestantism*, the movement away
from Rome by those whose watchword was *Sola Scriptura*, or
"The Bible Alone" as the guide to faith and practice.

I wonder, though, what Martin Luther would have done if he had
the resources of the online world at his disposal. My personal
feeling is, yes, he would have posted his 95 theses on the Net
and probably would have organized his church there. In much
the same way, I believe John Wesley, who helped start the
Methodist Church 200 years after Luther, would be organizing
study groups online.

Back to the Reformation . . . Less than 20 years after Luther's
split with Rome, Henry VIII of England launched a reformation of
his own. When Pope Clement VII would not grant Henry an
annulment from his marriage to his first wife, Catherine of
Aragón, the king withdrew the English Catholic Church from
Rome. This English church eventually became the Anglican
Church, whose American branch is called the Episcopal Church.

In the nearly 500 years since the dawn of the Reformation, well over 500 churches, sects, and schisms have sprung up. The spiritual heirs of Luther both agree and disagree with his theology, although almost all have divorced themselves from the practices of Rome that Martin Luther most objected to: salvation by merit and the sale of "indulgences."

The differences between the Lutherans, Methodists, Baptists, and Presbyterians may seem to be nuances, but to the churches involved they are major and important. Baptists dissented from Luther over the question of infant baptism, holding that only those who can understand the ceremony should be baptized. The Presbyterians, under leaders such as Jean Chauvin (a.k.a. John Calvin) in Geneva and John Knox in Scotland, refined the concept of salvation to include *predestination*, the idea that God preordains who shall be saved. Methodists and others, from John Wesley forward, dissented from the Calvinist model, suggesting that "whosoever will" may be redeemed.

From these groups, like tributaries from a river, many branches have spun off from the main Protestant movements. The Methodists spawned the Wesleyans, the Presbyterians splintered into many directions, and there are about as many different kinds of Baptists as there are Baptists. The latter is an exaggeration, of course, but Baptists have followed an independent course, particularly in the past 150 years, with the Civil War coming between northern and southern Baptist congregations.

During the intervening years from Luther's day to ours, dozens of independent churches and movements have augmented Protestantism, including the Christian and Missionary Alliance and the Church of the Nazarene. Starting with the Azusa Street revival in Los Angeles in 1906, a separate faction called the Pentecostal movement was born. Coming from this has been the Assemblies of God, and other churches have come from this movement, covering the globe with their messages. The Assemblies of God message, in a nutshell, is the Pentecostal message that grew out of the Azusa Street revival — that the gifts of the Holy Spirit are still active today in the church.

Other churches have often been grouped under the Protestant banner, even if they don't exactly follow or even acknowledge the Reformation tradition. Therefore, I will include a look at some of these groups here along the way, including the Seventh-Day Adventist Church.

While you wander around the general Protestant universe, please know that far more lurks out there than I could possibly contain in a book of this nature — at least without equaling the size of a major metropolitan area phone book. Therefore, the sites included here are intended as a *representative guide* to the features within this vast area of the Web. I encourage you to utilize some of the links found at the sites listed here and to investigate other search engines such as Yahoo, InfoSeek, and Lycos. That said, let's begin our survey of this arena with a look at the major denominations.

Major Protestant Denominations Online

Let's begin our tour with the Lutherans, because, after all, the Reformation began with Martin Luther. In the United States, that means the Evangelical Lutheran Church in America and the Lutheran Church-Missouri Synod.

Lutherans

The Evangelical Lutheran Church was formed in 1988 after a convention that united three of the North American Lutheran Church bodies: the American Lutheran Church, the Association of Evangelical Lutheran Churches, and the Lutheran Church in America. The Evangelical Lutheran Church's home page (`http://www.elca.org`) is illustrated in Figure 17-1 and offers a full series of links to documents of church history, beliefs, and individual church home pages. I was impressed by a couple of elements on the ELCA site, among many. The site contain a link to not only other Lutheran organizations but to other Lutheran denominations and churches — now *that's* a show of charity. Also, the church home page (`http://www.elca.org/hompage.html`) includes a link to an excellent guide for creating church home pages. This is "constituent service" of the highest order.

In December 1995, the ELCA Web people designated the Good Shepherd Evangelical Lutheran Church in Madison, Wisconsin, (`http://www.execpc.com/~goodshep/`), as their "distinctive site of the month." With a variety of links to areas within the congregation's Web site and out on the Web in general, shown in Figure 17-2, you can easily see why.

The Lutheran Church-Missouri Synod is a more conservative Lutheran denomination, and you can find its home page at `http://www.cuis.edu/www/lcms/lcms.html`, a location maintained at Concordia University in River Forest, Illinois. This page, illustrated in Figure 17-3, offers both links to the Concordia University system, the *Lutheran Hour* radio and television ministry, and Missouri Synod member church home pages.

One nice example of these is the home page for Faith Lutheran Church in Hastings, Nebraska (`http://www.tcgcs.com/~faithlth/welcome.html`). As shown in Figure 17-4, not only does this page present a nice representation of the church building (I'm partial to line drawings), but it also has a clear statement of who the congregation represents and links to subsections of the Web site.

Figure 17-1: The Evangelical Lutheran Church in America home page.

Figure 17-2: The Good Shepherd Lutheran Church home page.

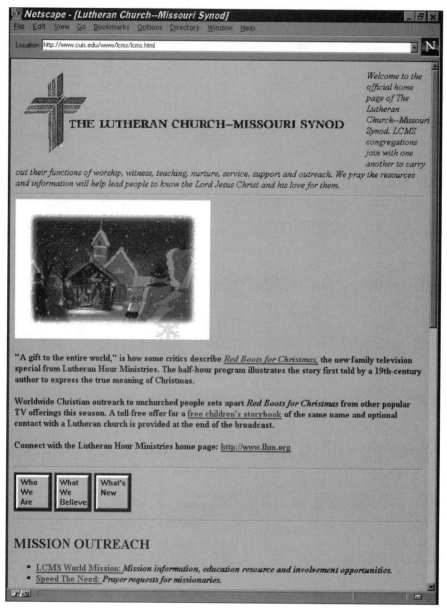

Figure 17-3: The Lutheran Church-Missouri Synod home page, maintained at Concordia University, has numerous links to LCMS sites, ministries, organizations, and church home pages.

Figure 17-4: The Faith Lutheran Church, in Hastings, Nebraska, home page.

The Lutheran tradition has spawned a great number of institutions and organizations: many of these have now gone online. Starting with the denominational sites I've listed, you'll find plenty of links to explore.

Anglicans and Episcopalians

From the Lutherans, our attention shifts to the Anglican communion, and its American cousin, the Episcopal Church. From the time of Henry VIII, the church has grown to embrace not only Britain and its Commonwealth but has also taken hold in the United States, where in 1994, some 2,471,880 claimed membership in the denomination, worshipping in over 7,300 churches.

As of this writing, the Episcopal Church in the United States did not yet have an official home page, but two unofficial sites are worth visiting. One is the *unofficial* home page maintained by Michael I. Bushnell, who is a member of the Brotherhood of St. Gregory, an Episcopal order. The home page, at `http://www.ai.mit.edu/people/mib/anglican/` and illustrated in Figure 17-5, offers several links to various Anglican sites as well as to various Episcopal-related home pages.

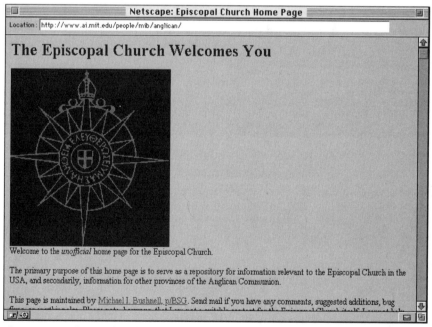

Figure 17-5: The unofficial Episcopal Church in the USA home page, as maintained by Michael I. Bushnell.

The other, very important site is Anglicans Online!, possibly the most astonishing site I've visited in this journey. It is edited and maintained by Tod Maffin, a certifiable technology "nerd" and avid Anglican from Canada. His site (`http://infomatch.com/~haibeck/anglican.html`) offers the finest look at a denomination that I've seen. This page contains plenty of very elegant links to the worldwide Anglican communion, foundational documents, scripture programs, and tons of sites. CBS Radio called it a "kind of a weekly newsmagazine"; I'll call it a weekly newsmagazine, very well edited and laid out. The illustration in Figure 17-6 doesn't begin to do the site justice (for one, we're publishing it in black and white). This is one site you *must* see for yourself.

From both the unofficial Episcopal Church home page and Anglicans Online!, you can jump to a variety of Episcopal and Anglican dioceses and parishes. These links will aid anyone interested in Anglicanism to understand more about this important denomination.

Baptists

"I have some relatives who aren't Baptists," one old preacher once admitted, "and I feel sorry for them." There are easily 30 million Baptists of all stripes in the United States, with the majority of these being members of the Southern Baptist Convention, which has close to 16 million congregants. The Southern Baptists claim Billy Graham as their own, and popular TV preachers Charles Stanley and Richard Lee. Baptist churches generally feature aggressive missionary and evangelistic efforts.

The Southern Baptist Convention does not yet have its own official Web site. Rather, SBCNet, a feature of CompuServe, contains news from Baptist Press, the denomination's news service, and a worldwide electronic prayer network called CompassionNet. If you subscribe to CompuServe (discussed in Chapter 5), you can enter the service by typing **Go SBCNet**; otherwise, contact CompuServe for signup details.

The Baptist Press news service is also available on the Internet, via the GOSHEN Web site (`http://www.goshen.net/BaptistPress`), which is part of a vast collection of Christian resources. The BP news dispatches a mix of official church pronouncements with features about everyday Baptist life. I particularly remember many intimate, informative stories from Baptist missionaries in Kobe, Japan after the devastating 1995 earthquake there. Baptist Press makes the lives of Baptists accessible to all of us, which makes it a valuable, interesting service.

At press time, the prestigious Yahoo directory listed nearly 80 home pages for individual Baptist churches, Southern Baptist, and the like. More will doubtless come online in the months to come because Baptists have never been reticent about sharing their faith in a variety of forums. Figure 17-7 shows the home page of Community Baptist Fellowship, which is a growing church in Pueblo, Colorado.

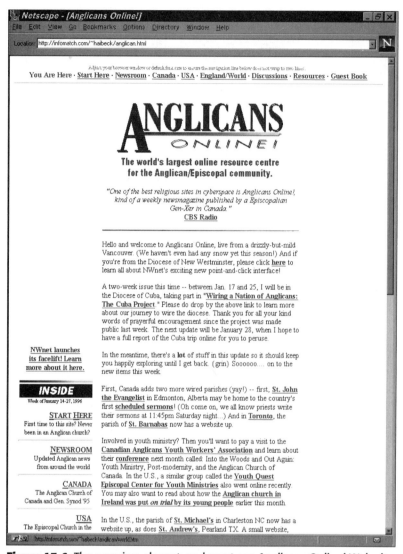

Figure 17-6: The amazing, elegant, and must-see Anglicans Online! Web site.

Also worth noting in discussing Baptist churches are sites for BaptistNet, which is sponsored by Smith & Helwys Publishing (`http://www.helwys.com/bnet1.htm`), a publisher of religious books and other materials. Baptist-Net is part of that firm's "Connected Christianity" site, which offers a wide number of links to various interdenominational resources. The Baptist Bible Fellowship International, whose home page is illustrated in Figure 17-8, offers information about the organization and ways for BBFI churches to build their own home pages.

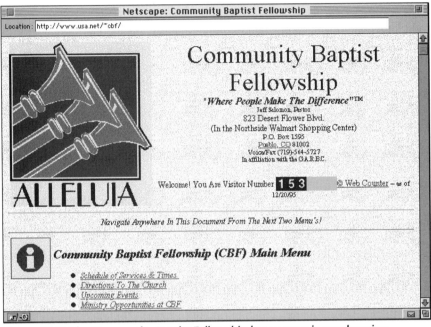

Figure 17-7: The Community Baptist Fellowship home page is a welcoming, informative site.

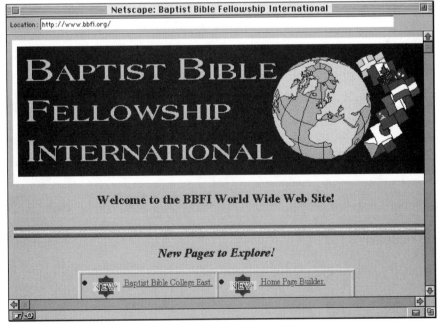

Figure 17-8: The Baptist Bible Fellowship International home page.

Presbyterians

Whoever says that the Presbyterians, those spiritual descendants of John Calvin and John Knox, lack a sense of humor had best stay away from the home page of the Presbyterian Church USA, `http://www.pcusa.org/pcusa.html`. Right on that home page is a link to Eculaugh, a service that offers "good, clean religious humor." The home page, illustrated in Figure 17-9, offers much in the way of substance, however, including In the One Spirit, a denomination-wide Bible study of the apostle Paul's First Letter to the Christians in Corinth. This page offers a file containing resources made available to PCUSA churches along with suggestions for their use. I found this a useful innovation that other denominations can easily adopt and use.

Among Presbyterian church home pages, the site for Calvary Presbyterian Church is a good representative site. It offers links to other PCUSA sites and pages describing the church, its leadership, and ministries. This site, illustrated in Figure 17-10, does so in a concise, clear, and colorful layout.

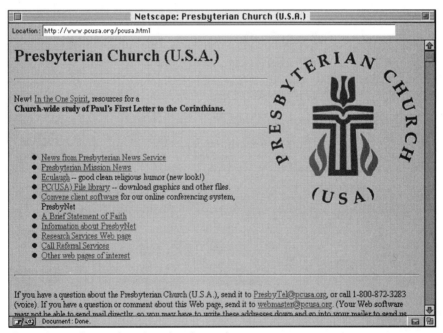

Figure 17-9: The Presbyterian Church USA home page.

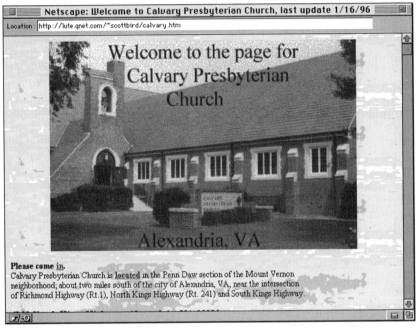

Figure 17-10: The Calvary Presbyterian Church in Alexandria, Va.

United Methodists

The United Methodist Church is the spiritual home to roughly 9 million Americans, including Hillary Rodham Clinton, who credits her Methodist upbringing for her interest in social causes. At http://www.umc.org/, you will find the official home page of the church (Figure 17-11), which the church's communications department maintains.

The site is not just a quarter for press releases, however, but also for information about the church's beliefs; a devotional; and links to college and university sites, relief organizations, and local churches. Among the local churches, Mulberry Street United Methodist Church in Mt. Vernon, Ohio, is a bit more than typical: the congregation takes its outreach to the Web, including a clear statement of the Gospel message and an invitation to respond. The site is well-designed, promotional without being pushy, and one worth a look. The URL is http://ecrknox.com/rbuch/homepag2.htm, and the page is illustrated in Figure 17-12.

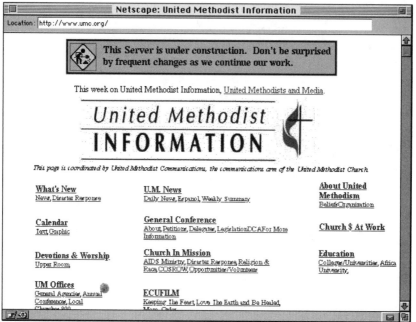

Figure 17-11: The United Methodist Church official home page.

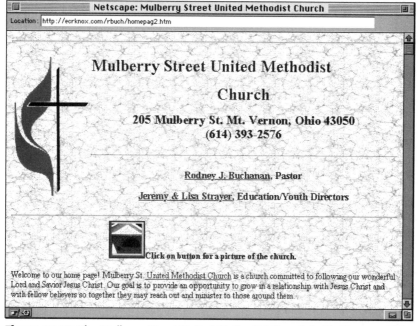

Figure 17-12: The Mulberry Street United Methodist Church in Mt. Vernon, Ohio, home page.

The Quakers

Today, there aren't much more than 100,000 members of churches which claim a Quaker heritage in the United States. Of these, the largest is known as the Religious Society of Friends, with the "Quaker" name derived from the Friends' practice of speaking in a meeting only when stirred by the Holy Spirit.

Quakerism was founded in the seventeenth century by George Fox, a pious Englishman who was not satisfied with the Anglican and Catholic churches of his day. Fox found a spiritual message which resonated throughout England and led to the establishment of the Quaker movement. The church maintained that Jesus, who had been present in the flesh, had risen from the dead and now come in the Spirit, acting in the hearts of followers, purifying and empowering them.

The fledgling movement was persecuted both by Oliver Cromwell and the restoration government of Charles II. Quakers, under the leadership of William Penn, became established in the United States. Though relatively small in numbers, the Quakers exerted influence in American life, largely through their non-violence and conscientious objection to military service. At least two Americans of Quaker descent — Herbert Hoover and Richard M. Nixon — were elected President.

Spiritually, Quaker ideas about the "priesthood of the believer," where so-called lay members have equal status and can perform church functions, as well as their views of the need for a personal experience of God, have touched other denominations. The late Elton Trueblood, a Quaker theologian, has been revered and read throughout American Christian communities as a source of inspiration and thinking.

Today, the Religious Society of Friends stresses its work for social justice, civil rights, and non-violence as much as its spiritual side. While honoring Christian tradition, the Friends state they are a non-creedal church, which leaves members free to form their own beliefs.

A home page for the Religious Society of Friends is found at `http://www.quaker.org/`. As shown in Figure 17-13, the church is planning a North American conference this year, about which details can be found at `http://www.quaker.org/fgc/gathering96/`.

United Church of Canada

Nearly two million Canadians claim membership in the United Church of Canada, which brought together Presbyterian, Methodist, Evangelical, and Congregational Churches based in Canada, with the aim of forming a distinctly Canadian church. The denomination is non-creedal, and has within it a wide range of viewpoints. No official home page for the denomination yet exists, but the home page of First United Church — Figure 17-14 — is a good starting place, and features links to other UCC sites.

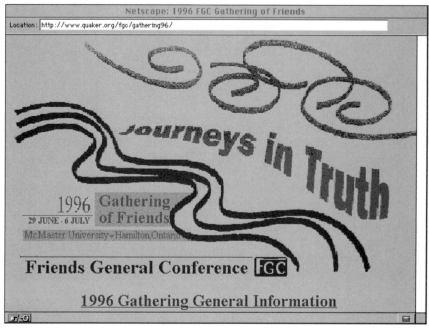

Figure 17-13: Friends Gathering 96 Home Page.

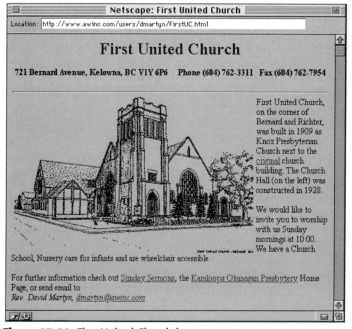

Figure 17-14: First United Church home page.

Missionary Updates

[Jesus] said to them, "Go into all the world and preach the good news to all creation."

— Mark 16:15, New International Version

The missionary imperative of Christians began with this command from Jesus and continues to this age. Millions around the world are learning about the Christian faith because people have forsaken lives of comfort and convenience to help fulfill this declaration. In this latter part of the twentieth century, even America is becoming a missionary target: missionaries from Korea, China, and Africa are reaching their brothers and sisters emigrating to the United States.

Overseas, missionary efforts are transmogrifying into new forms and venues. In many nations where religious efforts are not allowed, encouraged, or welcome, "tentmaker" missionaries — teachers, doctors, engineers, and businessmen — are often working at secular jobs by day and sharing their faith when off work. Additionally, the mission field is becoming a place where second-career and retired couples are finding opportunities for service.

Now, the Internet is becoming perhaps the greatest wave of missionary endeavor. Just as people encountered Paul and the apostles in the marketplaces and gathering spots of old, the Net is becoming today's Mars Hill. The casual Net surfer can find Christian messages with a few clicks, and the presence of Christian movements online aids in getting the word out.

These two streams converge when Internet sites support and promote missionary endeavors. Many denominations and churches offer pages of individual missionary efforts, and more are coming online. The Woman's Missionary Union, a Baptist organization, maintains an active, extensive Web site, `http://www.wmu.com/wmu/`, which features links to its catalog of publications and to opportunities for involvement. Figure 17-15 illustrates the page.

Another organization supporting missionary endeavors is Servants Missionary Service, which connects those in the field with supporters at home by maintaining mailing lists and preparing regular letters for mailing. From the SMS home page, illustrated in Figure 17-16 (`http://www.scsn.net/~sms/`), you can find information on the SMS service.

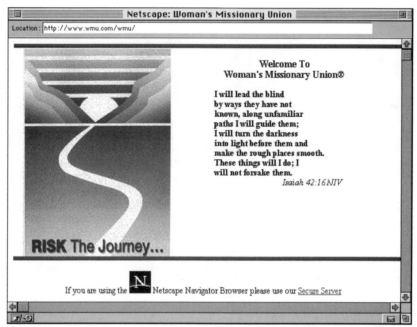

Figure 17-15: The Woman's Missionary Union home page.

Figure 17-16: The Servants Missionary Service home page.

Web users can also find out about the activities of a given missionary with the click of a few keys. Typical of such displays is that of Jerry & Barb Manderfield (Figure 17-17), who are missionaries to Cali, Colombia (`http://users.aol.com/cybershoe/homepage.htm`). This multilayered Web site offers newsletters from the Manderfields reporting on the results of their ministry in Colombia.

Figure 17-17: The home page for Jerry & Barb Manderfield, missionaries in Colombia.

One of the largest evangelical missionary organizations is Wycliffe Bible Translators (`http://www.wycliffe.org/WBT-USA/home.htm`), which has labored for decades to translate scriptures into the most obscure languages, thereby making the Gospel available to remote peoples. Figure 17-18 shows the home page for their U.S. branch, which contains information about this important — and sometimes persecuted — work.

Figure 17-18: The Wycliffe Bible Translators-USA home page.

One additional missionary resource worth noting here is Fingertip-Missions on the Internet, which is a project of the Student Mission Advance in Hamilton, Ontario, Canada. Figure 17-19 illustrates its home page (`http://www.netaccess.on.ca/ fingertip`). Though the site is obviously aimed at Canadian resources, it is an interesting way of presenting missionary information that people in other countries can easily duplicate.

These selections are but a sample of the missionary resources available online. Be sure to check denominational home pages for additional links.

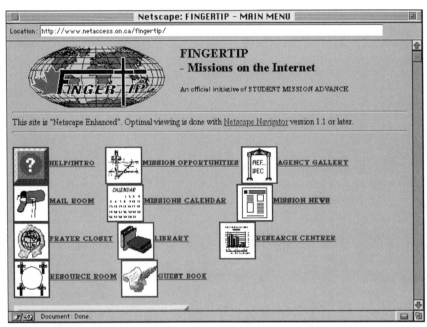

Figure 17-19: Fingertip-Missions on the Internet home page.

Theological and Biblical Studies

"...They received the word with all readiness of mind and searched the scriptures daily, whether those things were so."

— Acts 17:11, King James (Authorized) Version

From the earliest days of the Christian Church, followers of this religion have by and large been diligent Bible students. Studying the Bible led Martin Luther away from the practices of the Roman Church, and scripture study brought leaders such as Tyndale, Wycliffe, and Calvin to the fore. In our age, evangelist Billy Graham credits Bible study as a key to his effectiveness in ministry: anyone who's heard Graham preach knows that "The Bible says . . ." is a frequently used phrase.

The believer with access to the Internet can gain access to a wide range of theological resources, from seminaries and colleges to individualized Bible studies. I personally believe that this will be one of the great assets of Internet-related sites for Christians: the ability to access vast stores of knowledge in an instant, from the comfort of your home or office.

In this section, I'll cover some of the highlights of this burgeoning field and offer some resources for you to consider. As with other sections in this chapter, please know that more theological and Bible study resources will most likely crop up on the Net as time goes by.

Seminaries

An increasing number of theological seminaries are turning to the Internet as a venue for students, faculty, and prospective students. Fuller Theological Seminary, one of the nation's premiere evangelical post-graduate schools, maintains its site at `http://www.fuller.edu/` and offers information on both its graduate school of theology as well as continuing and extended education. Figure 17-20 illustrates the site's home page, which is representative of the sites many schools are creating.

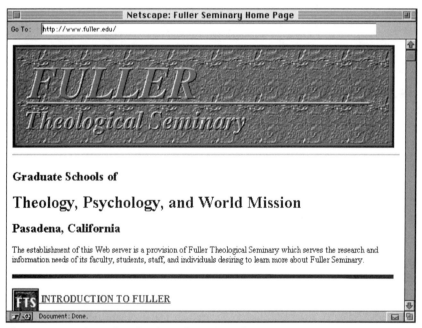

Figure 17-20: The Fuller Theological Seminary home page.

You'll find a more involved site at the home page for Dallas Theological Seminary. This school has spawned many evangelical leaders, including Dr. Charles R. Swindoll, its current president, author, and radio speaker whose books are perennial bestsellers in the Christian book market and beyond. The home page, `http://www.bible.org/dts/dts.htm` (illustrated in Figure 17-21), offers links to the main departments of the school in addition to *Bibliotheca Sacra*, the theological journal published by the school, from which you can download many articles.

Figure 17-21: The Dallas Theological Seminary home page.

Internauts may also want to discover a project created by Dale Lature, a student at United Theological Seminary in Cincinnati: the Internet Theological Seminary is an online venture that promises several links to useful sites. The URL is `http://www.iac.net/~dlature/itseminary/its.html`. This provides a good start for making online theology available for the student.

Bible study

The good news and bad news of Bible Study online is that many good resources are available online. Unfortunately, most search engines will combine these with sites that may be less reliable as far as evangelical and mainline Christians are concerned.

Many will locate Bible study resources on their denominational home pages, as we saw with the Presbyterian Church USA home page described earlier in this chapter. By connecting with a denominational source, you can be reasonably assured of the veracity of the material provided. Similarly, established schools (Concordia University in the Lutheran Church, Dallas Theological Seminary, and others) often have extension courses that may be more advanced than a regular Bible study but less involved than a formal college course.

Among the general Bible study resources out there, I can recommend the Online Bible Institute as a reliable source (`http://www./brigadoon.com/psrnet/sbl/obihome.htm`), with an illustration of the home page in Figure 17-22. Among the first of its course offerings is "How to Hear God's Voice In Scripture," a 10-lesson package that introduces students to the basic teachings of the Bible.

Figure 17-22: The Online Bible Institute offers electronic courses.

Another good starting point is the BibleNet Study Guides page, found at `http://www.isstb.com/biblenet/study.html` and illustrated in Figure 17-23. This site is impressive for its offering of a variety of study resources. It's a site worth watching.

One other Bible study site will commend itself to many readers: *Our Daily Bread*, a popular evangelical study guide, is available online through the Gospel Communications Network (`http://www.gospelcom.net/rbc/odb/odb.html`). You can read today's devotional, with a hypertext link to the scripture passage being discussed, and read those entries for the month. The site also offers an archive of earlier pages. By making a bookmark for this excellent site, you can start (or end) your day with a devotional thought.

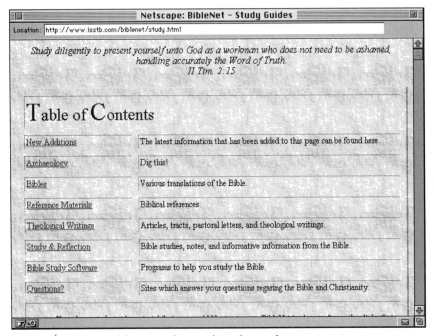

Figure 17-23: The BibleNet study page has plenty of resources.

Evangelical Web Sites

As you can clearly see from the references in this chapter, the evangelical movement in Protestant Christianity has been among the most aggressive users of the Internet as both an outreach tool and one for edification. You can also see this from the wide variety of evangelical Web sites that are out there and waiting for your inspection.

Perhaps the premiere umbrella site for evangelicals is the Gospel Communications Network (http://www.gospelcom.net/), whose home page is illustrated in Figure 17-24. This Web site is organized under the aegis of Gospel Films, Inc., a leading producer of evangelical movies.

The GospelCom site offers links to home pages of several major Christian ministries, including the following:

- ◆ InterVarsity Christian Fellowship
- ◆ International Bible Society
- ◆ The Navigators
- ◆ Radio Bible Class
- ◆ Fellowship of Christian Athletes

The Billy Graham Center archives at Wheaton College

Located in the suburbs of Chicago, Wheaton College (not to be confused with a similarly named institution in Massachusetts) is an evangelical college that boasts numerous Christian leaders as alumni and faculty. Perhaps the most well-known is Billy Graham, who was a student there before his evangelistic career. The Billy Graham Center's archives are a repository of historical documents and materials on the preaching of the Christian Gospel around the world.

What is it like to hold a crusade? To be the only Christian missionary in a given location? To be the son or daughter of a missionary? Or to blend your evangelism with social activism?

Using the Internet resource *gopher*, this site contains the transcripts of oral history interviews with Consuella Batchelor York, a pastor and prison chaplain; Eleanor Ruth Elliott, a missionary to China and the Philippines; and evangelist and social activist John Perkins of Mississippi. You can reach the Billy Graham Center archives from the Wheaton College home page (http://www.wheaton.edu), illustrated in the figure that follows, or by using gopher (gopher://gopher.wheaton.edu:70/11/College/Departments/BGC/BGCarch). Either way, you can access the unfiltered recollections of those who were (and in some cases still are) on the front lines of Christian evangelism.

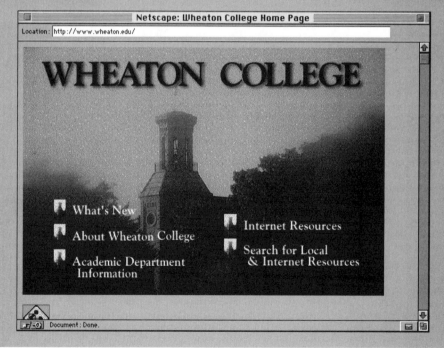

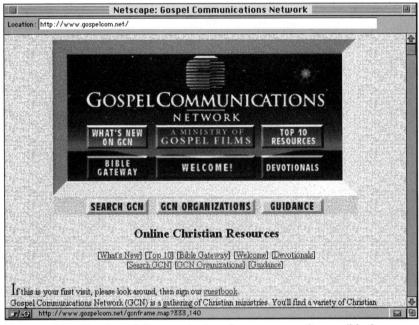

Figure 17-24: The Gospel Communications home page: quite possibly the premiere evangelical Christian Internet site.

I've mentioned *Our Daily Bread,* the RBC daily devotional. The GospelCom site also includes links to the Bible Gateway, an online lookup of verses in several translations. The Navigators, a tremendous organization devoted to the discipling of Christian believers, also has a homepage linked to this site: here you'll find its excellent magazine, *Discipleship Journal.*

In addition, the GospelCom page features a site of particular interest to Christian computer users: *Internet for Christians* is both a book and a Web site. Each was created by Quentin J. Schultze, Ph.D., a communications professor at Calvin College in Grand Rapids, Michigan. Dr. Schultze's book and site are decidedly evangelical in focus, although each lists general Christian sites as well. The site is a good place to start when Web-wandering is the order of the day.

For some people, however, a visit to the Gospel Communications Web site won't be a trolling stop for more links. Rather, they're facing a crisis and need some guidance. The Gospel Communications people have several interactive pages that offer that guidance (Figure 17-25) along with hyperlinks to the scripture verses that support these pages. It's a terrific resource that many will find of interest and benefit.

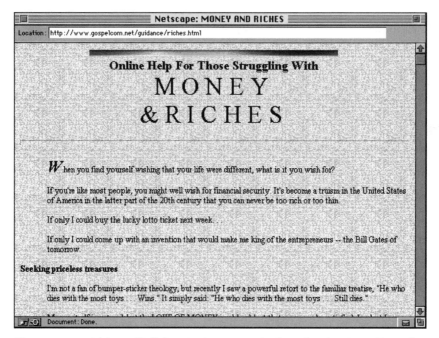

Figure 17-25: Advice, with links to scripture, can be found at the GospelCom site.

You also won't go too far wrong if you point your browser to GOSHEN — not the Biblical land, but rather the Global Online Service Helping Evangelize Nations (`http://www.goshen.net`), which is a truly amazing collection of links to a wide variety of Catholic, mainline Protestant, evangelical, and Pentecostal sites. You'll find links to a whole host of organizations, ministries, and publications, all starting from the home page illustrated in Figure 17-26.

Similarly situated, but also with a presence on CompuServe, is the Christian Interactive Network (`http://www.gocin.com`), whose home page, shown in Figure 17-27, also contains a large number of links, both here and overseas. The site also offers Web storage services to Christian ministries and a salvation message: "God has a Free Gift for You."

As you wander these Web sites and link to the vast array of ministries that will catch your eye, may I direct your attention to two interesting sites? First, Jews for Jesus have been at once controversial and commended: controversial among some Jews, many of whom have hurled all sorts of invectives and accusations against them, and commended by other Jews, who investigate their claims and indeed find Yeshua, the Jewish messiah whose name is also rendered as Jesus. Check out the Jews for Jesus home page: `http://www.jews-for-jesus.org/index.html`, shown in Figure 17-28.

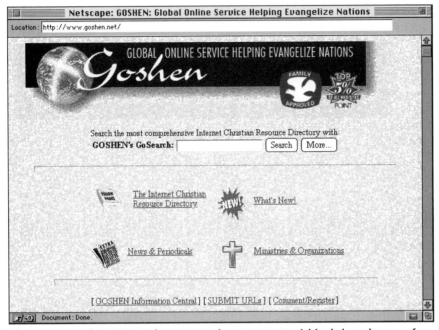

Figure 17-26: The GOSHEN home page, host to an astonishingly broad range of Christian links.

Figure 17-27: The Christian Interactive Network.

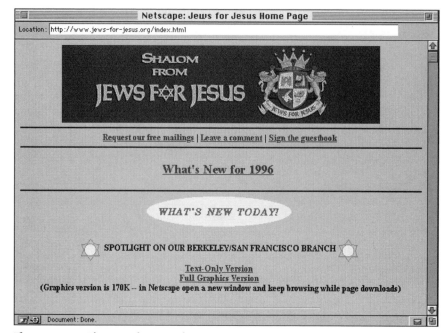

Figure 17-28: The Jews for Jesus home page.

Another important, aggressive, and impressive organization aimed at promoting Yeshua among Jewish believers is the Messianic Jewish Ministries International, whose Web page, `http://www.messiah.net/` offers links to a page describing the movement and its extensive catalog of Messianic Jewish resources.

A Pentecostal Potpourri

Among the fastest growing denominations in the world today are the various Pentecostal churches, led by the Assemblies of God (A/G), which is one of the most rapidly growing churches in the world. Indeed, of the ten largest individual church congregations in the world today, seven are A/G churches, including the huge Yoido Full Gospel Church, in Seoul, Korea, pastored by the charismatic David Yonggi Cho. Among the distinctive features of A/G worship are a full acceptance of the gifts of the spirit, including speaking in tongues and healing.

The A/G's home page, `http://www.ag.org/`, is a dynamic, well-organized and expanding Web site, aimed at introducing people to the denomination and providing other links. It's shown in Figure 17-29.

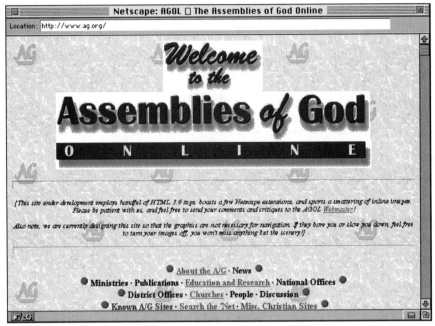

Figure 17-29: The Assemblies of God home page.

Among sites with a less direct connection to the Assemblies of God is CBN — The Christian Broadcasting Network (http://www.the700club.org/), which offers details of this popular television program and the ministry behind it. Although not officially part of the A/G, CBN founder Rev. Pat Robertson and his staff certainly appear to be in alignment with the A/G's teachings on spiritual gifts.

You can find local A/G churches just about anywhere; no longer are they largely the province of America's "Bible Belt." This home page from Evangel Assembly of God, in the Chicago suburb of Schaumburg, Illinois (http://www.mcs.com/~bradc/evangel.html), offers a good sense of a local A/G church page, as seen in Figure 17-30.

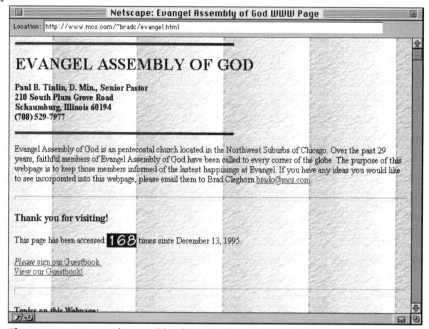

Figure 17-30: Evangel Assembly of God, Schaumburg, Illinois.

Music and Youth Resources

Christian music and ministries aimed at young people could each fill a book of their own — even if the discussion is limited to Internet resources. Because of the wide range of interests in each of these fields, I'll present only a couple of links, but these will lead the pilgrim in many profitable ways.

Neil C. Gilliand, a student at Auburn University, hosts the C4 Ministries home page, http://www.auburn.edu/~gillinc, shown in Figure 17-31. You'll find links to several contemporary Christian music sites and magazines. Yes, the young lady in the lower right of the screen *is* Amy Grant. Arguably the most successful contemporary Christian musician of all time, Grant has crossed over from Christian to pop and back, and, yes, this page contains links to Amy Grant sites.

As to youth resources, readers will again want to look at various denominational sites along with more general ones. You'll find Youth For Christ at Gospel Communications (see the discussion earlier in this chapter) and Youth Dynamics (http://www.whidbey.net/~samyd/), another organization that serves the needs of unchurched youth in rural areas.

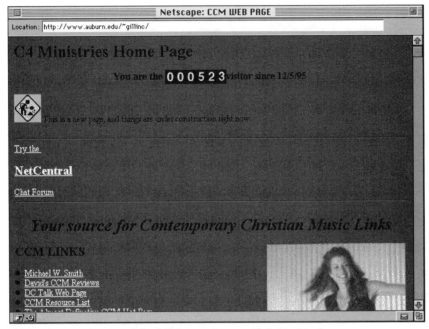

Figure 17-31: The C4 Ministries Contemporary Christian Music page.

The Salvation Army: marching along the InfoBahn

Founded in 1865, The Salvation Army (http://www.SalvationArmy.org) is an evangelical part of the Christian church that adds a clear gospel message to its social services. The organization formally opened in the United States in 1880 and has become a cherished part of the American scene: raising roughly $750 million in 1994, it is the nation's top charity.

At the heart of the Army's work is soul-saving, not fund-raising. As noted on its international home page (shown in the first figure), the Army is an evangelical organization. Wander through its Web site, and you'll see Salvation Army activity all over the world, such as in Johnsonville, a suburb of Wellington, New Zealand (http://lumeria.actrix.gen.nz/users/awestrup/), shown in the second figure.

The Army's doctrines and teachings are accessible through the home page, as are a lively discussion forum and search engines for other Salvation Army-related sites. During the next year, you can expect to see much more from this dynamic movement as territories around the world come online to spread the word in this new open air of cyberspace. Just recently, the Salvation Army unit in Australia's Eastern Territory opened its Web site. Drop by sometime at http://www.ozemail.com.au/~salvoest.

(continued)

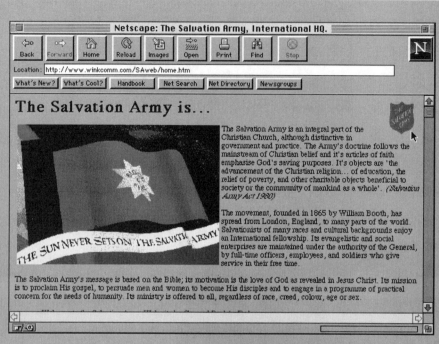

The Salvation Army is...

The Salvation Army is an integral part of the Christian Church, although distinctive in government and practice. The Army's doctrine follows the mainstream of Christian belief and it's articles of faith emphasise God's saving purposes. It's objects are 'the advancement of the Christian religion... of education, the relief of poverty, and other charitable objects beneficial to society or the community of mankind as a whole'. *(Salvation Army Act 1980)*

The movement, founded in 1865 by William Booth, has spread from London, England, to many parts of the world. Salvationists of many races and cultural backgrounds enjoy an International fellowship. Its evangelistic and social enterprises are maintained under the authority of the General, by full-time officers, employees, and soldiers who give service in their free time.

The Salvation Army's message is based on the Bible; its motivation is the love of God as revealed in Jesus Christ. Its mission is to proclaim His gospel, to persuade men and women to become His disciples and to engage in a programme of practical concern for the needs of humanity. Its ministry is offered to all, regardless of race, creed, colour, age or sex.

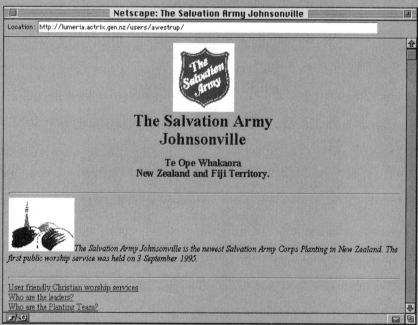

The Salvation Army
Johnsonville

Te Ope Whakaora
New Zealand and Fiji Territory.

The Salvation Army Johnsonville is the newest Salvation Army Corps Planting in New Zealand. The first public worship service was held on 3 September 1995.

User friendly Christian worship services
Who are the leaders?
Who are the Planting Team?

Something More: Additional Christian Web Sites

It's noted elsewhere in this book — in the Foreword and as I close in Chapter 19 — that the Internet is a constantly evolving entity, and thus any book attempting to list religious resources is a "work in progress." How true: In the closing days before this volume went to press, your author became aware of several worthwhile sites that should be included, even at the last minute.

A tip of the quill, however, must go to Gleason Sackman, who shares his discoveries of Christian-related Internet sites with a large number of people, including Internet curmudgeon Daniel P. Dern, who kindly passed these along to me!

ChristianWeb: Another location aimed at disseminating information across a wide spectrum of Christian traditions is ChristianWeb, which offers its services as a Web space provider to organizations and congregations, as well as to Christian businesses. Located at http://www.christianweb.com/ and illustrated in Figure 17-32, ChristianWeb's resources are impressive: the list of church home pages covers the United States and a tremendous number of links — you're very likely to find something in your neighborhood!

Seventh-Day Adventist General Conference: Back in Chapter 10, we discussed the *Adventist Information Ministry* home page, which offers a lot of background information on this American-founded church. Now, the General Conference of Seventh-Day Adventists, the denomination's governing body, has established a Web site of its own: http://www.cuc.edu/sdaorg/gc, shown in Figure 17-33. The General Conference page is very well organized, very informative and offers Bible studies from the famed "Voice of Prophecy" broadcast. Included is a link to the denomination's news service, which features weekly news releases of SDA activities. It's a site worth a visit; and, by the way, it's maintained at Columbia Union College, an Adventist higher education facility in suburban Washington, D.C.

FaithNet: Here's a novel idea from the northwestern United States which others might want to emulate: FaithNet, currently under development as this book goes to press, hopes to be a place where various faith communities can come together and present their materials. This could be a useful venture for small congregations and other groups to get together and gain more exposure than they might otherwise gain. The service hopes to attract sponsors so it can offer content for free; a subscription method is also being considered. The address is http://casconn.com/faithnet/faithnet.htm and it's illustrated in Figure 17-34.

Figure 17-32: The Christian Web home page is a burgeoning site, containing much useful information and many good links to other sites.

Figure 17-33: The Seventh-Day Adventist General Conference home page.

Figure 17-34: FaithNet, a communications project in the making.

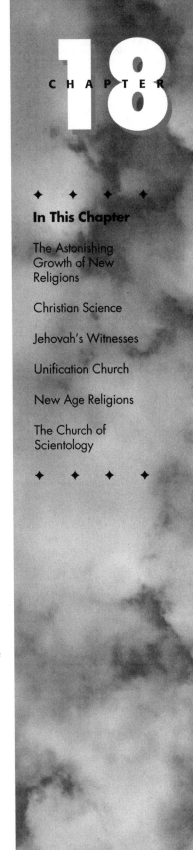

"New" Religions Online

The Astonishing Growth of New Religions

Some 20 or 30 years ago, you'd have had difficulty finding a Baha'i in many cities; today, you may be working next to one. The New Age movement was unheard of in 1965; today, the people who consider themselves devotees number in the millions. And although the Unification Church, headed by Rev. Sun Myung Moon, has encountered a great deal of hostility, this group has undoubtedly grown and prospered in the United States, maturing into a denomination in its own right.

The astonishing growth of new religions in the United States has taken some observers by surprise. In a scientific age, with electron microscopes capable of parsing the tiniest of particles, why should people put stock in Tarot cards, crystals, or the preaching of this or that individual? Why should they defect from the mainline churches that have built this country into sects with precepts that many have called into question? And many parents have asked why their children have forsaken the faith of their fathers for a new one.

More than one religious leader has suggested that the growth in new religions represents the "unpaid debts" of more established faiths. Disaffected members of a group seek a new spiritual home only when they're extremely dissatisfied or haven't been properly fed by the parent group. Others bemoan a lack of "Biblical literacy," claiming that those who easily believe the claims of new groups don't understand the faith they're leaving.

Others view the growth of new religions as part of a society's spiritual evolution. As the Christian world moved from one brand of orthodoxy to Roman Catholicism and Eastern Rite churches and then into Protestantism and its descendants, the rise of new religions represented some people's search for a compatible community of belief. This view has been expressed somewhat by scholars, such as Harvard University's Harvey Cox, who have chronicled the rise of many new religious groups and movements.

Like the street corner and Chautauqua of old, the Internet represents a new marketplace of ideas. Advocates for many belief systems are taking to Cyberspace in an effort to reach their own followers and new disciples, and those looking for a spiritual pathway are finding information there. This fact has both pleased and dismayed some, in the same way as the arrival of new religions.

The First Amendment to the U.S. Constitution provides that Congress shall not make any law "respecting the establishment of religion or prohibiting the free exercise thereof." The beauty of the United States is that anyone can set up any church or movement he or she desires and seek disciples or followers at will, and everyone can follow any religion they desire.

In turn, the Internet, which is so largely based in the United States, has become the new open air where you or I can set up our soapboxes and preach. As an advantage, perhaps, we can do this on a 24-hour, seven-day a week basis without physically having to stand on a real street corner for that length of time. Electronic mail compresses time, allowing people to make inquiries and receive answers quickly and easily: for example, to send an e-mail in the morning and have an answer when you return home from work. Mailing lists, which consist of Internet messages passed back and forth among participants, can yield a steady stream of faith-related information and fast answers to questions.

Of course, these advantages pertain to so-called mainline denominations as well as to new religions. These technologies only require a group and its members to take advantage of them.

Christian Science

Following a miraculous recovery from illness in 1866, Mary Baker Patterson Glover Eddy founded the Church of Christ, Scientist. She wrote the book *Science and Health with Key to the Scriptures,* which set forth her theory that "There is no life, truth, intelligence, nor substance in matter. All is infinite Mind and its infinite manifestation, for God is All-in-all."

Keeping things in perspective

The views expressed by the organizations and individuals listed in this chapter (and probably in other chapters as well) are bound to offend *someone*. This seems as good a place as any to say again that a listing in this book of *any* Internet or online resource *does not imply endorsement or recommendation of the views, theology, or tenets of any specific individual or group* by this writer or IDG Books Worldwide, Inc. Rather, we offer these listings merely as a guide and remind readers that *caveat lector* — "Let the reader beware" — is the watchphrase here. Examine everything you read, and test what you find against what you know and against reliable references from history, scripture, and other sources.

That said, let me also point out that while I may or may not endorse any or all of the views expressed by those listed here, I will defend their right to express those views. Recent reports from various parts of the world reveal that some governments are trying to restrict the free expression of religious belief, using tax laws, laws concerning "unauthorized practice of medicine," and other ambiguous statutes to clamp down on unpopular spiritual movements. I would be impolite to criticize those nations of which I am not a citizen, but these recent and continuing examples should serve as a warning to those who love freedom and who want their *own* beliefs respected and protected.

You may not agree with what Group X believes, and Group X may not agree with your beliefs. However, if you don't protect the rights of Group X, watch out. Martin Niemoller, an evangelical pastor who resisted Hitler and the Nazis, put it best. After reciting a list of groups for which he did not "stand up" because he was not a Jew, a communist, or a radical, he said that he looked for someone to come to his aid when the Nazis came for him. "There was no one left to stand up," he reported.

End of sermon. Thank you for your attention.

This theology, including a reliance on prayer and spiritual treatment of illness, spawned a movement that grew to an estimated peak membership of two million members. (Official figures are not released by the church as a matter of policy.) In its infancy, the movement was the talk of a nation, unusual both because of its spiritual healing emphasis and for having a woman as its leader. Eddy was at once celebrated and vilified in print. Mark Twain wrote a satirical book about the movement, but many famous people — including the Smucker family (of jam and jelly fame) and C.W. Post (who founded the breakfast food company) — embraced the faith.

Christian Science not only affected the thinking of a nation, but it may also have changed the course of religion in the United States. Many observers and historians link Eddy's movement to a succession of "new thought" movements — from Unity, which was started by two former Christian Scientists, down to today's New Age disciplines. To cite two examples: the Women's National Book Association named Mary Baker Eddy as author of one of the 75 most influential books written by a woman, and in 1995, the National Hall of Fame honored Eddy with a place in its ranks as the founder of a religion.

In addition, Christian Science has stood at the boundaries of the fight for religious freedom, winning the right for parents to select the course of treatment for their children, albeit engendering some opposition from those who say minor children should not be deprived of medical care on the basis of their parent's faith. Indeed, recent attacks on the privileges long enjoyed by Christian Science parents have spawned a religious freedom home page (`http://www.religious-freedom.org/rf`) that is nondenominational and emphasizes the commonality of religious freedom needs around the world.

Just as this book went to press, the First Church of Christ, Scientist, the "Mother Church" of the Christian Science movement, unveiled its own home page, `http://www.tfccs.com/` (Figure 18-1), which offers a good introduction to the church, its founder, and its teachings. Links from that page take the viewer to questions and answers about Christian Science, Mary Baker Eddy, and her book, *Science and Health*.

In my tour of the Christian Science pages, I was impressed by the organized layout and the easily accessible presentation of information, which are hallmarks of a good Web site. One good example of such a page is that for the Christian Science Center, a 14-acre campus in the Back Bay section of Boston that is stunning in its architecture. You can get a glimpse of the Center at `http://www.tfccs.com/GV/TMC/TMCMain.html` (see Figure 18-2). Included are tour schedules and a picture of the two oldest buildings on the campus (the original Mother Church and the Extension building), and you can download a QuickTime movie of the *Mapparium*, a beautiful, stained glass map of the world (correct as of its construction in 1935). You can view the movie with a QuickTime player, widely available for both Macintosh and Windows.

Christian Science is perhaps best known for its daily newspaper, *The Christian Science Monitor*, which Mary Baker Eddy founded in 1908. Apart from a daily religious article, the paper is decidedly secular in outlook, although its editorials are influenced by Eddy's credo for the paper: "To Injure No One, But To Bless All Mankind." At the writing of this book, only a limited version of the paper, covering the crisis in Bosnia, is online at `http://www.freerange.com/csmonitor/`, as shown in Figure 18-3. According to the church, a more robust version of the *Monitor* should be online as this book first reaches stores. At around the same time, the church will also place online *The Christian Science Sentinel*, a weekly religious publication.

These pages will obviously attract those interested in the brand of metaphysics offered by the Christian Science movement. In my opinion, however, this site has much to commend itself to those who are neither Christian Scientists nor potential converts. An elegant design, clear organization, and plenty of links to useful information give us an example of a quality site.

Figure 18-1: The Church of Christ, Scientist home page.

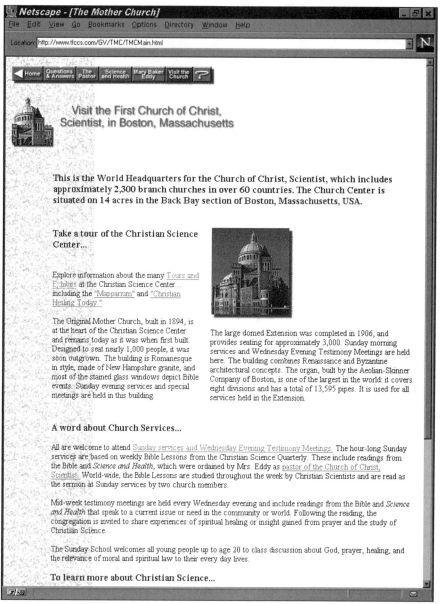

Figure 18-2: Christian Science Center page.

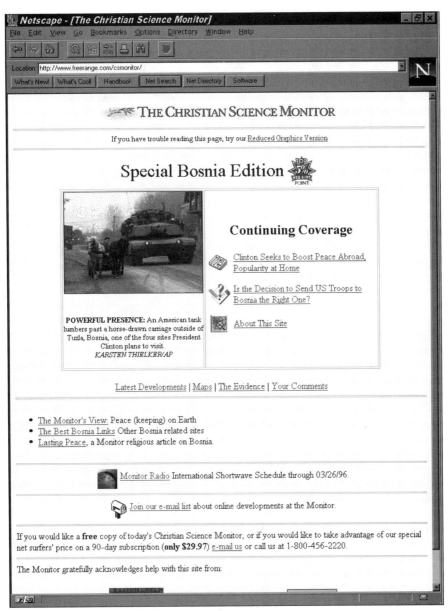

Figure 18-3: A special Bosnia online edition of *The Christian Science Monitor*.

Jehovah's Witnesses

Founded in Pittsburgh by a young clothing store owner disenchanted with his Presbyterian upbringing, the Watchtower Bible and Tract Society blanketed the United States, England, and much of the rest of the world. The organization carried the *Scripture Studies* of Charles Taze Russell with it and warned people of an apocalyptic climax to world events, circa 1914. Though the date has shifted through the years and now is somewhat nebulous according to the group's literature, two aspects of the organization remain true to its roots:

✦ The door-to-door preaching by its members

✦ A firm belief that "millions now living will never die"

After Russell's death, the movement's name was changed to Jehovah's Witnesses by Joseph Franklin "Judge" Rutherford, a one-time, circuit-riding substitute judge in Missouri who served as Russell's lawyer. The movement's leaders shifted the emphasis from setting 1914 as the date for the "end of the world" toward viewing 1914 as the date when the final countdown began.

The movement claims over two million members worldwide (half of which are found in North America), and has boasted achievements outside the theological realm. Many of these have involved civil liberties issues in the United States, including the right to go from house-to-house spreading their message, the right to exempt oneself from being required to pledge allegiance to the American flag, and the right to refuse blood transfusions. The latter two stem from the Jehovah's Witnesses' core beliefs and were won under often trying circumstances, including numerous court challenges.

In their early days, the Jehovah's Witnesses were pioneers in several media. They claim to be among the first to use a motion picture in preaching efforts and were among the first to operate a radio station with the goal of spreading their message. The volume of printed material emanating from the Watchtower (as it is now called) headquarters in New York, and elsewhere, is staggering, numbering in the tens of millions of copies each year.

Curiously, however, the Watchtower Bible and Tract Society (which today is the official name of the movement's main organization) does not see itself as a candidate for Cyberspace. In a January 1996 telephone interview, a spokesman said, "I don't believe we would be involved at all" with online efforts, despite the movement's background of firsts in other media.

Individual members of the movement do maintain information on the World Wide Web, however. For example, an Australian member who signs himself as "Tony" (http://www.magna.com.au/~tony/j_w/) offers simple information about the movement and some of its basic doctrines (Figure 18-4).

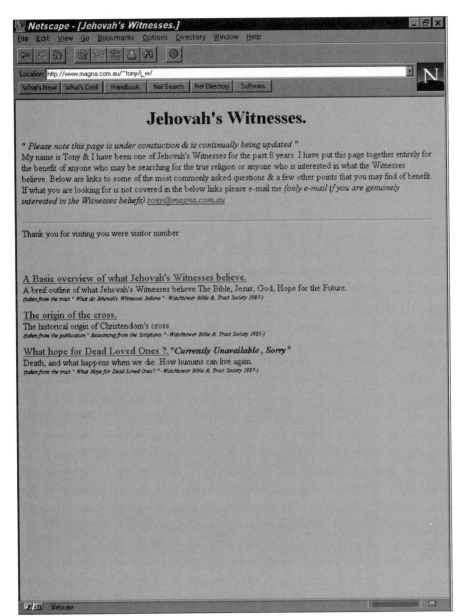

Figure 18-4: Home page from "Tony," a Jehovah's Witness.

Lynn D. Newton, an engineer in the Motorola Computer Group's system test unit, has written the *Glossary of American English Hacker Theocratese* (http://www.eecs. umich.edu/~lnewton/glossary/readme.html), which he intends "as entertainment, not weighty teaching material." It's a listing of words commonly used by Jehovah's Witnesses in the United States, and it offers some insight into the teachings and thinking of the movement.

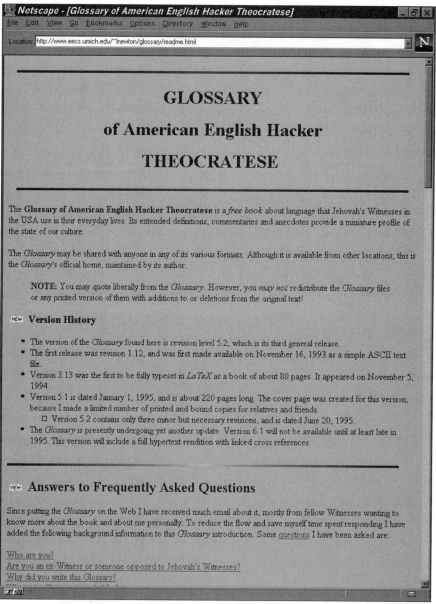

Figure 18-5: *Glossary of American English Hacker Theocratese,* by Lynn D. Newton.

A fair number of opponents to the Watchtower have Web sites expounding their beliefs and differences with Jehovah's Witnesses. Perhaps the most elaborate comes from *The Watchtower Observer,* http://www.nano.no/~telemark/DnSEng.html/, which publishes some remarkable research about the Witnesses and historical events (Figure 18-6).

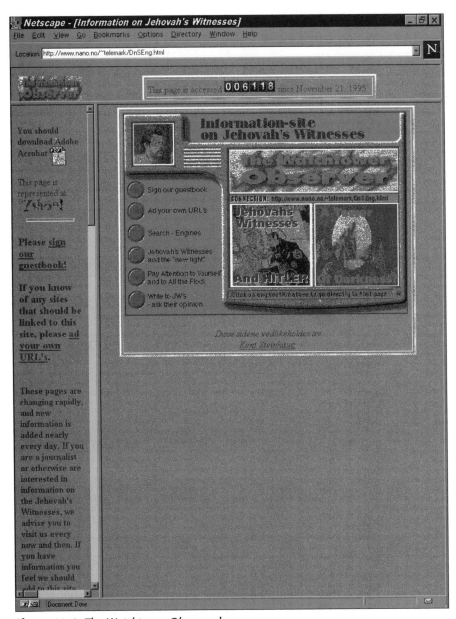

Figure 18-6: *The Watchtower Observer* home page.

Unification Church

Founded in 1954 by Rev. Sun Myung Moon, a Korean who said he had a vision from God, the Unification Church came to the United States in force in 1972, with a series of Moon's heavily advertised public speeches. His message, which posits Korea as a new focus for prophetic events and as the nation from which the next Messiah must come, was embraced by some, shunned by others, and ridiculed in the general media.

After the movement broke onto the American scene, Rev. Moon became controversial first for his staunch support of President Richard M. Nixon during the Watergate crisis and then in a controversial tax case. Accused of evading roughly $8,000 in income taxes, Moon and an aide were convicted on May 18, 1982. The Korean evangelist was sentenced to 18 months in prison, much of which he served doing menial jobs at a federal penitentiary in Danbury, Connecticut. Many religious leaders from mainline Protestant churches and other affiliations condemned the prosecution as vindictive and wrong.

Following his release from custody, Rev. Moon returned to oversee the Unification Church, which has a solid core of membership in the United States and has a seminary in upstate New York. Members of the church own a variety of businesses, including *The Washington Times*, a daily newspaper.

Since 1991, this author — who is not a Unificationist — has contributed a weekly computer column to *The Washington Times*.

The church does not currently maintain an official Web presence, but member Damian Anderson has spearheaded a pioneering effort to place Unification materials on the Web. Starting from his privately sponsored Unification Home Page (`http://www.cais.com/unification/`), Anderson has posted many documents and offers links to Unification literature in seven different languages (Figure 18-7). He is also an avid participant in Internet newsgroups and has written numerous messages explaining Unification thought, which are indexed and available through this site.

Admittedly controversial in its history and theology, the Unification Church has stood the test of 25 years in the United States. Its members have been "mainstreamed" into American society, and its achievements are worth pondering, as is Anderson's Web page.

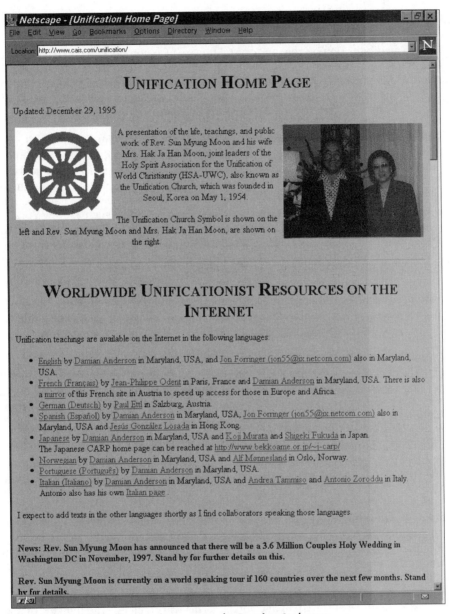

Figure 18-7: The Unification home page, by Damian Anderson.

New Age Religions

Do you meditate? Do you rely on "crystal power"? Do you believe you have an "aura" or are "psychic"? Does "channeling" mean more to you than using a TV remote control? Are you under the strong impression that you have lived before? How's your ESP? To many millions of people, these are not flip questions or jokes good for a laugh at parties. Instead, they are touchstones for believers in New Age religions.

The term *New Age* is an umbrella phrase for many different philosophies and organizations. Popularized in the 1980s, particularly in books by actress Shirley MacLaine and others, New Age generally encompasses more avant-garde trends in spirituality. Today, New Age books occupy their own section in major bookstore chains. In major cities, annual or semiannual expositions draw thousands for seminars and exhibits about chakras, auras, and past life regression. In major cities such as New York, Washington, Los Angeles, and San Francisco, massive publications are devoted to practitioners and teachers of New Age arts. Even the once-sleepy tourist town of Sedona, Arizona, is now celebrated as a New Age center. (However, it's *not* true that the local cable system features a channel channel!)

As with some other religious and spiritual movements, New Age religion has no mother church, largely because the movement is so diffuse. Some online guides to the New Age do exist, however, and they have links of their own to other sites.

One such introductory site is the Protree Alternative Information Center WWW (http://www.protree.com/kiwi/Spirit.html#subjects), which is a simple page offering a variety of links to New Age sites (Figure 18-8). It's typical of many general New Age pages, offering links eclectic and perhaps eccentric, but definitely interesting — for those who wish to explore further.

You'll find a more detailed — and more global — Spirit-WWW Web site (http://www.spiritweb.org/), which was started in 1993 and now has three "mirror" sites: one in Mountain View, California; another in Ravenna, Italy; and a third in Canberra, Australia. Figure 18-9 illustrates part of the home page.

According to a message from site creator/maintainer René K. Müller, "I'm really surprised by all of the positive responses and support I received." This really shouldn't come as a surprise though. Even with my 17-inch portrait (vertical) display monitor, it took three full screens to display all of the contents of the Spirit-WWW home page. Items such as channelings, UFO phenomena, reincarnation, theosophy (along with an event calendar), metaphysical resources, and even a spiritual glossary (whose definitions of Christian and Judaic terms will challenge the thinking of mainstream adherents of those faiths) are all there. It's well organized, multidimensional, and intriguing. I especially appreciated seeing links to other networks, sites, and Internet mailing lists, offering yet another avenue for seekers.

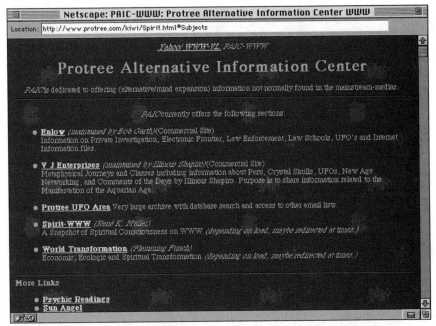

Figure 18-8: The Protree Alternative Information Center WWW home page.

New Age students will doubtless find another interesting site in the Celestine home page (`http://www.maui.net/~shaw/celes/celestine.html`). This page is a private venture maintained by Sandy Craig Shaw, a computer programmer at the Mees Solar Observatory, which is one of the University of Hawaii's Haleakala Observatories. This site is dedicated to students of *The Celestine Prophecy*, a book by James Redfield that has gained a wide following in the United States and elsewhere. It details a series of insights that Redfield suggests are common to all of us at this end-of-the-millennium age. Shaw's home page details some of the things people are doing with Redfield's teachings, in discussion groups, tours, and workshops. Figure 18-10 shows the Shaw page.

Figure 18-9: The Spirit-WWW home page, which is mirrored on three sites around the world.

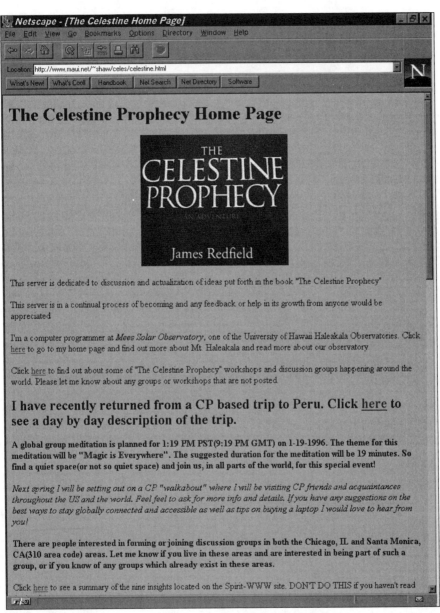

Figure 18-10: The Celestine home page, maintained by Sandy Craig Shaw, discusses teachings found in *The Celestine Prophecy,* by James Redfield.

The Church of Scientology

One of the most controversial movements, certainly in terms of the Internet, is the Church of Scientology International, which is based in Los Angeles and operates in the United States and around the world. Founded by L. Ron Hubbard, a noted writer of science fiction, the church posits a theory that a person must deal with negative memories and mental images before one can be a "clear" individual.

Scientology operates on principles set forth by Hubbard in *Dianetics*, a book that has sold multiple millions of copies since its first publication over 40 years ago. Scientologists are trained in "auditing" their peers and helping to discover the mental blockages that prevent the state of "clear."

Many people disagree with Scientology's teachings, despite testimonials from celebrities such as actors John Travolta and Ann Archer, and musicians Chick Corea and Mark Isham, among others. This opposition has taken political form in some countries and legal form in others. Through it all, the Scientologists say they are merely asking for the right to practice their religion, something guaranteed in the United States under the First Amendment and in other countries under either local laws or the United Nations' "Declaration of Human Rights."

Perhaps nowhere today has the controversy over Scientology been as strong as on the Internet. In recent years, those who dissent from the teachings of Scientology have posted files containing church teachings on the Net in an effort to document their assertions about what they consider negative aspects of Scientology. The Church of Scientology and its affiliated organizations, which hold copyrights to the writings of L. Ron Hubbard and trademark registrations of several names and symbols used in the religion, have gone to court seeking to block transmission of these materials, claiming infringement of "religious trade secrets." Courts have supported the Scientologists, who then used marshals to recover computers and data files from some active opponents. Courts have also ruled against the Scientology movement, as in 1995 when a federal district court supported *The Washington Post*'s bid to publish certain items obtained from public court records.

The battles between the Scientologists and their opponents will most likely continue for some time to come. According to an article in *Insight on the News*, a magazine published by *The Washington Times*, the Church of Scientology sees itself as the cyberspace equivalent of the sheriffs of America's Wild West. Those who oppose the church believe they have the First Amendment on their side.

Those who are interested in seeing the Scientologists' side of the story can start with http://www.theta.com/goodman, a page created by Leisa Goodman, the Media Relations Director of the Church of Scientology International in Los Angeles. She offers links to many articles and documents describing the teachings of Scientology and its benefits, as well as a discussion of the issues surrounding the posting of Scientology materials on the Internet.

Ron Newman of Somerville, Mass., best represents the opposing side. You can find his page, *The Church of Scientology vs. the Net* at http://www.cybercom.net/~rnewman/scientology/home.html. It is updated on a regular basis and contains link after link to sites of interest as well as articles relative to the controversy.

Tying It All Together (More or Less)

What You've Learned So Far

Your journey through the religious and spiritual resources of the Internet and online services has just about reached the end . . . at least for this book. We've traveled, you and I, from the basics of computers and online services to a plethora of Web sites and online locations.

What have we learned? I might be presumptuous to speculate on your behalf, but let's recap just a bit. We've seen the vast array of online services and the spectacular assortment of Internet sites and resources. We've been introduced to exhibits and file libraries on several continents, and we've "met" various religious movements and groups that we may not have known otherwise.

We've also seen what you need to do to get online, and we've seen the amazing results of people finding faith online. All this, and real-life examples of people gaining personal benefit from finding their spiritual bearings online.

As you'll see in this chapter — as I believe we have seen throughout these pages — where we have been and what we have seen is just the beginning. The use of the Internet for religious exploration, edification, and fellowship will only grow.

In this chapter, you'll look at some additional resources for using the Internet, a personal perspective on designing a Web page, some last-minute additions, and some final thoughts. As much as is possible for an ever-changing subject such as the Internet, this chapter represents an effort to help you keep up with the latest available information.

As mentioned elsewhere in this book, this is very much a living document: Check out my home page, `http://www.reston.com/kellner/kellner.html`, and you'll see links to update pages for this volume. It's my way of maintaining a commitment to this project, and to you.

Additional Internet Resources

By now, if you're surfing the Net, you are using a browser of one stripe or another: Netscape, Mosaic, or the AOL, eWorld, Interchange, Microsoft, Netcom, or Prodigy browsers, among others. There are additional resources you can use to make your Internet work more enjoyable.

Eudora

This is one of the great electronic mail packages, published by Qualcomm, Inc., and you can often get it for free or as part of a bundle. It's a deceptively simple e-mail program with which you can send, receive, and forward e-mail; enclose files of all sorts; and add a *signature* that automatically includes your name, e-mail address, home page, phone number, or other information. You can maintain an address book with Eudora, which keeps your contact list in order.

Eudora is a quick and easy way to manage your e-mail. The free version is called Eudora Lite, and it runs on Windows and Mac systems. Point your browser over to `http://www.qualcomm.com/` and you can learn about Eudora and download a copy for your use. (If you want to order the full version of the program, the price of which starts at $65 — less for students of degree-granting institutions — the Qualcomm home page will provide you with that information.)

I've used a lot of e-mail software, and for Internet e-mail, Eudora is one of my favorites. It's compact, complete, and convenient — there's not much more you can ask for in such a program. Along with the Web site, you can contact Qualcomm at (800) 2-EUDORA or (619) 597-5113.

CyberFinder

This little beauty is for Mac users only, for now, but what a wonderful program it is. From Aladdin Systems, you can organize the URLs for your favorite Web sites in folders by category or other selection, with each URL becoming a bookmark. These URLs are easily accessible from any application (word processor, spreadsheet, database, you name it) with one click to start up your browser, dial the Internet, and reach your desired site. The program costs $30 from Aladdin and runs on any Mac SE or later model.

As with many of Aladdin's fine products, you can download a demo version of CyberFinder 2.0 from Aladdin's Web site (`http://www.aladdinsys.com/`), where you will also find information on Aladdin's great data compression/extraction utility called StuffIt and some other extremely useful Aladdin applications for Macintosh and PC platforms.

Designing Your Own Web Page

Creating an Internet home page, which announces your presence on the Internet and serves as a point of contact between you and the rest of the world, isn't too difficult. In fact, it can be rather automatic, as I found recently with Adobe Systems Inc.'s PageMill product.

In the early days of the Internet, you needed a good command of HTML, the Hypertext Markup Language used to create a Web page by hand. Now, all you need is a good command of your credit card: Adobe Systems Inc., of Mountain View, California, offers PageMill, a $99 program for Macintosh and Power Mac computers that includes drag-and-drop placement of elements for a Web page, the chance to preview your page, and a convenient format in which you can upload the page to the service hosting your Web page. A Windows 95 version is due later in 1996, Adobe says.

I found PageMill easy to use, a delight in fact. The program has a miniature word processor, which allowed me to type in the text for my home page and select a format for the headings and other elements. When I wanted to separate the main headline from the text, I could easily add a rule, or line, to accomplish this, just by clicking on an icon representing the rule and dragging it onto the screen.

Placing a picture on a page is equally simple: click on the icon and then drag a picture frame onto the page. Associate the frame with a disk image and the illustration appears on the Web page. With the mouse, you can resize the image and move it on the page.

As you build your page, you will probably want to add links to other Internet sites and a click-on device so that people can send you electronic mail. These are both drag-and-drop functions: you can select a link icon, apply it to a highlighted section of text, and type the location of the Internet in another section of the screen. The link is created and will show up in testing for confirmation. An e-mail link is similar: highlight your e-mail address (or other text), select the option, and your page will contain a command to invoke the e-mail functions of a Web browser.

PageMill also contains tools that can create forms for people to fill out online and then send back to you. This is a nice plus for mail order publishers and others who savor interactive communications. You can create multiple pages with the program and, by creating links between each one, design a whole Web site. Overall, PageMill is a valuable tool for Web page authoring if you don't want to become an HTML programmer. Get information from Adobe at (800) 411-8657 or `http://www.adobe.com/Apps/Applications.html`.

Along with PageMill, at least three other tools commend themselves to users interested in Web authoring:

- ◆ **HoTMetaL** is HTML editing software from SoftQuad, Inc., Toronto. On UNIX, Windows, and Mac platforms, the program imports text from most major word processors, includes templates, and features "automatic rule checking," to make sure that your pages conform to HTML standards. The price tag is $195, and you can download a trial version for Windows and Mac users from the firm's home page. Contact SoftQuad at (416) 239-4801 or point your browser to `http://www.sq.com/products/hotmetal/hmp-org.htm`.

- ◆ **America Online's NaviPress** unit offers free demos of its HTML editing software for Macintosh and Windows platforms and space on a server to demonstrate the finished product for 30 days. The software is available for Macintosh, Windows, and UNIX. For information, call (800) 879-6882 or point your browser to `http://www.naviservice.com/index.htm`.

- ◆ **FrontPage**, now from Microsoft Corp., bills itself as an easy-to-use Web site designing package for Windows. A Macintosh version is due this year. FrontPage contains an editor, a graphics manager, and something called WebBots, which implements the most common Web server functionality, such as text searches, feedback forms, and threaded discussion forums. With WebBots, you don't need any programming or complex setup wizards and templates to create personal and business Web pages in a task-oriented manner. The list price is $695, and you can obtain information by calling Microsoft at (800) 426-9400 or by catching the company at its Internet address: `http://www.microsoft.com/msoffice/frontpage/index.htm`.

Some Last-Minute Additions

Even as this book was rushing toward completion, I kept learning about some useful and interesting sites. And, I'll confess, this is a good place to add at least one or two that might well have appeared elsewhere. I've listed them all here and, with the cooperation of this book's indexer, you'll be able to find them at least in one fashion or another.

Baha'is Online

The Baha'i faith is a religion derived primarily from the teachings of Bahá'u'lláh that seeks to unite people of all faiths in a common goal of global unity. Stating that both mankind and religion are one and that divisions are artificial constructs, Baha'is preach a message of peace, equality, and the elimination of prejudice. The movement has gained a great number of adherents, and more than two dozen Baha'i home pages are available on the World Wide Web. One of these is at `http://oneworld.wa.com/bahai/magazine/homepage.html`, and it serves as a good place to begin an investigation of this movement. You may also want to investigate Baha'i Resources on the Internet, which contains a great number of related links. The address is `http://www.bcca.org/services/srb/resource.html`.

Catholic Kiosk

The Archdiocese of Cincinnati, Ohio maintains a site at `http://www.erinet.com/aquinas/arch/dio.html`, which is illustrated in Figure 19-1. This site is elegant in its design, friendly in its approach, and useful in its content. It contains daily mass readings for the faithful and links a-plenty. It's worth investigating for both Catholics and others.

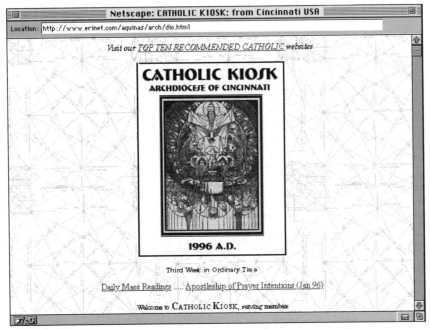

Figure 19-1: Catholic Kiosk, from the Archdiocese of Cincinnati, Ohio.

Druids

This pre-Celtic religion was centered on the worship of nature and the construction of stone circles for this purpose, of which Stonehenge in England is one of the most famous. The Order of Bards, Ovates, & Druids, based in England, offers a book of teachings of Druid tradition at its Web site: `http://www.raccoon.com/~aiko/obod.html`. This site offers the argument that Druidism is "in tune with the spirit of our times."

Unitarian Universalist Association

The UUA serves members of this church, which describes itself as a "liberal religion" rooted in Judaism and Christianity but "non-creedal." The site contains links to various UU resources, including church home pages. It does not appear to be updated on a frequent basis, but the site `http://uua.org/` is a starting point for investigation.

Some Final Thoughts about "Cyber-Religion"

If I were a great prognosticator, you'd find me on Wall Street — or perhaps at a race track — picking the winners I see — or foresee, in this case — coming down the pike. But having studied this subject for many years, I offer some observations that you may want to ponder as we all face the dawn of the Cyber Age.

◆ **Online religion won't go away.** This seems obvious, but its implications may not be. I have stated elsewhere that this is not merely a revolution in communication. The availability of religious information online, the potential for fellowship across the miles via computer, and quick access to texts from virtually every faith on the planet will all have an impact on the way religions connect to people, and vice versa.

◆ **Online religion will make it easier for "seekers" to find new spiritual homes**. Those pilgrims and strangers the old hymn spoke of will tarry at Web sites and drink in much. Organizations that present a compelling message, update their sites, and respond quickly to inquiries will gain greatly from the online world.

◆ **This new era will flatten the levels of denominational structures, whether the denomination wants it or not.** The experience of the Worldwide Church of God, whose dissidents largely organized online, is instructive. So, too, are the experiences of other movements and other leaders. When the lowliest person can e-mail the individual at the top — or those close to him — the leader ignores the *vox populi* at his own peril. I don't suggest that churches and movements will become weathervanes, blowing this way and that, but rather that leadership will have to become more adept at listening to its constituents and responding to them.

On the plus side, communication will be faster and broader than before. On the down side, this instantaneous communication may render some levels of organizational government obsolete. That may not be a great loss, however: many organizations wish they had additional field resources, and a flattening of bureaucracy will free those up.

◆ **We're only at the *beginning* of a worldwide trend toward religion being available online.** I hope this book, and others, will inspire people to delve into the online world, contend for their views, and share their knowledge. We will all be richer, and in this, we will all find opportunity and hope.

Glossary

The Internet, like religion, has a particular terminology all its
own. Here's a glossary of terms for both religion and computers.

address
An *electronic mail address* is the string of characters that you
must give an electronic mail program to direct a message to a
particular person. See also *Internet address*.

ARCHIE
A system for locating files that are publicly available by anonymous FTP.

ARPANET
Advanced Research Projects Agency Network: A pioneering long-
haul network funded by ARPA. It served as the basis for early
networking research as well as a central backbone during the
development of the Internet. The ARPANET consisted of individual packet-switching computers interconnected by leased
lines.

ASCII
American Standard Code for Information Interchange. Text
formatted in ASCII is "plain" text that can be read by or on
almost any computer with virtually any word processor or text
editor.

atheism
The belief that there is no God, which was the official philosophy
of the Soviet Union and many other Communist states before the
collapse of that empire. It is also held as a private belief by many
people in the West.

B
Byte: One character of information, usually eight bits wide.

b
Bit — binary digit: The smallest amount of information that may
be stored in a computer.

Bible
Generally the Old and New Testaments, as canonized by Rabbinical
and/or Church authorities. Differences exist in the canons
accepted by the Catholic and Protestant wings of Christianity.

BITNET
Because It's Time Network: BITNET has several thousand host computers, primarily at universities and in many countries. It is managed by EDUCOM, which provides administrative support and information services. There are three main constituents of the network: BITNET in the United States and Mexico, NETNORTH in Canada, and EARN in Europe. There are also AsiaNet in Japan and connections in South America.

bps
Bits per second: A measure of data transmission speed.

Buddhism
A religion centered on the teachings on Gautama Buddha.

Christianity
A religion centered on the teachings and life of Jesus of Nazareth, also called Jesus Christ; today, it is represented by three main divisions: Roman Catholic, Eastern Orthodox, and Protestant.

DARPA
U.S. Department of Defense Advanced Research Projects Agency: The government agency that funded the ARPANET and later started the Internet.

DECNET
Digital Equipment Corporation network: A networking protocol for DEC computers and network devices.

dedicated line
A permanently connected private telephone line between two locations.

default route
A routing table entry that is used to direct any data addressed to any network numbers not explicitly listed in the routing table.

DNS
Domain Name System: A mechanism used in the Internet for translating names of host computers into addresses. The DNS also allows host computers not directly on the Internet to have registered names in the same style.

download
To transfer files from one computer to another.

e-mail
The vernacular abbreviation for electronic mail.

FAQ
Frequently Asked Questions: A list of common questions with their answers. Most mailing lists and all network newsgroups provide FAQ postings on a regular basis.

Flame
An Internet posting, usually on a newsgroup or via e-mail, that offers a negative, sometimes profane, response to another posting. You may receive flames in your Internet activity, but it is wise not to respond in kind.

FTP
File Transfer Protocol: The Internet standard high-level protocol for transferring files from one computer to another.

gateway
A special-purpose dedicated computer that attaches to two or more networks and routes packets from one network to the other. In particular, an Internet gateway routes IP datagrams among the networks it connects. Gateways route packets to other gateways until they can be delivered to the final destination directly across one physical network. See *router*.

GB
Gigabyte: A unit of data storage size that represents one billion characters of information.

Gb
Gigabit: One billion bits of information (usually used to express a data transfer rate, as in 1 gigabit/second = 1Gbps).

Gopher
A menu-based system for exploring Internet resources.

header
The portion of a packet, preceding the actual data, containing source and destination addresses and error-checking fields.

Hebrew
Language of ancient and modern Israel used for Jewish scriptures and prayer books.

Hinduism
Religion based on the Vedic traditions of India.

Holy Koran
Main scripture of Islam.

host number
The part of an Internet address that designates which node on the (sub)network is being addressed.

Internet
The global collection of interconnected regional and wide-area networks that use IP as the network layer protocol.

Internet address
An assigned number that identifies a host on an internet. It has two or three parts: network number, optional subnet number, and host number.

internetwork
Any connection of two or more local- or wide-area networks.

IP
Internet Protocol: The network layer protocol for the Internet. It is the datagram protocol defined by RFC 791.

Islam
Religion founded by Mohammed, centered on the Koran and five pillars of observance.

Jehovah's Witnesses
Sect founded in 19th Century, based largely on prophecy and end-time speculation.

Judaism
Religion centered on revelation of God as seen in the Hebrew scriptures (Old Testament). Three main branches represent Judaism today: Orthodox, Conservative, and Reform.

KB
Kilobyte: A unit of data storage size that represents 1,024 characters of information.

Kb
Kilobit: 1,024 bits of information (usually used to express a data transfer rate, as in 1 kilobit/second = 1Kbps).

knowbot
An experimental information-retrieval tool; a "knowledge robot" or "robot librarian."

LAN
Local area network: A network that takes advantage of the proximity of computers to offer relatively efficient, higher speed communications than long-haul or wide-area networks.

Latter-Day Saints, Church of Jesus Christ of
Also known as the Mormons, the LDS Church posits itself as a restoration of primitive Christianity.

MB
Megabyte: A unit of data storage size that represents one million characters of information.

Mb
Megabit: One million bits of information (usually used to express a data transfer rate, as in 1 megabit/second = 1Mbps).

modem
A piece of equipment that connects a computer to a data transmission line (typically a telephone line).

Muslim
Literally, "follower of Islam."

network number
The part of an internet address that designates the network to which the addressed node belongs.

NFS
Network File System: A network service that lets a program running on one computer use data stored on a different computer on the same internet as if it were on its own disk.

NIC
Network Information Center: An organization that provides network users with information about services provided by the network.

NII
National Information Infrastructure.

NSFNET
National Science Foundation Network: A high-speed internet that spans the country, and is intended for research applications. It is made up of the NSFNET Backbone and the NSFNET regional networks. It is part of the Internet.

NSFNET Backbone
A network connecting 21 sites across the continental United States. It is the central component of NSFNET.

NSFNET Mid-Level
A network connected to the highest level of the NSFNET that covers a region of the United States. It is to mid-level networks that local sites connect. The mid-level networks were once called "regionals."

NSFNET Regional
A network connected to the NSFNET Backbone that covers a region of the United States. Local sites connect to the regionals.

Occult
Practices involving non-Judeo-Christian religious traditions, including witchcraft, astrology, and Satanism.

packet
The unit of data sent across a packet switching network. The term is used loosely. Although some Internet literature uses it to refer specifically to data sent across a physical network, other literature views the Internet as a packet switching network and describes IP datagrams as packets.

Pagan
Practitioner of ancient non-Judeo-Christian religion.

PPP
Point-to-Point Protocol: provides a method for transmitting datagrams over serial point-to-point links.

protocol
A formal description of message formats and the rules two computers must follow to exchange those messages. Protocols can describe low-level details of machine-to-machine interfaces (for example, the order in which bits and bytes are sent across a wire) or high-level exchanges between allocation programs (for example, the way in which two programs transfer a file across the Internet).

RFC
The Internet's Request for Comments documents series: The RFCs are working notes of the Internet research and development community. A document in this series may be on essentially any topic related to computer communication, and may be anything from a meeting report to the specification of a standard.

router
A special-purpose dedicated computer that attaches to two or more networks and routes packets from one network to the other. In particular, an Internet gateway routes IP datagrams among the networks it connects. Gateways route packets to other gateways until they can be delivered to the final destination directly across one physical network.

server
A computer that shares its resources, such as printers and files, with other computers on the network. An example of this is a Network Files System (NFS) server that shares its disk space with a workstation that does not have a disk drive of its own.

SLIP
Serial Line Internet Protocol: SLIP is currently a de facto standard, commonly used for point-to-point serial connections running TCP/IP. It is not an Internet standard but is defined in RFC 1055.

SMTP
Simple Mail Transfer Protocol: The Internet standard protocol for transferring electronic mail messages from one computer to another. SMTP specifies how two mail systems interact and the format of control messages they exchange to transfer mail.

SNMP
Simple Network Management Protocol: The SNMP (RFC 1157) is the Internet's standard for remote monitoring and management of hosts, routers, and other nodes and devices on a network.

subnet
A portion of a network, that may be a physically independent network, which shares a network address with other portions of the network and is distinguished by a subnet number. A subnet is to a network what a network is to an internet.

T1
A term for a digital carrier facility used to transmit a DS-1 formatted digital signal at 1.544 megabits per second.

T3
A term for a digital carrier facility used to transmit a DS-3 formatted digital signal at 44.746 megabits per second.

Taoism
Religion based on teachings of Tao Te Ching.

TCP
Transfer Control Protocol: A transfer layer protocol for the Internet. It is a connection-oriented, stream protocol defined by RFC 793.

TCP/IP
Transfer Control Protocol/Internet Protocol: A common shorthand that refers to the suite of application and transfer protocols that run over IP. These include FTP, Telnet, SMTP, and UDP (a transfer layer protocol).

Telnet
The Internet standard protocol for remote terminal connection service. Telnet allows a user at one site to interact with a remote time-sharing system at another site as if the user's terminal were connected directly to the remote computer.

The Salvation Army
Evangelical movement founded by William Booth in 1865.

UNIX
An operating system developed by Bell Laboratories that supports multiuser and multitasking operations.

WAIS
Wide Area Information Server: An Internet service for looking up specific information in Internet databases.

WAN
Wide Area Network.

WESTNET
One of the National Science Foundation-funded regional TCP/IP networks that covers the states of Arizona, Colorado, New Mexico, Utah, and Wyoming.

Wiccan
Ancient pagan/witchcraft traditions, revived in recent years.

WWW
World Wide Web.

Index

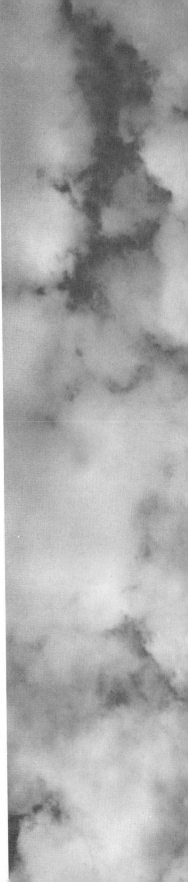

✦ C ✦

✦ **I** ✦

(continued)

✦ N ✦

✦ O ✦

✦ P ✦

✦ Q ✦

✦ R ✦

✦ S ✦

(continued)

✦ X ✦

✦ **Y** ✦

✦ **Z** ✦

The Fun & Easy Way™ to learn about computers and more!

Windows® 3.11 For Dummies® 3rd Edition
by Andy Rathbone
ISBN: 1-56884-370-4
$16.95 USA/
$22.95 Canada

Mutual Funds For Dummies™
by Eric Tyson
ISBN: 1-56884-226-0
$16.99 USA/
$22.99 Canada

DOS For Dummies® 2nd Edition
by Dan Gookin
ISBN: 1-878058-75-4
$16.95 USA/
$22.95 Canada

The Internet For Dummies® 2nd Edition
by John Levine & Carol Baroudi
ISBN: 1-56884-222-8
$19.99 USA/
$26.99 Canada

Personal Finance For Dummies™
by Eric Tyson
ISBN: 1-56884-150-7
$16.95 USA/
$22.95 Canada

PCs For Dummies® 3rd Edition
by Dan Gookin & Andy Rathbone
ISBN: 1-56884-904-4
$16.99 USA/
$22.99 Canada

Macs® For Dummies® 3rd Edition
by David Pogue
ISBN: 1-56884-239-2
$19.99 USA/
$26.99 Canada

The SAT® I For Dummies™
by Suzee Vlk
ISBN: 1-56884-213-9
$14.99 USA/
$20.99 Canada

Here's a complete listing of IDG Books' ...For Dummies® titles

Title	Author	ISBN	Price
DATABASE			
Access 2 For Dummies®	by Scott Palmer	ISBN: 1-56884-090-X	$19.95 USA/$26.95 Canada
Access Programming For Dummies®	by Rob Krumm	ISBN: 1-56884-091-8	$19.95 USA/$26.95 Canada
Approach 3 For Windows® For Dummies®	by Doug Lowe	ISBN: 1-56884-233-3	$19.99 USA/$26.99 Canada
dBASE For DOS For Dummies®	by Scott Palmer & Michael Stabler	ISBN: 1-56884-188-4	$19.95 USA/$26.95 Canada
dBASE For Windows® For Dummies®	by Scott Palmer	ISBN: 1-56884-179-5	$19.95 USA/$26.95 Canada
dBASE 5 For Windows® Programming For Dummies®	by Ted Coombs & Jason Coombs	ISBN: 1-56884-215-5	$19.99 USA/$26.99 Canada
FoxPro 2.6 For Windows® For Dummies®	by John Kaufeld	ISBN: 1-56884-187-6	$19.95 USA/$26.95 Canada
Paradox 5 For Windows® For Dummies®	by John Kaufeld	ISBN: 1-56884-185-X	$19.95 USA/$26.95 Canada
DESKTOP PUBLISHING/ILLUSTRATION/GRAPHICS			
CorelDRAW! 5 For Dummies®	by Deke McClelland	ISBN: 1-56884-157-4	$19.95 USA/$26.95 Canada
CorelDRAW! For Dummies®	by Deke McClelland	ISBN: 1-56884-042-X	$19.95 USA/$26.95 Canada
Desktop Publishing & Design For Dummies®	by Roger C. Parker	ISBN: 1-56884-234-1	$19.99 USA/$26.99 Canada
Harvard Graphics 2 For Windows® For Dummies®	by Roger C. Parker	ISBN: 1-56884-092-6	$19.95 USA/$26.95 Canada
PageMaker 5 For Macs® For Dummies®	by Galen Gruman & Deke McClelland	ISBN: 1-56884-178-7	$19.95 USA/$26.95 Canada
PageMaker 5 For Windows® For Dummies®	by Deke McClelland & Galen Gruman	ISBN: 1-56884-160-4	$19.95 USA/$26.95 Canada
Photoshop 3 For Macs® For Dummies®	by Deke McClelland	ISBN: 1-56884-208-2	$19.99 USA/$26.99 Canada
QuarkXPress 3.3 For Dummies®	by Galen Gruman & Barbara Assadi	ISBN: 1-56884-217-1	$19.99 USA/$26.99 Canada
FINANCE/PERSONAL FINANCE/TEST TAKING REFERENCE			
Everyday Math For Dummies™	by Charles Seiter	ISBN: 1-56884-248-1	$14.99 USA/$22.99 Canada
Personal Finance For Dummies™ For Canadians	by Eric Tyson & Tony Martin	ISBN: 1-56884-378-X	$18.99 USA/$24.99 Canada
QuickBooks 3 For Dummies®	by Stephen L. Nelson	ISBN: 1-56884-227-9	$19.99 USA/$26.99 Canada
Quicken 8 For DOS For Dummies® 2nd Edition	by Stephen L. Nelson	ISBN: 1-56884-210-4	$19.95 USA/$26.95 Canada
Quicken 5 For Macs® For Dummies®	by Stephen L. Nelson	ISBN: 1-56884-211-2	$19.95 USA/$26.95 Canada
Quicken 4 For Windows® For Dummies® 2nd Edition	by Stephen L. Nelson	ISBN: 1-56884-209-0	$19.95 USA/$26.95 Canada
Taxes For Dummies™ 1995 Edition	by Eric Tyson & David J. Silverman	ISBN: 1-56884-220-1	$14.99 USA/$20.99 Canada
The GMAT® For Dummies™	by Suzee Vlk, Series Editor	ISBN: 1-56884-376-3	$14.99 USA/$20.99 Canada
The GRE® For Dummies™	by Suzee Vlk, Series Editor	ISBN: 1-56884-375-5	$14.99 USA/$20.99 Canada
Time Management For Dummies™	by Jeffrey J. Mayer	ISBN: 1-56884-360-7	$16.99 USA/$22.99 Canada
TurboTax For Windows® For Dummies®	by Gail A. Helsel, CPA	ISBN: 1-56884-228-7	$19.99 USA/$26.99 Canada
GROUPWARE/INTEGRATED			
ClarisWorks For Macs® For Dummies®	by Frank Higgins	ISBN: 1-56884-363-1	$19.99 USA/$26.99 Canada
Lotus Notes For Dummies®	by Pat Freeland & Stephen Londergan	ISBN: 1-56884-212-0	$19.95 USA/$26.95 Canada
Microsoft® Office 4 For Windows® For Dummies®	by Roger C. Parker	ISBN: 1-56884-183-3	$19.95 USA/$26.95 Canada
Microsoft® Works 3 For Windows® For Dummies®	by David C. Kay	ISBN: 1-56884-214-7	$19.99 USA/$26.99 Canada
SmartSuite 3 For Dummies®	by Jan Weingarten & John Weingarten	ISBN: 1-56884-367-4	$19.99 USA/$26.99 Canada
INTERNET/COMMUNICATIONS/NETWORKING			
America Online® For Dummies® 2nd Edition	by John Kaufeld	ISBN: 1-56884-933-8	$19.99 USA/$26.99 Canada
CompuServe For Dummies® 2nd Edition	by Wallace Wang	ISBN: 1-56884-937-0	$19.99 USA/$26.99 Canada
Modems For Dummies® 2nd Edition	by Tina Rathbone	ISBN: 1-56884-223-6	$19.99 USA/$26.99 Canada
MORE Internet For Dummies®	by John R. Levine & Margaret Levine Young	ISBN: 1-56884-164-7	$19.95 USA/$26.95 Canada
MORE Modems & On-line Services For Dummies®	by Tina Rathbone	ISBN: 1-56884-365-8	$19.99 USA/$26.99 Canada
Mosaic For Dummies® Windows Edition	by David Angell & Brent Heslop	ISBN: 1-56884-242-2	$19.99 USA/$26.99 Canada
NetWare For Dummies® 2nd Edition	by Ed Tittel, Deni Connor & Earl Follis	ISBN: 1-56884-369-0	$19.99 USA/$26.99 Canada
Networking For Dummies®	by Doug Lowe	ISBN: 1-56884-079-9	$19.95 USA/$26.95 Canada
PROCOMM PLUS 2 For Windows® For Dummies®	by Wallace Wang	ISBN: 1-56884-219-8	$19.99 USA/$26.99 Canada
TCP/IP For Dummies®	by Marshall Wilensky & Candace Leiden	ISBN: 1-56884-241-4	$19.99 USA/$26.99 Canada

Title	Author	ISBN	Price
The Internet For Macs® For Dummies® 2nd Edition	by Charles Seiter	ISBN: 1-56884-371-2	$19.99 USA/$26.99 Canada
The Internet For Macs® For Dummies® Starter Kit	by Charles Seiter	ISBN: 1-56884-244-9	$29.99 USA/$39.99 Canada
The Internet For Macs® For Dummies® Starter Kit Bestseller Edition	by Charles Seiter	ISBN: 1-56884-245-7	$39.99 USA/$54.99 Canada
The Internet For Windows® For Dummies® Starter Kit	by John R. Levine & Margaret Levine Young	ISBN: 1-56884-237-6	$34.99 USA/$44.99 Canada
The Internet For Windows® For Dummies® Starter Kit, Bestseller Edition	by John R. Levine & Margaret Levine Young	ISBN: 1-56884-246-5	$39.99 USA/$54.99 Canada

MACINTOSH

Title	Author	ISBN	Price
Mac® Programming For Dummies®	by Dan Parks Sydow	ISBN: 1-56884-173-6	$19.95 USA/$26.95 Canada
Macintosh® System 7.5 For Dummies®	by Bob LeVitus	ISBN: 1-56884-197-3	$19.95 USA/$26.95 Canada
MORE Macs® For Dummies®	by David Pogue	ISBN: 1-56884-087-X	$19.95 USA/$26.95 Canada
PageMaker 5 For Macs® For Dummies®	by Galen Gruman & Deke McClelland	ISBN: 1-56884-178-7	$19.95 USA/$26.95 Canada
QuarkXPress 3.3 For Dummies®	by Galen Gruman & Barbara Assadi	ISBN: 1-56884-217-1	$19.95 USA/$26.99 Canada
Upgrading and Fixing Macs® For Dummies®	by Kearney Rietmann & Frank Higgins	ISBN: 1-56884-189-2	$19.95 USA/$26.95 Canada

MULTIMEDIA

Title	Author	ISBN	Price
Multimedia & CD-ROMs For Dummies® 2nd Edition	by Andy Rathbone	ISBN: 1-56884-907-9	$19.99 USA/$26.99 Canada
Multimedia & CD-ROMs For Dummies® Interactive Multimedia Value Pack, 2nd Edition	by Andy Rathbone	ISBN: 1-56884-909-5	$29.99 USA/$39.99 Canada

OPERATING SYSTEMS:

DOS

Title	Author	ISBN	Price
MORE DOS For Dummies®	by Dan Gookin	ISBN: 1-56884-046-2	$19.95 USA/$26.95 Canada
OS/2® Warp For Dummies® 2nd Edition	by Andy Rathbone	ISBN: 1-56884-205-8	$19.99 USA/$26.99 Canada

UNIX

Title	Author	ISBN	Price
MORE UNIX® For Dummies®	by John R. Levine & Margaret Levine Young	ISBN: 1-56884-361-5	$19.99 USA/$26.99 Canada
UNIX® For Dummies®	by John R. Levine & Margaret Levine Young	ISBN: 1-878058-58-4	$19.95 USA/$26.95 Canada

WINDOWS

Title	Author	ISBN	Price
MORE Windows® For Dummies® 2nd Edition	by Andy Rathbone	ISBN: 1-56884-048-9	$19.95 USA/$26.95 Canada
Windows® 95 For Dummies®	by Andy Rathbone	ISBN: 1-56884-240-6	$19.99 USA/$26.99 Canada

PCS/HARDWARE

Title	Author	ISBN	Price
Illustrated Computer Dictionary For Dummies® 2nd Edition	by Dan Gookin & Wallace Wang	ISBN: 1-56884-218-X	$12.95 USA/$16.95 Canada
Upgrading and Fixing PCs For Dummies® 2nd Edition	by Andy Rathbone	ISBN: 1-56884-903-6	$19.99 USA/$26.99 Canada

PRESENTATION/AUTOCAD

Title	Author	ISBN	Price
AutoCAD For Dummies®	by Bud Smith	ISBN: 1-56884-191-4	$19.95 USA/$26.95 Canada
PowerPoint 4 For Windows® For Dummies®	by Doug Lowe	ISBN: 1-56884-161-2	$16.99 USA/$22.99 Canada

PROGRAMMING

Title	Author	ISBN	Price
Borland C++ For Dummies®	by Michael Hyman	ISBN: 1-56884-162-0	$19.95 USA/$26.95 Canada
C For Dummies® Volume 1	by Dan Gookin	ISBN: 1-878058-78-9	$19.95 USA/$26.95 Canada
C++ For Dummies®	by Stephen R. Davis	ISBN: 1-56884-163-9	$19.95 USA/$26.95 Canada
Delphi Programming For Dummies®	by Neil Rubenking	ISBN: 1-56884-200-7	$19.99 USA/$26.99 Canada
Mac® Programming For Dummies®	by Dan Parks Sydow	ISBN: 1-56884-173-6	$19.95 USA/$26.95 Canada
PowerBuilder 4 Programming For Dummies®	by Ted Coombs & Jason Coombs	ISBN: 1-56884-325-9	$19.99 USA/$26.99 Canada
QBasic Programming For Dummies®	by Douglas Hergert	ISBN: 1-56884-093-4	$19.95 USA/$26.95 Canada
Visual Basic 3 For Dummies®	by Wallace Wang	ISBN: 1-56884-076-4	$19.95 USA/$26.95 Canada
Visual Basic "X" For Dummies®	by Wallace Wang	ISBN: 1-56884-230-9	$19.99 USA/$26.99 Canada
Visual C++ 2 For Dummies®	by Michael Hyman & Bob Arnson	ISBN: 1-56884-328-3	$19.99 USA/$26.99 Canada
Windows® 95 Programming For Dummies®	by S. Randy Davis	ISBN: 1-56884-327-5	$19.99 USA/$26.99 Canada

SPREADSHEET

Title	Author	ISBN	Price
1-2-3 For Dummies®	by Greg Harvey	ISBN: 1-878058-60-6	$16.95 USA/$22.95 Canada
1-2-3 For Windows® 5 For Dummies® 2nd Edition	by John Walkenbach	ISBN: 1-56884-216-3	$16.95 USA/$22.95 Canada
Excel 5 For Macs® For Dummies®	by Greg Harvey	ISBN: 1-56884-186-8	$19.95 USA/$26.95 Canada
Excel For Dummies® 2nd Edition	by Greg Harvey	ISBN: 1-56884-050-0	$16.95 USA/$22.95 Canada
MORE 1-2-3 For DOS For Dummies®	by John Weingarten	ISBN: 1-56884-224-4	$19.99 USA/$26.99 Canada
MORE Excel 5 For Windows® For Dummies®	by Greg Harvey	ISBN: 1-56884-207-4	$19.95 USA/$26.95 Canada
Quattro Pro 6 For Windows® For Dummies®	by John Walkenbach	ISBN: 1-56884-174-4	$19.95 USA/$26.95 Canada
Quattro Pro For DOS For Dummies®	by John Walkenbach	ISBN: 1-56884-023-5	$16.95 USA/$22.95 Canada

UTILITIES

Title	Author	ISBN	Price
Norton Utilities 8 For Dummies®	by Beth Slick	ISBN: 1-56884-166-3	$19.95 USA/$26.95 Canada

VCRS/CAMCORDERS

Title	Author	ISBN	Price
VCRs & Camcorders For Dummies™	by Gordon McComb & Andy Rathbone	ISBN: 1-56884-229-5	$14.99 USA/$20.99 Canada

WORD PROCESSING

Title	Author	ISBN	Price
Ami Pro For Dummies®	by Jim Meade	ISBN: 1-56884-049-7	$19.95 USA/$26.95 Canada
MORE Word For Windows® 6 For Dummies®	by Doug Lowe	ISBN: 1-56884-165-5	$19.95 USA/$26.95 Canada
MORE WordPerfect® 6 For Windows® For Dummies®	by Margaret Levine Young & David C. Kay	ISBN: 1-56884-206-6	$19.95 USA/$26.95 Canada
MORE WordPerfect® 6 For DOS For Dummies®	by Wallace Wang, edited by Dan Gookin	ISBN: 1-56884-047-0	$19.95 USA/$26.95 Canada
Word 6 For Macs® For Dummies®	by Dan Gookin	ISBN: 1-56884-190-6	$19.95 USA/$26.95 Canada
Word For Windows® 6 For Dummies®	by Dan Gookin	ISBN: 1-56884-075-6	$16.95 USA/$22.95 Canada
Word For Windows® For Dummies®	by Dan Gookin & Ray Werner	ISBN: 1-878058-86-X	$16.95 USA/$22.95 Canada
WordPerfect® 6 For DOS For Dummies®	by Dan Gookin	ISBN: 1-878058-77-0	$16.95 USA/$22.95 Canada
WordPerfect® 6.1 For Windows® For Dummies® 2nd Edition	by Margaret Levine Young & David Kay	ISBN: 1-56884-243-0	$16.95 USA/$22.95 Canada
WordPerfect® For Dummies®	by Dan Gookin	ISBN: 1-878058-52-5	$16.95 USA/$22.95 Canada

For scholastic requests & educational orders please call Educational Sales at 1. 800. 434. 2086

FOR MORE INFO OR TO ORDER, PLEASE CALL ▶ **800. 762. 2974**

For volume discounts & special orders please Tony Real, Special Sales, at 415. 655. 3048

Fun, Fast, & Cheap!™

The Internet For Macs® For Dummies® Quick Reference

by Charles Seiter

ISBN:1-56884-967-2
$9.99 USA/$12.99 Canada

Windows® 95 For Dummies® Quick Reference

by Greg Harvey

ISBN: 1-56884-964-8
$9.99 USA/$12.99 Canada

Photoshop 3 For Macs® For Dummies® Quick Reference

by Deke McClelland

ISBN: 1-56884-968-0
$9.99 USA/$12.99 Canada

WordPerfect® For DOS For Dummies® Quick Reference

by Greg Harvey

ISBN: 1-56884-009-8
$8.95 USA/$12.95 Canada

Title	Author	ISBN	Price
DATABASE			
Access 2 For Dummies® Quick Reference	by Stuart J. Stuple	ISBN: 1-56884-167-1	$8.95 USA/$11.95 Canada
dBASE 5 For DOS For Dummies® Quick Reference	by Barrie Sosinsky	ISBN: 1-56884-954-0	$9.99 USA/$12.99 Canada
dBASE 5 For Windows® For Dummies® Quick Reference	by Stuart J. Stuple	ISBN: 1-56884-953-2	$9.99 USA/$12.99 Canada
Paradox 5 For Windows® For Dummies® Quick Reference	by Scott Palmer	ISBN: 1-56884-960-5	$9.99 USA/$12.99 Canada
DESKTOP PUBLISHING/ILLUSTRATION/GRAPHICS			
CorelDRAW! 5 For Dummies® Quick Reference	by Raymond E. Werner	ISBN: 1-56884-952-4	$9.99 USA/$12.99 Canada
Harvard Graphics For Windows® For Dummies® Quick Reference	by Raymond E. Werner	ISBN: 1-56884-962-1	$9.99 USA/$12.99 Canada
Photoshop 3 For Macs® For Dummies® Quick Reference	by Deke McClelland	ISBN: 1-56884-968-0	$9.99 USA/$12.99 Canada
FINANCE/PERSONAL FINANCE			
Quicken 4 For Windows® For Dummies® Quick Reference	by Stephen L. Nelson	ISBN: 1-56884-950-8	$9.95 USA/$12.99 Canada
GROUPWARE/INTEGRATED			
Microsoft® Office 4 For Windows® For Dummies® Quick Reference	by Doug Lowe	ISBN: 1-56884-958-3	$9.99 USA/$12.99 Canada
Microsoft® Works 3 For Windows® For Dummies® Quick Reference	by Michael Partington	ISBN: 1-56884-959-1	$9.99 USA/$12.99 Canada
INTERNET/COMMUNICATIONS/NETWORKING			
The Internet For Dummies® Quick Reference	by John R. Levine & Margaret Levine Young	ISBN: 1-56884-168-X	$8.95 USA/$11.95 Canada
MACINTOSH			
Macintosh® System 7.5 For Dummies® Quick Reference	by Stuart J. Stuple	ISBN: 1-56884-956-7	$9.99 USA/$12.99 Canada
OPERATING SYSTEMS:			
DOS			
DOS For Dummies® Quick Reference	by Greg Harvey	ISBN: 1-56884-007-1	$8.95 USA/$11.95 Canada
UNIX			
UNIX® For Dummies® Quick Reference	by John R. Levine & Margaret Levine Young	ISBN: 1-56884-094-2	$8.95 USA/$11.95 Canada
WINDOWS			
Windows® 3.1 For Dummies® Quick Reference, 2nd Edition	by Greg Harvey	ISBN: 1-56884-951-6	$8.95 USA/$11.95 Canada
PCs/HARDWARE			
Memory Management For Dummies® Quick Reference	by Doug Lowe	ISBN: 1-56884-362-3	$9.99 USA/$12.99 Canada
PRESENTATION/AUTOCAD			
AutoCAD For Dummies® Quick Reference	by Ellen Finkelstein	ISBN: 1-56884-198-1	$9.95 USA/$12.95 Canada
SPREADSHEET			
1-2-3 For Dummies® Quick Reference	by John Walkenbach	ISBN: 1-56884-027-6	$8.95 USA/$11.95 Canada
1-2-3 For Windows® 5 For Dummies® Quick Reference	by John Walkenbach	ISBN: 1-56884-957-5	$9.95 USA/$12.95 Canada
Excel For Windows® For Dummies® Quick Reference, 2nd Edition	by John Walkenbach	ISBN: 1-56884-096-9	$8.95 USA/$11.95 Canada
Quattro Pro 6 For Windows® For Dummies® Quick Reference	by Stuart J. Stuple	ISBN: 1-56884-172-8	$9.95 USA/$12.95 Canada
WORD PROCESSING			
Word For Windows® 6 For Dummies® Quick Reference	by George Lynch	ISBN: 1-56884-095-0	$8.95 USA/$11.95 Canada
Word For Windows® For Dummies® Quick Reference	by George Lynch	ISBN: 1-56884-029-2	$8.95 USA/$11.95 Canada
WordPerfect® 6.1 For Windows® For Dummies® Quick Reference, 2nd Edition	by Greg Harvey	ISBN: 1-56884-966-4	$9.99 USA/$12.99/Canada

For scholastic requests & educational orders please call Educational Sales at 1. 800. 434. 2086

FOR MORE INFO OR TO ORDER, PLEASE CALL ▶ **800 . 762 . 2974**

For volume discounts & special orders please call Tony Real, Special Sales, at 415. 655. 3048

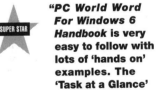

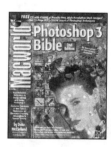

10/31/95

"*Macworld Complete Mac Handbook Plus CD* covered everything I could think of and more!"

Peter Tsakiris, New York, NY

"**Very useful for PageMaker beginners and veterans alike—contains a wealth of tips and tricks to make you a faster, more powerful PageMaker user.**"

Paul Brainerd, President and founder, Aldus Corporation

"**Thanks for the best computer book I've ever read—*Photoshop 2.5 Bible*. Best $30 I ever spent. I *love* the detailed index....Yours blows them all out of the water. This is a great book. We must enlighten the masses!**"

Kevin Lisankie, Chicago, Illinois

"*Macworld Guide to ClarisWorks 2* is the easiest computer book to read that I have ever found!"

Steven Hanson, Lutz, FL

"**...thanks to the *Macworld Excel 5 Companion*, 2nd Edition occupying a permanent position next to my computer, I'll be able to tap more of Excel's power.**"

Lauren Black, Lab Director, Macworld Magazine

Macworld® QuarkXPress 3.2/3.3 Bible
by Barbara Assadi & Galen Gruman
ISBN: 1-878058-85-1
$39.95 USA/$52.95 Canada
Includes disk with QuarkXPress XTensions and scripts.

Macworld® PageMaker 5 Bible
by Craig Danuloff
ISBN: 1-878058-84-3
$39.95 USA/$52.95 Canada
Includes 2 disks with PageMaker utilities, clip art, and more.

Macworld® FileMaker Pro 2.0/2.1 Bible
by Steven A. Schwartz
ISBN: 1-56884-201-5
$34.95 USA/$46.95 Canada
Includes disk with ready-to-run data bases.

Macworld® Word 6 Companion, 2nd Edition
by Jim Heid
ISBN: 1-56884-082-9
$24.95 USA/$34.95 Canada
NEWBRIDGE BOOK CLUB SELECTION

Macworld® Guide To Microsoft® Word 5/5.1
by Jim Heid
ISBN: 1-878058-39-8
$22.95 USA/$29.95 Canada

Macworld® ClarisWorks 2.0/2.1 Companion, 2nd Edition
by Steven A. Schwartz
ISBN: 1-56884-180-9
$24.95 USA/$34.95 Canada

Macworld® Guide To Microsoft® Works 3
by Barrie Sosinsky
ISBN: 1-878058-42-8
$22.95 USA/$29.95 Canada

Macworld® Excel 5 Companion, 2nd Edition
by Chris Van Buren & David Maguiness
ISBN: 1-56884-081-0
$24.95 USA/$34.95 Canada
NEWBRIDGE BOOK CLUB SELECTION

Macworld® Guide To Microsoft® Excel 4
by David Maguiness
ISBN: 1-878058-40-1
$22.95 USA/$29.95 Canada

Microsoft is a registered trademark of Microsoft Corporation. Macworld is a registered trademark of International Data Group, Inc.

or scholastic requests & educational orders please ll Educational Sales, at 1. 800. 434. 2086

FOR MORE INFO OR TO ORDER, PLEASE CALL ▶ 800 762 2974

For volume discounts & special orders please call Tony Real, Special Sales, at 415. 655. 3048

Official Hayes Modem Communications Companion

by Caroline M. Halliday

ISBN: 1-56884-072-1
$29.95 USA/$39.95 Canada

Includes software.

1,001 Komputer Answers from Kim Komando

by Kim Komando

ISBN: 1-56884-460-3
$29.99 USA/$39.99 Canada

Includes software.

PC World Excel 5 For Windows® Handbook, 2nd Edition

by John Walkenbach & Dave Maguiness

ISBN: 1-56884-056-X
$34.95 USA/$44.95 Canada

Includes software

PC World WordPerfect® 6 Handbook

by Greg Harvey

ISBN: 1-878058-80-0
$34.95 USA/$44.95 Canada

Includes software.

PC World DOS 6 Command Reference and Problem Solver

by John Socha & Devra Hall

NATIONAL BESTSELLER

ISBN: 1-56884-055-1
$24.95 USA/$32.95 Canada

Client/Server Strategies™: A Survival Guide for Corporate Reengineers

SUPER STAR

by David Vaskevitch

ISBN: 1-56884-064-0
$29.95 USA/$39.95 Canada

Internet SECRETS™

by John Levine & Carol Baroudi

ISBN: 1-56884-452-2
$39.99 USA/$54.99 Canada

Includes software.

Network Security SECRETS™

by David Stang & Sylvia Moon

ISBN: 1-56884-021-7
Int'l. ISBN: 1-56884-151-5
$49.95 USA/$64.95 Canada

Includes software.

PC SECRETS™

by Caroline M. Halliday

ISBN: 1-878058-49-5
$39.95 USA/$52.95 Canada

Includes software.

IDG BOOKS WORLDWIDE

Here's a complete listing of PC Press Titles

Title	Author	ISBN	Price
BBS SECRETS™	by Ray Werner	ISBN: 1-56884-491-3	$39.99 USA/$54.99 Canada
Creating Cool Web Pages with HTML	by Dave Taylor	ISBN: 1-56884-454-9	$19.99 USA/$26.99 Canada
DOS 6 SECRETS™	by Robert D. Ainsbury	ISBN: 1-878058-70-3	$39.95 USA/$52.95 Canada
Excel 5 For Windows® Power Programming Techniques	by John Walkenbach	ISBN: 1-56884-303-8	$39.95 USA/$52.95 Canada
Hard Disk SECRETS™	by John M. Goodman, Ph.D.	ISBN: 1-878058-64-9	$39.95 USA/$52.95 Canada
Internet GIZMOS™ For Windows®	by Joel Diamond, Howard Sobel, & Valda Hilley	ISBN: 1-56884-451-4	$39.99 USA/$54.99 Canada
Making Multimedia Work	by Michael Goodwin	ISBN: 1-56884-468-9	$19.99 USA/$26.99 Canada
MORE Windows® 3.1 SECRETS™	by Brian Livingston	ISBN: 1-56884-019-5	$39.95 USA/$52.95 Canada
Official XTree Companion 3rd Edition	by Beth Slick	ISBN: 1-878058-57-6	$19.95 USA/$26.95 Canada
Paradox 4 Power Programming SECRETS™, 2nd Edition	by Gregory B. Salcedo & Martin W. Rudy	ISBN: 1-878058-54-1	$44.95 USA/$59.95 Canada
Paradox 5 For Windows® Power Programming SECRETS™	by Gregory B. Salcedo & Martin W. Rudy	ISBN: 1-56884-085-3	$44.95 USA/$59.95 Canada
PC World DOS 6 Handbook, 2nd Edition	by John Socha, Clint Hicks & Devra Hall	ISBN: 1-878058-79-7	$34.95 USA/$44.95 Canada
PC World Microsoft® Access 2 Bible, 2nd Edition	by Cary N. Prague & Michael R. Irwin	ISBN: 1-56884-086-1	$39.95 USA/$52.95 Canada
PC World Word For Windows® 6 Handbook	by Brent Heslop & David Angell	ISBN: 1-56884-054-3	$34.95 USA/$44.95 Canada
QuarkXPress For Windows® Designer Handbook	by Barbara Assadi & Galen Gruman	ISBN: 1-878058-45-2	$29.95 USA/$39.95 Canada
Windows® 3.1 Configuration SECRETS™	by Valda Hilley & James Blakely	ISBN: 1-56884-026-8	$49.95 USA/$64.95 Canada
Windows® 3.1 Connectivity SECRETS™	by Runnoe Connally, David Rorabaugh & Sheldon Hall	ISBN: 1-56884-030-6	$49.95 USA/$64.95 Canada
Windows® 3.1 SECRETS™	by Brian Livingston	ISBN: 1-878058-43-6	$39.95 USA/$52.95 Canada
Windows® 95 A.S.A.P.	by Dan Gookin	ISBN: 1-56884-483-2	$24.99 USA/$34.99 Canada
Windows® 95 Bible	by Alan Simpson	ISBN: 1-56884-074-8	$29.95 USA/$39.99 Canada
Windows® 95 SECRETS™	by Brian Livingston	ISBN: 1-56884-453-0	$39.99 USA/$54.99 Canada
Windows® GIZMOS™	by Brian Livingston & Margie Livingston	ISBN: 1-878058-66-5	$39.95 USA/$52.95 Canada
WordPerfect® 6 For Windows® Tips & Techniques Revealed	by David A. Holzgang & Roger C. Parker	ISBN: 1-56884-202-3	$39.95 USA/$52.95 Canada
WordPerfect® 6 SECRETS™	by Roger C. Parker & David A. Holzgang	ISBN: 1-56884-040-3	$39.95 USA/$52.95 Canada

For scholastic requests & educational orders please call Educational Sales, at 1. 800. 434. 2086

FOR MORE INFO OR TO ORDER, PLEASE CALL ▶ 800. 762. 2974

For volume discounts & special orders please c Tony Real, Special Sales, at 415. 655. 3048